EXPERIENCE
MATTERS

ED HOFFMAN

EXPERIENCE MATTERS

(HERE'S MINE)

LIBERTY HILL PRESS

Xulon Press
2301 Lucien Way #415
Maitland, FL 32751
407.339.4217
www.xulonpress.com

Library of Congress Control Number: 2021915977

Paperback ISBN-13: 978-1-6628-2500-2
Dust Jacket ISBN-13: 978-1-6628-2501-9
Ebook ISBN-13: 978-1-6628-2502-6

TABLE OF CONTENTS

Introduction vii
Chapter 1 1
Chapter 2 17
Chapter 3 23
Chapter 4 33
Chapter 5 39
Chapter 6 45
Chapter 7 57
Chapter 8 67
Chapter 9 75
Chapter 10 85
Chapter 11 97
Chapter 12 113
Chapter 13 119
Chapter 14 129
Chapter 15 139
Chapter 16 153
Chapter 17 167
Chapter 18 179
Chapter 19 191
Chapter 20 207

Chapter 21. 219

Chapter 22. 227

Chapter 23. 249

Chapter 24. 259

Chapter 25. 275

Chapter 26. 289

Chapter 27. 319

Chapter 28. 337

Chapter 29. 343

Endnotes 347

INTRODUCTION

"I'm the only friend you've got. I'm making you money."[1]
- Other People's Money, 1991

THEY SAY THERE are two rules for marriage:

- Rule #1: Your wife is always right.
- Rule #2: If you feel your wife is wrong, slap yourself and read Rule #1 again.

For the past 15 years, my wife has been saying that I should write a book.

I'm a simple man, so my obvious follow-up was usually: "About what?"

"All your experiences," she would say. "All the things that you've seen and done, and the lessons that you've learned."

"Okay," I'd say. "I'll get right on that." And then I didn't, until now.

Maybe it was because I saw the need to add some clarity to the conversation, based on the experiences that helped form my common sense viewpoint. Or, maybe it was because I finally slapped myself and re-read Rule #1.

This book will be filled with life lessons; you'll see them in every chapter. The first one, and the one that you'll come to understand as the theme of this book, is this: *Experience is the best teacher, especially when it's someone else's experience.*

If you're only trying to learn from your own experience, then you're wasting your time doing all the wrong things — just so you can later come to the conclusion that you should have done things differently, after it's already too late. How does that help you? It doesn't. That's why you want to learn from the experiences of others: to make the right decisions, when they count.

The Old Ways

Maybe this isn't what your grandmother told you, so get ready: *Sometimes, the old ways are not necessarily the best ways.*

Some of us are doing things a certain way in life, just because that's the way it's always been done by whoever we consider our "establishment." If there's any time in history for us to change that, it's now. Whatever you believe about the COVID pandemic (I happen to believe it was not worthy of shutting down the American economy, but I digress), you can at least acknowledge that it was a time when Americans changed the way they lived — and many of those changes are here to stay. So why not change the way we think, too?

There are old ways of thinking about life: You go to school, do your homework, graduate, go to college (or some other specialized educational destination) and head toward your career. There, you'll have only one type of retirement plan someone else devised for you. You'll let someone else manage it and say a prayer that when the time comes, it will be enough. As years go by, you might vote for people who make promises based on the short-sighted goals of the young (maybe because you believe it's virtuous, or maybe just because your kids seem to love you more if you do). And eventually, you die.

That's the way it's always been done. But that doesn't mean it's right.

If you agree, maybe your response is: "Well, someone should say what we've all been thinking." Someone did, and that's why almost 63,000,000 people voted for him in 2016. He wasn't a great politician, but that's not why they voted for him. They voted for him because he was saying the things they were already thinking. I'm not even talking about issues like illegal immigration.

I'm talking about simple principles, like the crazy notion that people should have to work hard in life.

But apparently, that's not the way we're supposed to present it anymore. Not to kids, not to teenagers, not to young adults...not even to older adults. We're supposed to let everyone believe they're a victim. It's shameful.

Understanding Agendas

What's also shameful is standing by silently while our more vulnerable family members, friends and neighbors allow themselves to be spoonfed. Democrats may have invented the term "fake news" as a cheap shot at Fox News and conservative talk radio — but thankfully, Republicans co-opted the term in a way that actually made sense. The truth is, there's fake news everywhere.

You don't need me, any cable news channel, your favorite spin-heavy political blog, Democrats *or* Republicans to determine what the truth is. It's our responsibility to look at all sides, and then make our own determinations about what makes sense to us individually. Understand this: *All of them have an agenda*.

It doesn't make them evil. It makes them normal, because *everyone* has an agenda.

If you're young, then what makes sense to you right now was probably formed by some combination of your own experiences and what you were told growing up (by parents and teachers who formed their opinions the same way). That's fine, but there's a key piece missing there: the varied experiences of others. This book is designed to share my experiences with you, so you can take them into account when forming and questioning your own views.

Everyone has an agenda, and I'm no different. My agenda is to help people understand how agendas affect our decisions. Some of the agendas we encounter in life include the following.

Sales Agendas

When you walk into an appliance store, a car lot or a real estate agent's office, the people who work there all have an agenda.

The problem is, it's usually the wrong one. The agenda *should* be to help you find the right appliance, vehicle or house for you. Unfortunately, it's actually to help themselves sell whatever appliance, vehicle or house they've been told to find a buyer for that particular month. Their agenda is to sell you what *they* want you to have, so *they* can close a sale.

Support Agendas

When you walk into a church, the agenda of everyone responsible for presenting the service should be to bring you closer to God, from wherever you are spiritually in that moment. Unfortunately, too many people have decided to *stop* walking into a church — because they feel like the only thing that matters to that church is the money they walk in with. And because the spiritual side impacts the physical side, those people will suffer in more ways than one.

Institutional Agendas

When you talk with a university recruiter (or sometimes, even a trade school), the agenda of that school should be to help you find the right educational program for what you want to do with your life. But now, higher education is not even about education. It's about enrollment and money. "But that's okay, right? At least I'll have a degree." That would be true, if your agenda was to get a degree. But if you're being honest with yourself, your agenda is not the degree. Your agenda is a lifestyle.

Lifestyle Agendas

To expand on that: Most of the time, our personal agendas boil down to security, a retirement when we're older and a nice lifestyle on the way there. So if you aren't passionate about what that pricey institutional degree is in, do you really need it to achieve your agenda? We'll talk more about the college myth later on — but for now, just understand that you (or your kids) may not need additional schooling to afford a comfortable lifestyle.

Investment Agendas

Maybe you already understand that a lifestyle can be attained without a college degree, and you're breaking into investing (that's good, because we'll be talking about it a lot throughout the book). But *when* you're investing, are you strategizing based on what you think is the hot commodity — or, what you know will give you a high return? It should be the latter. If your strategy is to invest in the sexy stock of the moment "just because" it seems like everyone else is, or to own properties in certain areas "just because" everyone's talking about them, then you're doing it wrong.

Remember, you're not investing to be popular. You're investing to make money: cash flow, long term appreciation and an eventual goal of either liquidation of the asset or long-term, passive income for retirement.

Use the Guidance, Take the Baby Steps, Reach the Rocket

Unfortunately, there's bad information out there that pushes new investors to take big steps too quickly. But when you're starting out with $10,000, you can't afford to buy a $5 million apartment building in a prestigious area — so, don't worry about it. Just buy properties that will appreciate, when the market cycle is in the right phase for it. How will you know what the right phase is? We'll get there. Just keep reading. One thing you can do now, even before we take a deep dive into the market cycle, is to start watching for trends. As I write this introduction (summer 2021), we are still in a Seller's Market 2, with buyers being priced further out of the market — but the good news is, that means the Buyer's Market 1 phase is right around the corner. Even without fully knowing what those terms mean, you can probably guess that Buyer's Market 1 is the one that's most favorable to you as an investor.

Sometimes, new investors are so excited about breaking into real estate that they think they have to start out with commercial investments, because "that's where the big money is." Well, I'm here to tell you that leaping straight into the commercial market is rarely an option. But that's okay! So you can't afford to buy a commercial strip mall — once again, don't worry about it. If we've learned anything throughout the COVID pandemic, it's that people can do just about anything from home. The markets are already starting to reflect that reality. Soon, all the strip malls you had your eye on are going to be bulldozed. What's going up to replace them? Most likely, multi-family housing complexes (AKA apartment buildings). By the time it happens, you may be on your way to having access to an investment like that...but only if you follow my guidance and take the baby steps to reach that goal.

The same applies when you're starting out with stocks. Most likely, you can't afford to invest in Tesla yet — so, don't worry about it. Just buy stocks that have growth potential at your accessibility level. If you care more about what product a company sells than how much money you can make from investing in it, you're praying the Prayer for the Dead. That's what it's called in the movie I quoted at the beginning, *Other People's Money*. As Danny DeVito's character in the film says:

"Lest we forget, that's the only reason any of you became stock-holders in the first place. You want to make money. You don't care if they manufacture wire and cable, fried chicken or grow tangerines! You want to make money!"

Don't worry about what the product is. Can you make money from it? That's the only question you need to ask.

When you choose wisely, buy what you can afford and transfer the appreciation into a nest egg, you'll eventually be able to invest bigger. That's what I did, and I'll be explaining how you can do it later in the book. All you need is some guidance as you take the necessary baby steps from the launch pad to the rocket. That's what I'll give you as you move through this book.

Other Ways to Learn from Experience

You'll notice that every chapter of the book begins with a quote from a feature film. That's because I believe movies are a way to learn from other people's successes and failures in a creative, entertaining way. If you only watch a movie once, you'll miss all the pearls of wisdom and enlightenment that are tucked into movie dialogue. There's a lot more on that to come in the next chapter. My hope is that you'll see how movies can be your friends and teachers. Teachers of what? Say it with me: *experience*.

You can also learn from the experience (or lack thereof) of those in power. The saying goes, "How do you know a politician is lying? His mouth is moving." Well, that's somewhat true. If something sounds like a tall promise that's short-sighted, then it probably is. Trust your instincts; be smart enough to understand what some lofty campaign promise (usually for some form of "free money") will mean for your future. Almost inevitably, it will mean higher taxes, and not just if you reach "the top one percent of earners."

What has it meant for those countries that our colleges and universities use as examples — you know, the ones they talk about when they brainwash our kids into hating America? Usually, their favorite example is Sweden. Well, Sweden's top personal tax rate is 57%. In the United States, our top personal tax rate is around 37% (although the gaffe machine currently occupying the White House may soon raise it to 43%, presumably to pay for all the COVID relief he's authorized). Those are the long-term ramifications of the government giving out free money. What will that mean for your future, and the future of your loved ones? I'm not concerned for myself anymore. I'm concerned for my kids and grandkids, and you should be concerned for yours too (yes, even if you're young).

Ask yourself:

- Does spoiling people with endless waves of COVID relief make long-term sense?
- Does Universal Basic Income – an idea championed by populist Democrats like Bernie Sanders and Andrew Yang (both of whom will continue to run for president until they die, and Yang has a lot longer to go than Bernie does) – make long-term sense?
- Stopping the construction of an oil pipeline may *sound* like it makes sense for the environment (even though it's on largely unoccupied land), but does $5 for a gallon gasoline make sense? Raising the price of a gallon of gas

to $5 is more taxation than anything the IRS could possibly impose on you as a middle class American.

- Getting paid $15 an hour to work at Target may seem like a great idea, but does paying twice as much for the stuff you buy there make sense in the long-term (or even the short-term)?

- The campaign to defund the police may appear virtuous at first; after all, the media has portrayed the small percentage of police who abuse their power as the norm. So the tagline sounds great, until you see that the cities that actually tried it experienced massive spikes in crime (who would've guessed that weakening law enforcement would result in more criminals committing more crimes?). As it turns out, criminals were watching. They know they're being catered to right now, and they know how to capitalize on bad decisions born out of inexperience.

The things being hailed as virtuous and good to our young people will end up biting them in the ass big time, unless they are willing to start learning from experiences that are not their own.

My hope for you is that after reading this book, you see the immense value of learning from the experiences of others. Let them get embedded in your psyche. Use them to learn how to recognize good opportunities and red flags. Let them influence your thought process as you make physical, financial, relational and spiritual decisions. Allow them to help you discern what the truth is, vs. what's just a distraction designed to evoke some kind of emotion inside you so that you buy what's being advertised, vote for what's being promised or invest in someone else's dream.

If this becomes your way of thinking, then the common sense, logic and integrity you gain will help you succeed in whatever your ultimate agenda is. As we get further into my personal experiences, you'll see that there are lessons you can apply to your career, your parenting, your personal development and maybe even your politics.

It's true that "Experience is the best teacher" is a pretty commonplace belief. But it's the second part — "especially when it's someone else's experience"— that can make all the difference in your life.

Hopefully, you're ready to learn from mine. Let's do this.

CHAPTER 1

*"You haven't seen enough movies.
All of life's riddles are answered in the movies."*[2]
- Grand Canyon, 1991

THESE DAYS, LOTS of people are TV bingers. Others are podcast bingers. Most people aren't book bingers (but hopefully, some still are). Personally, I'm a movie binger. I was binging movies long before binging was a trend. Movies have been my "thing" since childhood. Here's why I believe they're important.

I love the experience of going to the movies; however, I'm writing this chapter in the middle of a pandemic-related lockdown that prevents movie theaters from being open. Luckily, I love more than the experience of the theater. I also love movies because of what they can teach us — especially the ones that teach us something new every time we watch. Some movies have to be watched dozens of times to extract all the lessons they contain. Learning from the experiences of others is easy to do when you watch movies, because movies are living pictures of other people's experiences. But here's the thing: Somewhere, there's a movie in *all* of our lives. Here's an example of someone who proved that.

If you attend enough sales conferences, you'll get to hear a lot of motivational speakers. One of the speakers who provided me with the most clarity is Rudy Ruettiger.

Rudy Ruettiger was a high school football player from Illinois who had a dream to play for Notre Dame. After two years in the Navy (or in the movie version, a steel mill), he decided it was time to

1

apply to his dream school – but unfortunately, he was rejected because of his low GPA. He didn't give up, though, enrolling in nearby Holy Cross College instead and re-applying to Notre Dame four times over the next two years as he worked to build a better academic profile. On his fourth try, he was accepted into Notre Dame; after a great deal of hard work, he was accepted onto the football program's scout team (which basically meant he was used as a crash dummy).

But Rudy was undeterred to make the roster of players who would actually play on the field, and his day finally came in the last game of his senior year: Notre Dame vs. Georgia Tech. He wasn't looking to go pro; all he wanted was to play in one game to impress his dad, and he needed to be on the field for at least one play in order to go on record as having been on the team. And that's what he got to do, sacking the Georgia Tech quarterback in the final play of the game. His teammates then carried him off the field, something that had never happened in Notre Dame football history up to that point. The game happened in 1975; about 15 years later, Rudy Ruettiger successfully sold his story to be made into a feature film. In 1993, the film *Rudy* was released. It raked in $22.8 million at the box office and it lives on in cable today.

When I had the opportunity to hear him speak, something Rudy said struck a powerful chord with me: "I only played for 27 seconds. If they hadn't gotten The Hobbit (Sean Astin, not technically "The Hobbit" but someone who played *a* hobbit in Tolkien's universe) to play me and put it on the screen, no one would even know who I am."[3]

There's a movie in all of our lives.

The next morning, I had a one-on-one with Rudy for about 10 minutes. Sean Astin is 5'7". The real Rudy is reportedly 5'6", but in person he looks about 5'3" (this is relevant because he was told his height would always prevent him from playing college football).

Rudy was an ordinary guy who had an extraordinary experience. He went after something and did it with heart. The movie captured that small piece of his life – a piece that some people wouldn't think of as a great experience. But to him, it was. And it obviously resonated with a lot of people, because it consistently ranks high on "best sports movie" lists to this day.

What moment of *your* life is a movie waiting to happen? Everybody has one.

We Can Be Heroes

The story of Rudy reminds me of another movie: *Hero*, from 1992. His story perfectly exemplifies this line: "I think we're all heroes if you catch us at the right moment."[4]

Whether you're watching a sports movie, a military movie or a movie about a college kid overcoming some challenge, you're watching somebody overcome adversity. Technology changes, but truths about life don't change. You can see those truths in the movies.

I can teach someone something over and over and it doesn't sink in until they see it in a different context. Often, that context is in the movies. If you're a parent or a teacher or an employer or a coach, you can teach people lessons with movies. If you're trying to teach a concept and it hasn't broken through yet, here's an idea: Find a movie that teaches it and show it to them. In my experience, this can work.

This is why I love recommending movies to other people. I want them to get the same lessons I get, and I know they'll probably find a few lessons I may have missed. Take a movie like *Draft Day* from 2014. If you think of it as just another football movie, you're missing the point. Just like *Rudy*, it's not a football movie; it's a movie about character. *The Devil Wears Prada* isn't a fashion movie or a chick flick; it's a movie about business. For anyone who wants to be a real leader in their field, I suggest using any free time you have to rewatch your favorite movies and write down the lessons you find in them. You can use them to teach your people and continue to grow yourself.

The Way it Used to Be

Don't let that header fool you; this won't be a section on how much better movies used to be. If anything, movies have gotten better.

You may or may not be old enough to remember, but there was a time when watching a movie dozens of times was almost impossible. You could see a first-run movie in the theater once, maybe twice before it was pulled. If you had a second-run theater nearby, you could go see it six months later when it was no longer new (and pay a lot less for your ticket). If you wanted to see it again after that, you'd have to wait up to a year for it to air on prime-time TV — and if the movie was a hit, that was always a big deal.

In the mid-80s, we had the video revolution. With the innovation of Betamax and VHS, you could all of a sudden watch your favorite movies on demand at home. It sounds quaint now that "on demand" doesn't require you to put a giant tape into a machine, but it was pretty exciting at the time. Every time a Disney movie, a family favorite like *The Wizard of Oz* or a classic like *Rocky* was released on video, people literally celebrated. It's pretty funny that most of us thought that technology would last forever.

By the late 90s, DVDs were invented; by the early 2000s, we all had DVD players. Pretty soon, the expectation was that you could see a movie in the theater and own the DVD six months later. Like you, I have a ton of DVDs I never watch anymore because of digital streaming (and, like you, I'm pondering whether I should start getting rid of them. I'd have a lot more wall space if I did).

Movies are an entertainment product, but the process of making them involves so many technical arts that we don't fully appreciate. When we watch the Academy Awards, most of us outside of the film industry are only interested in Best Actor, Best Actress, Best Picture...maybe Best Director. But we should probably care about Best Cinematography, Best Lighting, or Best Sound too. Those are the motion picture arts that require the most technical skill, yet they get the least amount of glory.

Personally, I have zero technical film experience. But I learned a lot when I started watching the people I would hire to edit movie clips for my presentations. I would start to notice that when you're clipping a scene from a movie for some other purpose, it's hard to communicate the entire message without including some of the dialogue that preceded it. Sometimes, it would take hours to piece together someone else's work into *my* piece of work (by the way, my "piece of work" only involved inserting a movie scene into a business presentation. I'm not talking about illegally reproducing an entire film). Then, in response to the rampant video piracy that happened in the 80s and 90s, every movie came equipped with copy protection built in and the whole thing got even harder (thankfully, we now have YouTube!).

The point is, it was during those video editing sessions that I learned about all the work that goes into making movies. The process is intricate and intense. Recently, I read that a typical Hollywood drama is now made with a 1:20 shooting ratio; that means roughly 20 minutes of footage is shot for every one minute used. So, in a 120-minute feature, about 38 hours of footage goes unused in the final product. When you think about that, it makes you appreciate the talent it takes to be a good film editor.

Becoming a Connoisseur

Next, I began to realize the role that actors play in the quality of the final product. In one of my favorites, *A Few Good Men*, it's everything from the expression on Tom Cruise's face to Jack Nicholson's tone of voice. That film has dozens of lessons crammed into its dialogue. You can learn something new every time you watch it. To cite something a little more recent, it's the same thing with *The Big Short*. You can watch that movie 100 times and learn something new every time (not just about the mortgage crisis, either).

When I talk about learning from movie lines, I don't mean the memorable dialogue everyone quotes. In other words, I'm not referring to, *"You can't handle the truth!"*[5] I'm talking about the lines that are said more quietly as background notes, or more quickly during a fast-paced scene where two people are dialoguing, but nobody's voice is raised. Here are a few of my favorites:

- "You say the meek shall inherit the earth. And I say the only thing the meek can count on is getting the short end of the stick."[6]
  - *Leap of Faith*, 1992

- "It's supposed to be hard. If it wasn't hard, everyone would do it. The hard ... is what makes it great."[7]
  - *A League of Their Own*, 1992

- "The only thing that you regret in life are the risks you don't take."[8]
  - *Grumpy Old Men*, 1993

- "People want leadership...In the absence of leadership, they'll listen to anyone who steps up to the mic."[9]
  - *The American President*, 1995

- "Why do you feel that Truman's never come close to discovering the true nature of his world?"

- "We accept the reality of the world with which we're presented. It's as simple as that."[10]
  - *The Truman Show, 1998*

- "Life's a game of inches. So is football. Because in either game—life or football—the margin for error is so small. I mean, one half a step too late or too early and you don't quite make it."[11]
  - *Any Given Sunday*, 1999

- "Principles only mean something if you stick by them when they are inconvenient."[12]
  - *The Contender*, 2000

- "More jobs means fewer people looking for work. Means it's harder to find good people to fill those jobs. Means you got to raise wages to get them. Means inflation goes up. You got it?...No, I didn't think so. That's why I'm doing what I'm doing, and you're handing out

junk mail."[13]
- *The 25th Hour*, 2002

- "Great ambition and conquest without contribution is without significance."[14]
  - *The Emperor's Club*, 2002

- "The long way is easier. But it's longer. Much longer."[15]
  - *Big Fish*, 2003

- "Do you think a man can change his destiny? I think a man does what he can until his destiny is revealed."[16]
  - *The Last Samurai*, 2003

- "Now I'm gonna assume that by now you've learned that the world's not fair...and sometimes you get the short end. That's all you get. And if you don't do something personally to fix it, that's all you're *ever* gonna get."[17]
  - *Friday Night Lights*, 2004

- "You don't care about money because you've always had it."[18]
  - *The Aviator*, 2004

- "You failed, you failed, you failed, you failed, you failed. You want to be really great? Then have the courage to fail big and stick around. Make them wonder why you're still smiling."[19]
  - *Elizabethtown*, 2005

- "You come to see that a man learns nothing from the act of winning. The act of losing, however, elicits great wisdom. Not the least of which is how much more enjoyable it is to win. It's inevitable to lose now and again; the trick is not to make a habit of it."[20]
  - *A Good Year*, 2006

- "What was it that you used to say to your kids at Hillsdale High – that character is tested when you're up against it?"

- "That's not the problem here. He's got plenty of character."

- "Who said I was talking about him?"[21]
  - *Invincible, 2006*

- "We do what we have to do so we can do what we want to do."[22]
  - *The Great Debaters*, 2007

- "Marcus Aurelius hired a servant to walk behind him as he made his way through the Roman town square. And this servant's only job was to whisper in his ear when people praised him, "You're only a man. You're only a man."[23]
  - *Law Abiding Citizen*, 2009

- "Now, ya'll would guess that more often than not, the highest paid player on an NFL team is the quarterback. And you'd be right. But what you probably don't know is that more often than not, the second highest paid player is...a left tackle. Because, as every housewife knows, the first check you write is for the mortgage, but the second is for the insurance. The left tackle's job is to protect the quarterback from what he can't see comin'. To protect his blind side."[24]
  - *The Blind Side*, 2009

- "The medicine may be harsh but the patient requires it."[25]
  - *The Iron Lady*, 2011

- "There's a difference between fear and panic. Fear is healthy; panic is deadly."[26]
  - *Chasing Mavericks*, 2012

- "There are three types of people in this world: sheep, wolves and sheepdogs. Some people prefer to believe that evil doesn't exist in the world – and if it ever darkened their doorstep, they wouldn't know how to protect themselves. Those are the sheep. Then you've

got predators who use violence to prey on the weak. They're the wolves. And then there are those blessed with the gift of aggression, an overpowering need to protect the flock. These men are the rare breed who live to confront the wolf. They are the sheepdog."[27]
- *American Sniper*, 2014

- "You're doing this because you want to feel relevant again. Well guess what? There's an entire world of people out there trying to be relevant every single day."[28]
  - *Birdman*, 2014

- "Do you have any idea what you just did? You just bet against the American economy."[29]
  - *The Big Short*, 2015

- "I know what it's like to be in a place like this, let another man raise your children. When I was young, I was giving myself to something bigger. Jack, that something bigger's gone now."[30]
  - *13 Hours*, 2016

- "It's the actor's job to avoid impediments to their performance. It's the actor's job to strive for one hundred percent effectiveness. Naturally, we never succeed, but it's the pursuit that's meaningful."[31]
  - *Once Upon a Time in Hollywood,* 2019

My Movie History

We all have our own movie histories. Mine started when my parents took all four of us kids to the drive-in theater in their station wagon to see *The Ten Commandments*. My mom popped a bunch of popcorn at home and packed some sandwiches (no way could they afford concession stand prices for a family of six). My parents were in the front seat and my two sisters were in the middle seat. My brother Scott and I were lying down in the back of the station wagon, peering around their heads to see the screen.

At the time, I didn't know enough about the Bible to understand the plot. Even though the story is from the Torah and I came from a Jewish family, we weren't necessarily that religious (maybe that's one of the reasons I ended up rejecting it when I got older). So, what I ended up remembering about *The Ten Commandments* was 1) It was long, and 2) the special effects. But for a little kid, special effects are no small thing.

On the other hand, my next movie was the one that every kid who grows up in a Jewish family is required to see whether they like it or not. That would be *Fiddler on the Roof*, which every Jewish kid is forced to watch, and on every form in which it is released (I believe this is still the case today). In 1971, I was in that lucky first generation of kids who got to partake in this strange ritual. My parents were excited to see Jewish entertainment icon Chaim Topol (better known only as "Topal") in the lead role of Tevye, the pious and poor milkman who relies on the town matchmaker to find wealthy Jewish husbands for his five daughters.

I'm not sure if other families did *Fiddler* this way, but it was an all-day occasion for our family. That meant my parents drove us four kids to the Crest Theater in Long Beach, dropped us off and left; where they went, I don't know. When it was over, they picked us up, took us back home and left us there so they could go see the exact same movie we just saw. I'm not sure what that says about my family, but that's how we were introduced to *Fiddler*. Kids don't always question odd things while they're happening.

One year later, my buddies and I were riding our bikes to the Lakewood Center Theater to see *The Ra Expeditions*. Normally, a documentary doesn't motivate 11-year-old boys to ride their bikes three miles to the movie theater, but this one did. It was about adventurer and anthropologist Thor Heyerdahl, who attempted to cross the Atlantic in a papyrus boat with a crew he assembled from six different nations. We had seen the TV commercials and were ready to watch this guy sail from West Africa to Barbados on a vessel made of reeds. It was pretty cool. Back then, double features were the norm; you didn't pay to see one movie. You paid to see two. That day, the second feature was *The African Elephant*.

We did the same thing when *The Poseidon Adventure* came out. In fact, we did it at least three times. Over and over throughout the 1972 holiday season, someone would say, "We're going to see it again!"...and we did. Back then, you didn't get a ride from someone's mom or dad. Riding our bikes three miles each way was much cooler than asking one of our parents to drive, of course.

Today, the special effects of *The Poseidon Adventure* seem kind of cheesy — but back then, they were amazing. It was also the first time a movie got me so excited that I checked the book out at the library. There was something about that story that moved me. Everyone should have a movie that did that for them. If you don't remember what yours was, try thinking about it for a while until the memory comes back. It's important to remember what inspired you when you were young.

I'm still trying to remember what my first R-rated movie was. I thought it was *Billy Jack*, which is sort of a sequel to another film called *The Born Losers*. The reason I thought *Billy Jack* was rated R is because there's a scene that implies a woman is being raped. Turns out, that movie was actually rated GP (which is PG today; at some point, they just reversed the letters). I was the youngest kid tagging along with my brother and his friends, who were three years older. I remember seeing the actress tied up on the ground in that scene and innocently asking my brother, "What's he doing?" Scott and his friends just laughed.

But by ninth grade, I was ready for the 1970s version of what we now refer to as "adult content." A new movie called *Rocky* was coming out, and our English teacher Miss Brickey wanted us to discuss it in class. This was right after the week we had finished discussing "American Pie," the most popular song on KHJ and KEZY and every other pop music radio station in America. It had tons of cultural significance, and it's the reason the plane crash that killed Buddy Holly, The Big Bopper and Ritchie Valens is still called "the day the music died" (even though most people from my generation consider that day to be December 8, 1980, and I happen to agree. If you don't understand, Google the date).

Clearly, Miss Brickey was a cool teacher. So when she talked up this new movie about an underdog boxer, starring an unknown actor who also wrote the script himself, I knew I had to see it. She was passionate about the story and the showmanship. If she recommended we needed to see *Rocky*, I was going to.

So I did, and it changed me. That's how I know young boys get their lives molded by the things they see in movies. I had never seen a movie like that before, and I was never the same after seeing it. When you see a movie like that at a time when you're trying to figure out who you are and what you're capable of, it makes a lasting impression. The music becomes the soundtrack of your life, just like it did for me when I played it going into my first arm wrestling tournament. But now, the *Theme from Rocky* plays everywhere. So even young kids today get to say it's part of their life soundtrack, too.

When the story starts, Rocky isn't really serious about boxing. He's just doing it to make money. He meets Adrian, a nice looking lady, and he sees what's behind all her sweaters and glasses and hats. The scene where he walks her home at night became an endless source for my friends and I to quote the movie for the sole purpose of making each other laugh.

One kid, in particular, mastered this. His name was Walter Watinabe. Walter was great at making the most mundane scene in the entire film look like a hilarious comedy act. Thanks to him, lots of us kids can say that our favorite high school memory is goofing off with quotes from this single scene from *Rocky*. "Hey, it's the bum from the docks. Get a job, you bum!" and, "Look at this face, 64 fights. Look at that nose. See that nose? That nose ain't never been broken in 64 fights. I'm proud of that!" It was stupid and hilarious and meaningful. That's how I learned that the most significant movie lines are not always the best-known.

More importantly, Rocky has heart. He loses his confidence only to find it again. He figured out what he was capable of. And it helped me figure out what I was capable of, too.

Every Rocky Has a Lesson

If I like a movie, I watch the sequel. And if I like the sequel, I watch the whole series. I don't wait to hear what people have to say about it.

When *Rocky III* was released, my girlfriend and I had broken up (before we got back together, then got married, then broke up for good...probably should have seen the writing on the wall there). I saw it over and over, in the theater, by myself. It got me out of my own head and took me to a different place. Everyone should have a movie like that, too.

The entire *Rocky* series is about knowing who you are and pushing yourself. I think about the saying, "Don't ask God to lighten your burden; ask him to strengthen your back."[33] Rocky demonstrates how to do that, whether he's going against Apollo Creed, Thunderlips or Clubber Lang. No matter who the opponent is, he's overcoming. And no matter how big he got, he was still the underdog.

In *Rocky Balboa*, you see him start to pass on the wisdom he's acquired to his son, delivering an inspirational speech about what winning really is — while inside, he knows he's aging and doesn't see himself winning a title anymore. What parent can't relate to that?

I was challenged to extract one lesson from the summary of each *Rocky* film. Here goes:

- In *Rocky,* he's given a shot at a title. But he has so much respect for his opponent that he doesn't think he has a chance.
  - The lesson: *You have an opportunity. Take advantage of the opportunity. Can you do it? You won't know until you put all you have into trying.*
- In *Rocky II*, he had lost part of his eyesight and Apollo Creed was taking things more seriously. But Rocky won anyway, because of his heart in the ring.
  - The lesson: *You can overcome anything. You can overcome shots of one million to one.*

- In *Rocky III*, he had lost some of his intensity and street cred. He wants to beat Clubber Lang, but he gets his ass kicked. In a pivotal confrontation on the beach, Adrian makes him admit that he's afraid. The truth was, he was afraid to lose.
  - The lesson: *If you're not serious about it, you won't accomplish it. Whatever "it" is, go in all the way. If you're serious about it.*

- In *Rocky IV*, an aging Rocky tells Apollo, "That's not us anymore. We can't do it the way we did before."[34] But Apollo convinces Rocky to train him for the fight against Ivan Drago. Drago literally kills Apollo in the ring; now, Rocky wants revenge. When his painfully honest wife Adrian tells him he can't win, he replies: "No, maybe I can't win. Maybe the only thing I can do is just take everything he's got. But to beat me, he's going to have to kill me. And to kill me, he's gonna have to have the heart to stand in front of me. And to do that, he's got to be willing to die himself."[35] Drago does "have the heart," but so does Rocky. And on Drago's home territory, Rocky beats him.
  - The lesson is in Apollo's plea to Rocky: *"We always have to be in the middle of the action 'cause we're the warriors. And without some challenge, without some damn war to fight, then the warriors might as well be dead, Stallion."*[36] *Don't be dead. Fight the war.*

- In *Rocky V*, he's busted and broken. He has brain injuries. A young fighter named Tommy Gunn asks him for training and Rocky delivers. But when Tommy is stolen away by a big time promoter, everything Rocky invested in Tommy was thankless. In the end, Tommy gets humbled when Rocky defeats him in an impromptu street fight.
  - The lesson: *First, age doesn't matter. It's always heart. Second, show gratitude for the people who helped you get to where you are.*

14

- In *Rocky Balboa*, his son Robert is blaming his own life challenges on living in the "big shadow" of his dad. In the speech that won this film acclaim, Rocky tells him: "The world ain't all sunshine and rainbows. It's a very mean and nasty place...it will beat you to your knees and keep you there permanently if you let it. You, me, or nobody is gonna hit as hard as life. But it ain't about how hard you hit; it's about how hard you can *get* hit and keep moving forward...That's how winning is done!"[37]
  - The lesson: *Don't blame your parents, the economic status you were born into, your skin color or the world for your station in life. Nothing worth going after is going to be easy.*

Movies are more than entertainment. They can be some of our greatest sources of wisdom and inspiration, if we let them.

CHAPTER 2

"I don't give a damn what you think you are entitled to!"[38]
- A Few Good Men, 1992

BACK IN THE early 80s, you could make extra money twice a week by selling your plasma. That sounds worse than it actually was. Basically, you would lie down on a table for an hour and a half while someone extracted half a pint of blood from you. The first time you did it was $12. The second time was $17. If you went seven times in one month, you got a $50 bonus. I did it as often as possible. Why?

To pay for an American tradition. It's called college.

This tradition is based on the belief that as soon as a kid graduates from high school, their next step should be college (the more expensive, the better). Because of this ritual, too many young people feel they're entitled to higher education — and, too many parents are putting themselves into massive debt to accommodate that entitlement.

If your child is bent on going to college and you're willing to pay for it, be prepared to accept this reality:

They're not going there to get a career; they're going there to get an education (hopefully), and you might not like what they'll be taught.

Does that mean a college degree is worthless? I'm inclined to say yes, but with this caveat: College *will* prepare young people to think in a certain way. Now, those thinking styles could grow in a number of different directions — and again, parents may or may not like the outcome.

When You're Good at One Thing

When I decided to study engineering in college, it was a choice based on the only thing I understood about my thinking style after 13 years of school: I was good at math.

What do you do if you're good at math? Here are your choices:

- You can become a math teacher (pass. No offense to any math teachers out there, but that was not for me).
- You can go into finance (I did later, but not in the traditional sense).
- Or you can become an engineer, which looked exciting to me as a kid graduating in 1979, two years after the launch of the Apple II, when people who seemed like they knew what they were talking about said that computers were the future of engineering.

That's why the engineering field appealed to me (that, and what I had heard about salaries for that field. Money is always a great motivator).

But why did I like math — and more importantly, why should you *care* why I liked math? Because I believe you should like math too. Here's why.

Math = Logical Thinking Styles

I liked math because it was right or wrong, black or white, A or B. Math is for logical thinkers, people who don't like the color gray. If numbers intimidate you, that's okay. Math is much more than numbers.

Math is this: *If three is bigger than two and two is bigger than one, then three is bigger than one.* You might say, "Well, yeah." But that's more than an obvious formula. It's really a principle that means this: *To develop an opinion, you need to hear from more than one source.* Once you have heard from multiple sources, you can use your brain to put all the information together and form your own opinion.

In the movie quote we start out with above from *A Few Good Men*, Lt. Kaffee (Tom Cruise) used the testimony of various witnesses to pin Col. Jessup (Jack Nicholson) into a corner so that he would admit to ordering the "code red" — but ultimately, the jury had to reach their own conclusion. I love that, because it illustrates the process of using logic to generate an informed opinion. But logic isn't just good for impressing people.

What Logical Thinking Can Do

With logic on your side, you can negotiate just about anything. If you're a young adult, you can use logic to negotiate:

- The price of your first house;
- The terms of your first auto loan;
- The starting salary of your first corporate job;
- How many kids you and your spouse will have;
- Where you'll live, who will work, who's in charge of the house...

See the pattern? When my kids were young, I invested in their math abilities for this reason. Now they're both gainfully employed, pay their own bills and know how to take care of themselves. Did I send them to college? No. Do I regret it? Not for a second. I encouraged them to master mathematics, which taught them the logical thinking styles they needed to succeed; this cost a lot less than a college degree. No one had to donate plasma seven times a month, and everyone came out successful.

When you live by logical thinking, no one can pull the wool over your eyes. If you look back on your own life, you might recognize that some of your most painful experiences could have been avoided if you simply had the ability to look past people's bullshit.

- Maybe it's something in your marriage (or your divorce).
- Maybe it's those years you lived beyond your means.
- Maybe it's missing out on that job you should have said yes to — the one you chose over the job that *seemed*

too good to pass up, until you quickly figured out that it wasn't.

In any of those events, did someone pull the wool over your eyes? Logical thinking could have prevented it. That's what you want to pass on to your kids, and you can do it without sending them to an institution that costs more than their first house will.

Logic from a Young Lawyer

Back to my college experience. It started, but it didn't finish. Here's the story.

Before it was engineering, my first interest was law school. I thought with my proclivity for reasoning and legendary gift of gab, I could be Perry Mason. But as any honest attorney will tell you, TV law is bullshit. Not only is it impossible to solve a case in 30 to 60 minutes, it's also impossible to work on only one case at a time.

For me, all it took was one young lawyer at a school career day to burst the bubble. Addressing our class of clueless Lakewood High School juniors, he told us that in his career, "You should expect to carry a caseload of 120 files at any given time." Well, there went Perry Mason (or for anyone who wants to be an attorney today, there goes *Law & Order*).

As for law school, "You don't do anything but go to class and study," he said. "You don't have a job; you don't have a girlfriend. All you do is eat, sleep and crap law school; then, you go study for another six months to pass the bar exam." And *then*, after all that, he described how you dive into a career where your success is determined not by how many cases you won, but by how well you managed to balance the aforementioned 10 dozen caseloads at a time — and until you could afford to hire staff, you had to do it all yourself.

Talk about bursting a bubble.

Eventually, I started out in the mortgage business the same way this guy started out as a lawyer. I was on my own for a while before adding on a loan assistant and a partner. As we got better at juggling more and more loans at a time, it grew — and today, I juggle 120 clients at a time with a team of loan officers, loan officer assistants, loan processors, underwriters, doc drawers, funders and compliance people. But while listening to this lawyer at a high school career day, the younger me couldn't fathom carrying 10 dozen litigation clients at a time all by myself — especially if they were, as the majority of lawsuits are, boring as hell. Even as a criminal lawyer, you're not likely to unravel many mysteries and murders. Most likely, you'll spend most of your time prosecuting wife beaters or defending meth addicts.

Now, this poor guy probably had no idea whether any of the 17-year-olds he was trying to impress had future ambitions in the legal profession. He just wanted a captive audience to make him feel important, and why shouldn't he? He had earned it. But unlike him, I promptly decided "no thanks" to a future of no money, no girlfriends and no TV cases. And off I went to Cal State Long Beach to study electrical engineering. All I knew was that the technology and the salary seemed exciting. And unfortunately, that's the way a lot of young people choose their college majors today. If you're a young adult who thinks "going back to school" is your only hope, or you're a parent looking to send your kid to college right out of high school, you need to be aware of that.

CHAPTER 3

IF YOU AREN'T from California, then you might not know there are two state school systems here:

- You have your Cal State schools, also known as the CSU system. This includes Cal State Fullerton, Cal State Northridge, Cal State LA and Cal State Long Beach, among others. I landed at Long Beach, but it was not my first choice; more on that in a minute.
- Then there are UC schools, which are typically thought of as vastly superior to anything Cal State has to offer. They include UC Davis, UC Irvine, UC Riverside, UC Santa Barbara — and of course, UCLA.

If I was so smart, how did I end up in the CSU system? The answer was, as it is for most things, money. Paying my own way through college wasn't something I wanted to do on principle. I would have been happy to let my parents foot the bill, if they were able or willing — but unfortunately, they weren't.

If You Never Work Hard Enough

Here's a little historical backdrop to set the stage. In 1979, Americans were tired of waiting in line for hours just to put gas in their cars. Cut to President Peanut Farmer, whose solution was to lecture us on our so-called "crisis of confidence;" this was just presidential rhetoric for "stop driving so much, stop trying to improve your own lives, accept all these government-mandated solutions, live like wussies for a while and shut up."

During that time, lots of Americans were getting more aggressive about living better. This is what Carter was lecturing us about (how dare we have the audacity to own things!). My dad, Melvin Hoffman, always had a hard time staying on that upwardly mobile train. But as luck would have it, 1978-79 — the year I was tasked with figuring out my future for the first time — was the only year in his entire life that my dad worked *just* hard enough to dis-qualify his kids for any college grant money whatsoever.

Mel was an accountant, but not a CPA; instead, he was an "enrolled agent," or EA. An EA is an accountant who doesn't have much to do when it isn't tax season, and therefore never makes quite as much money as a CPA. My mom always blamed his lack of CPA credentialing on my older brother and sister, Scott and Rene; it was their fault our dad didn't continue his education, because their births somehow prevented it (my siblings must have been the first children in history to be delivered by stork).

The year before I graduated, my dad had taken over someone else's business. He would do this often, absorbing other tax pre-parer's clients when they retired or moved on to do something else (like earn a degree, become a CPA and make real money). He'd restart his own business with that influx, but usually not in a smart way, and very rarely in a way that benefited his family.

When Mel took over another EA's business before I graduated (we'll call that guy Jim), he got a brief cash infusion that would disqualify me for the Cal Grant or any other financial aid. Instead of investing in my education, he invested in remodeling his office. He thought it would impress these new clients — but what my dad didn't understand is that all people really care about is results. Naturally, it wouldn't take long before the new clients would realize that Mel wasn't Jim; Mel was just the guy Jim gave his business to, the guy with the newly furnished office. The next year, they'd take their business somewhere else. Instead of cor-recting his mistake, my dad would repeat the cycle.

The bottom line on my dad was this: He just never worked hard enough. If you *do* work hard enough at whatever it is you do, then opportunities present themselves. And if you use those opportunities wisely, that attracts *more* opportunities. You can keep that upwardly mobile cycle going for as long as you want — or, you can settle for where you are. My dad, after every office remodel, would settle for where he was.

Growing up, I never saw my dad finish anything he started. He'd install cabinets in the laundry room for my mom, but he wouldn't finish the job by putting handles on them. That's a small example, but the point is that he always settled for where he was, at everyone else in the family's expense.

From a young age, I was determined not to settle. I was determined to create my own opportunities. There was only one place I thought could teach me how, and that place was University of California, Los Angeles.

First Taste of College

Years before that young attorney dashed my dreams of starring in a legal drama of my own making — before I had any idea what kind of career I wanted at all, in fact — one thing I knew for sure was that I wanted to go to UCLA. My sister Rene, a straight A student, got in with no problem. When our family visited her there, I was still in junior high school: racing hormones, contorted body, and innocent enough to be in awe of everything I saw.

Maybe a dorm was just a room with two twin beds and a dresser, but that was just the place where you would sleep, study and change your clothes. You walked down a long hallway to a communal bathroom, and along the way there was ping pong... vending machines...*a pool table*! And from what I could tell, the party kept going after you left the residence halls. From my vantage point as an adolescent, college wasn't just a building; college was the entire city of Westwood. Everyone studied together, ate together, slept together, partied together (I wasn't exactly sure what partying *was* at that age, but I knew it was something fun). No wonder everyone talked about going to college!

25

From that point, I wanted in. Since this was my first time setting foot on any campus outside of Lakewood, I had no idea that there were, in fact, other universities one could go to. When it was time to start applying a few years later, I did the PSAT, SAT and whatever forms the guidance counselor put in front of me. It paid off; the class clown was accepted to UCLA.

Then came the great news that my dad had been successful for a single year of his career, which meant no grant money for college. And in those days, there wasn't a student loan to fit every kid and parent (maybe it should have stayed that way).

As much as I wanted to spend the next four years in the citywide utopia of UCLA, I had to accept that the much more affordable Cal State Long Beach was my next best option — because if college was meant to be, paying for it was up to me.

My Teenage Restaurant Career

I relied on lots of jobs to do this, and that was never a problem. I had already been working for years. Like a lot of you, my first "career" was in foodservice.

My first job was at a restaurant called Seafood Broiler (some of their locations became Red Lobster later on, while others became what's now the Market Broiler chain). I was 15, but it was well known at my school that the students who worked in the counselors' office during lunch time could doctor your work permit by "verifying" that your school records said you were 16. Usually, all you had to do was ask.

Most of the kids at Seafood Broiler started out as dishwashers before promoting to busboy, myself included. I think it's important to have fun at work; if you have fun while you work hard, you'll work harder to have *more* fun. And that's what we did there, competing for who could get the most tables bussed in one night.

Seafood Broiler had these huge wine containers that looked like barrels with big plastic tubs inside. It was always the job of one of us busboys to fill those monstrosities up (I guess this predates regulations for minors handling alcohol).

We'd have to take these big gallons of boxed wine (the kind that's in a plastic "bladder" bag inside the box) and pour the wine into the barrels. The way we made it fun was to leave a small amount of wine in the bottom of each bag so there'd be some for later. If the dumpsters were full (they usually were by that time of night), we could leave the boxes around the dumpster instead of tossing them in. That made them more accessible once the night was over. After work, we'd retrieve the boxes and drink whatever left-over wine we had intentionally left in there. Then you'd ride your bike home with a nice little buzz. This was fun, and we worked hard so we could have it night after night.

So clearly, not every hard working kid you hire is going to be your model employee. One night, the owner of Seafood Broiler showed up and announced we needed to clean up for a health department inspection. We stayed for hours after the place was closed, cleaning tiles, counters and floors. I was down on the floor wiping some baseboard tiles behind the salad bar. To support myself, I was leaning on the floor and hanging on the doorway that led from the kitchen to the salad bar. Unaware I was down there, the girl who had been working the salad bar came rushing through the door — and with an audible crunch sound, the hinges smashed through my fingers. The incident had started with me making it clear I was annoyed that we had to stay late on a school night, and it ended with all five of my hand digits throbbing in pain. At that point, I was bitching up a storm. The manager put me out of my misery by saying I was fired.

Lucky for me, getting fired at one mid-range restaurant doesn't always lead to an automatic ban from getting hired at any others. I worked at whatever restaurant would take me: Fiddlers Three, then Reuben's Plankhouse, and eventually back to Seafood Broiler. Ken, the manager, was willing to give me a second chance. "Well, you always were a good dishwasher," Ken told me (and I don't think it hurt that I was ripped enough to carry the highest stacks of plates). I worked my way back through the ranks there: dish-washer, busboy, kitchen prep, until I reached the coveted posi-tion of cook.

What was so prestigious about being a cook at a mid-level casual dining restaurant? At Seafood Broiler, it was the window. Through the window that separated the kitchen from the dining area, the customers could watch you grill their fish. That made the cooks the center of attention, which is a big deal for a kid. Now I had more money, more clout and a pretty cool job for a senior in high school. Then, shortly after graduation, I got fired a second time.

If you've been fired in the recent past, take comfort in the movie quote at the start of this chapter: *"Anybody who ever built an empire, or changed the world, sat where you are now. And it's because they sat there that they were able to do it."* Losing your job is not a failure; it's a rite of passage on the journey to success. If no one ever lost their job, no one would have the opportunity to grow. Sometimes, you *need* to change jobs in order to attain something better. And as much as it sucks, sometimes it has to happen by force.

Entering the World of Sales

That's certainly how it worked out for me, because being forced out of the restaurant world is what propelled me into the world of sales. I started at Montgomery Ward in the tire department.

What made mounting tires fun were the same things that made bussing tables fun: 1) the physicality, and 2) competing with your friends. The other tire busters and I would compete to see who was fastest at mounting and balancing four tires. We would set the clock and count down: "Ready, set, go!" You didn't stop until the tires touched the ground. The whole time I worked there, I held the record at 13 minutes. Like being watched behind the glass at Seafood Broiler, being the only white kid in this entry level staff of tire busters gave me added attention — so, I made sure to stand out for a different reason. Winning a silly tire mounting competition is how I chose to do that. Wherever you work, you can find a way to stand out for your accomplishments too. It sure beats standing out for your skin color or other traits you don't control.

Unfortunately, I got fired for something I *could* control: being an asshole. I could tell that Joe — my fat, moustache-faced, mullet-haired, weed-smoking-at-work boss — had been looking for a reason to fire me for quite some time, and eventually I gave him one. Sensing his dislike for me, I always had some smartass remark when Joe was around (my production was high, but my citizenship was unsatisfactory). He found some minor infraction and I was out.

At that point, I sensed a pattern:

- Something undesirable happened.
- I mouthed off.
- I got fired.

It was clear something about me needed to change at my next job. But I decided to stay with sales, and to stay with tires, because I had gotten pretty good at both. I found a job at Mark C. Bloome, a company whose slogan was, "How can you get the right tires if you don't have a choice?" Taglines were a little long back then.

At Mark C. Bloome, I made a better impression on the bosses. I started by mounting tires again, but was quickly promoted to tire sales person and then the management tracks; I was "third man" at the Long Beach store, then "second man" (more or less an assistant manager) at the Carson store. Then they moved me to Bellflower, which worked out because it was closer to my parents' house. They didn't send me around to other locations because I was a pain in the ass; they did it because they knew I could give each location a much-needed energy boost. I was being promoted up the line and everyone said I was upper management material. Things were looking good for me this time.

Then came one Sunday, when it all ended because of someone else's desperation. Another firing was about to go down, and this time it wasn't even my fault.

A guy named Randy and I were working the shop that day. Because this was back when people paid cash for things, we often had a lot of money in the register. That Sunday, we had too much cash on hand before the day was even halfway over. Ideally, you made the cash drops one at a time throughout the day; usually, you would do it every time the register count reached $500. But because things were rocking and rolling that day and neither of us paused to make a drop, we ended up with three drops totaling about $3,000. Not the best protocol, but these things happen when you get busy. Unfortunately, *this* thing didn't end there.

As the guy in charge that day, I told Randy, "Make a cash drop, but use separate envelopes so it looks like we made separate drops." That seemed logical. Here's how the drops worked (an important detail): You'd put your cash in a bank bag, open up the safe door and drop it into a chute in the floor. The chute closed on one end when you opened it up on the other. Randy put all the envelopes in at the same time and closed the door to the chute. We closed the shop, called it a day and went home, thinking nothing was amiss and proud that we had sold our asses off.

Unfortunately, neither of us knew the envelopes got stuck — but even that wasn't the real problem. The real problem was Alan, the cokehead who ran the mechanic department for the entire Mark C. Bloome chain. The managers trusted him, but those of us who worked the floor saw his addiction. After Randy and I closed the store, Alan and his addiction happened to stay behind...with three envelopes of cash stuck in the chute, unbeknownst to us. The next day, I got a call from a company vice president. When he told me to meet him at the corporate office in Torrance right away, I had no idea why. Here's how that meeting went:

Him: "So, yesterday you made your drops...1,2,3."
Me: "Yeah."
Him: "They totaled $3000."
Me: "Yeah."
Him: "What'd you do with it?"
Me: "What do you mean?"

It had all disappeared. I didn't steal it; Randy didn't steal it. Alan and his addiction stole it, all $3000. But they didn't believe me.

And so, at 18 years old, I was hooked up to a polygraph machine by my employer. Today, there's a polygraph scene in every crime show and movie — but in those days, nobody knew what a polygraph was (even today, people still call it a "lie detector test").

As a teenager in 1980, having electrodes connected over your entire upper body in order to detect your lies was pretty intimidating. They did the same thing to Randy, and we both knew it was Alan the cokehead who took the money. But guess who got fired? That's right.

My advice for someone in that position: If you have to handle that much money at work, prioritize the responsibilities you're tasked with. A management position requires you to protect more than just your paycheck. In today's world, kids would be lawyering up — but 40 years ago, that wasn't the case. After that, it took a while to get another job. As it turns out, accusations of theft can spread around and get you blacklisted (go figure).

Eventually, I was hired to work graveyard shifts at the AM/PM, getting paid under the table. I felt bad that it wasn't honest and I had to find time to sleep around the job and my classes — but since I was paying for my own gasoline, dates and school and no other tire shops would hire me, what choice did I have? Fortunately, this routine only lasted six months.

That's when the kid next door told me about Sears. He had a second job there and could help me get hired on in the tire department. They would listen to my side of the story and give me a chance. Never underestimate the power of personal testimony! The neighbor kid helped me get the interview, but I got myself the job. I told them the whole story: working my way up at the other stores, selling my ass off, loving my job and losing it because of Alan the cokehead.

They let me get my foot in the door as a tire buster. Within a month, I was moved up to the lube rack. The next month, I was promoted to a service writer (another "like an assistant manager" position). From 1982-86, I kept tons of customers happy and had fun doing it. In '84, I was promoted to assistant manager. That's the beginning of my Sears story, which led to the end of my college education and the beginning of my real adulthood.

CHAPTER 4

YOU MAY ONLY know Sears as a relic of the past that's been pushed into department store obscurity. But the Sears that's bankrupt and closing stores across the country today is not the Sears of the 70s and 80s; back then, there was nowhere more prestigious to have your tires replaced or your oil changed, not to mention where you bought your appliances and tools. Americans loved everything about Sears then, even if they didn't realize the tagline "Satisfaction Guaranteed" was etched in the glass above every door (which it was).

Lessons from Sears University

More than once, I was sent to management training at the West Coast corporate headquarters in Alhambra (Sears employees used to call it "The Cube," and architecture appreciators still call it "The Blue Cube").

At The Cube, Sears educated you for one week while you wore a tie. We learned management insights that weren't necessarily sexy, but they made sense. Here's one of the biggest takeaways I remember and employ regularly in my own business:

The average Sears customer will spend $48,000 here over their lifetime, on everything from Goodrich tires to DieHard batteries, *and from Craftsman tools to Kenmore appliances — so, we don't want to lose someone over a $100 brake job or a $50 battery.*

If someone is unhappy, just make them happy.
If they're unhappy with the tire you put on, give them a new one.
If they're unhappy with their oil change, refund their money.

Be the bigger person at all times.

Be the bigger person. That can be hard in some relationships — but in business, it's your lifeline. And that's what I still try to do today. If someone will be giving me repeat business over their lifetime, I don't want to ruin it over something trivial.

One time, legendary basketball coach Pat Riley came to speak to us at The Cube. He talked about what a difference Magic Johnson made to the Los Angeles Lakers when he was first drafted to the team in 1979 (it turns out that year wasn't only about my high school graduation and the Peanut Farmer's crisis of confidence lecture). By then, Kareem Abdul-Jabbar was at a point when he could have retired — but Magic infused enthusiasm, spirit and vitality to the team that gave the old timers the energy to keep going for several more years. In the end, Kareem kept going for another decade. It was an attitude thing, and Magic had it. I'm not a spectator sports guy, but I recognized the lesson: *Having the right attitude can change the environment you work in. Your attitude regulates your altitude.*

Another seminar we got at The Cube was given by Lou Ferrigno, star of The Incredible Hulk. Lou suffered so many ear infections as a child that he lost 80% of his hearing. It also prompted a lot of bullying: "They used to call me 'deaf Louie, deaf mute', because of my hearing and because of the way I sounded,"[41] he said. Bodybuilding was his escape — and because he couldn't afford to buy weights, he made his own with a broom and two buckets filled with cement. It was an attitude thing, and it helped him accomplish greatness.

You don't have to go to formal training to learn how to achieve, manage or lead. There were lots of colleagues I learned from along the way, too — ordinary guys I sold tires with, repaired flats with, goofed off with. One of them was Al Jones, a cool black guy with prescription sunglasses and Jheri curls. Al taught me that the easiest money was on the upsell. For example: For every Dunlap tire we'd sell them, we got a $3 bonus spiff (like a flat fee commission). Then we'd show them the next model up, which was a $6 spiff. We'd gently continue stepping them into the next level of product until they verbally told us to stop. Thanks to Al at Mark C. Bloome, who was twice my age, I learned a powerful sales strategy at 21 years old that I've never lost sight of. He also gave me this bit of wisdom:

When someone pulls a tire out of their trunk for a repair, you don't know who they are.

They might have one flat tire.
They might need a full set and this is just the tire that kept them from driving.
Or, all four tires might be flat.

Before you know which one it is, you treat everybody the same.

When a new customer or client walks in your door, you don't know what you'll be getting out of them. Before you find out what you're getting, treat everyone the same.

Good thoughts, good words, good deeds...no matter who you're dealing with.

At Montgomery Ward, the guys I learned from were Clay and Willie. One Thanksgiving morning, we worked a tire sale from 9 AM to noon. We were only busy for a short time, so there was plenty of time to talk. Willie would use any downtime at work to read the Bible, but Clay, who was black, loud and proud, declared that he would be going home to a barbeque when we were done. I was confused. "Don't you mean Thanksgiving dinner?" I said. "Turkey?"

"Man, that's for white people," Clay said. "I don't even like turkey."

At Sears, I had a manager named Bob Baine. Because Bob knew I was being looked at for management, he shared this bit of wisdom.

There are six things you have to learn in management:

- *Repeat, repeat, repeat...*
- *Remind, remind, remind.*

Having managed people for about three decades now, I can confirm that this is accurate.

When I was running a staff of more than 80 employees, I used this advice from Bob constantly. But it's the same whether you're managing 80 people or eight. You may have told an employee something last week, but that doesn't mean you'll never have to tell them again. Instead of blowing your top at them the first time they need a repeat, give them as many times as they need to let it soak in. It's the same with kids.

This applies whether you're managing salesmen, mechanics or people who pick up the trash. Everyone will do the minimum they can get away with to still keep their job. What you're looking for is the one person who doesn't have to be reminded all the time — the one who looks for ways to do more. That's who you want to promote.

Another Sears manager I learned from was George. He said this about success in sales: *If you don't ask for it, you don't get it.* It sounds obvious, but think of it this way: The guy who stands on the corner asking every woman who walks by if she wants to get laid, is at some point going to get laid. If you ask everybody, somebody will eventually say yes. He gets kicked, punched and screamed at (and rightfully so) — but he also gets laid more than anyone else.

Not a Model Employee

Just like I wasn't a model employee as a teenage busboy, I wasn't a model employee as a salesman. My production continued to be unusually high, but my attitude continued to be less-than-great. To elaborate:

- I was still a smart ass.
- When there was nothing to do, I'd hang out on the sales floor talking to people and distracting them from their work.
- I also had a problem with authority.

Does that sound like someone you'd hire? Probably not. But let's be honest: This is the attitude of most high achievers. It's also the same attitude that helped me realize I needed to be my own boss instead. I was the only one I could depend on to not fire me.

My attitude was, "You're my boss, cool. But when I'm not working, we're buds...equals in our downtime." Some of them were okay with that, some weren't. Maybe I didn't understand respect as well as I should have — but even now, I believe that if you say something in the heat of battle, it's alright. The important thing is that we understand each other at the end of the day.

I don't think most people want to work in an environment where anything they say could be reported to HR at any moment. People deserve to be themselves at work. The American workplace has lost that freedom, and I'm afraid it's never coming back.

CHAPTER 5

THE GOVERNMENT HAS no way of making you rich. If you want to be rich, it's *your* job to make that happen.

"But...but...what about that thing in the Declaration of Independence?"

Oh, *this* thing?

We hold these truths to be self-evident, that all men are created equal, that they are endowed by their Creator with certain unalienable Rights, that among these are Life, Liberty and the pursuit of Happiness.[43]

Yeah, what about it?

If you misunderstand its meaning, you're not alone. Constitutional scholars have been arguing the meaning of this "happiness principle" in the preamble for close to a century. More recently, liberal pundits in the last couple of decades have used it to add substance to their claims that the government should provide Americans with access to everything from:

- Free healthcare
- Affordable housing
- Universal basic income of $1,000 a month
- Free college

After all, don't those things make us happy? Well, not quite. These things make you feel secure, and security is certainly one piece of happiness.

But that wasn't the point of the happiness principle — or *any* part of the Declaration, for that matter. The Declaration isn't about all the things government *should* do; it's about all the things the government *shouldn't* do, or doesn't have to do. In other words, it's about *limiting* the responsibilities of government, which in turn limits the *power* of government.

Government only exists to 1) enforce the laws and 2) protect us from our enemies, from within and without. That's it. They're not in charge of creating happiness; they're in charge of creating an environment where we can pursue our own happiness. In turn, you get *more* happiness when you know you created it yourself.

So, the pursuit of happiness does *not* work like this:

- You're a person living in America, legally or otherwise.
- You receive ongoing government handouts for the achievement of existing in our society.
- You get happy.

It *does* work like this:

- You're a law abiding American citizen.
- You get your own job, start your own business, create your own opportunities.
- You make your own money, pay your own way, support your own family.
- If you want to make *more* money, you work harder, which creates more opportunities.
- In the process of doing those things, you become happy.

It's as simple as it sounds, and you won't only hear it from me. You can also hear it from the director of *Taxi Driver*, *Goodfellas*, *Gangs of New York*, *The Departed* and *The Wolf of Wall Street* (among many other films, but those are my favorites and I'd say that's a pretty good list). While promoting the last film in 2013, he said this:

"When I was growing up, I don't remember being told that America was created so that everyone could get rich. I remember being told it was about opportunity and the pursuit of happiness. Not happiness itself, but the pursuit."[44]

- Martin Scorsese

Makes sense? Here's a more academic take (that's not my thing, but maybe it's yours).

Philip Booth is a British economist who has studied the idea of the government playing a role in its citizens' happiness. "The government should focus on creating the meta-framework of institutions that give us the freedom to flourish and improve our wellbeing. In other words the government should not be trying to 'maximise happiness' but facilitating the pursuit of happiness," he said.[45]

It's a more scholastic way of phrasing something I say often: People are happiest when the government gets out of their way so they can conduct business in the free market and be in charge of their own prosperity (the free market always works. What *doesn't* always work is people).

They're happiest when they have the untethered ability to earn money. While some people may not realize this, getting hand-outs doesn't make them happy. The pursuit of happiness isn't about getting a check. It's about feeling like you're contributing to society, because God put you on this earth for a reason. They're happiest when they feel secure — and, in fact, they *need* to feel secure. As long as that security is coming from the government, it's not real. When you don't know how long your sense of security will continue, it's false.

When you know what people need, you can reverse engineer how to provide it. So, here's what you get when you reverse engineer security. To feel secure, people need the government to:

- **Stay calm.** This is something the legislative branch of the government has utterly failed at for the past four years, fueled by their endless quest to destroy the head

of the executive branch (the president — who, prior to the election fraud of 2020, was Donald Trump).
- **Keep the economy going.** When I began writing this, we were in month five of COVID-induced-quarantine-economic-shutdown-mass-hysteria. So, another government failure (and, one most likely fueled by the same motivations).

Lucky for Americans, government misconceptions about what people need to be happy are not unique to the United States. Our special friends across the pond suffer from the same illness.

Booth has written at length about former Prime Minister David Cameron's notorious obsession with the concept of making the British people happy. When growth figures were still promising before the economic crash of 2008-09, Cameron famously said this: "It's time we admitted that there's more to life than money, and it's time we focused not just on GDP but on GWB – general wellbeing."[46]

How inspiring. Unfortunately for the people of Great Britain, that's not the government's job.

It's too bad Cameron managed to get elected to the highest office in the United Kingdom without understanding that wellbeing is hard to sustain when you don't have any money to live on. Maybe that's one reason for the Brexit referendum of 2016, when British citizens voted 52% to 48% in favor of a mass exodus from the European Union. With more than 30 million people making their voices heard, it was the UK's highest voter turnout in 25 years.

Of course, the other reason behind their eagerness for change was their realization that unfettered immigration didn't deliver the utopia that was promised to them. All it took was around 700 terror attacks on their soil from 2006 to 2016 to figure that out (and it's too bad the Democrat party in the U.S. *still* hasn't figured it out). The British people had enough of their leaders permitting this, aided by the fact that their government belonged to yet *another* form of government above it in the EU. Some brave citizens asked the question, "When does it end?" and the people answered, "It ends *now*."

Four years before Brexit, Philip Booth wrote a message to Prime Minister Cameron and those who would govern like him: Government cannot make us happy, period.

He's absolutely right. But why...*why* can't government make us happy?

Booth believes it's because decisions about our happiness involve tradeoffs. "For one person, working longer hours and saving in order to get a deposit on a house — so he can have somewhere independent to live with his family — might improve that family's well-being."[47] Let's use this scenario and call it Decision A.

Meanwhile, the decision might be different for someone else. "For another person, spending more time with the family and less time at work might improve that family's well-being." We'll use this as another option and call it Decision B.

For me, happiness used to mean A (working longer hours to improve my family's well-being). Based on how I was brought up, I vowed to never put my family in the same position I grew up in by repeating the cycle of what I saw my dad to our family Now that I've improved their well-being many times over, happiness means B (spending less time at work to keep my wife happy. Personally, I love working — but "happy wife, happy life" is a mantra I take seriously. I highly recommend that!).

Because of the work I've built my livelihood on, I'm admittedly very biased — but I'll say it anyway, because it might help you: If you have not yet purchased a home, then doing something to change that could be one of your best decisions on the road to happiness. I'm pretty successful, but I'm not the only one you'll hear this from. When one of the top 10 mortgage lenders in the nation releases a consumer survey in its quarterly report that concludes homeownership leads to happiness, that's a pretty good indication that it does.

If you're like me — you've bought and sold many houses, already reached the apex of your career and need to spend *more* time at home rather than less — then for you, happiness may be achieved by winding things down a bit (unless you choose to work until your dying breath because you believe *that* will make you happy.

If so, that's your right as well. Try comparing these two ideas and see which one you identify with more:

1. "Whoever dies with the most toys wins."
2. "Whoever dies with the youngest body wins."

The way I see it is, what's the point of having the money if you don't take the time to enjoy it? Now, don't take this the wrong way; I'm not saying live like you have the money before you have it. The truth is, God won't give you the desires of your heart until you've earned them.

Personally, I plan to continue working but deliberately take more time off to enjoy the wealth I have now. For someone who isn't used to vacations, that's a big choice.

The decisions about what make us happy are deeply personal, and only we as individuals can make them for ourselves. Ultimately, it comes down to this: *Nobody knows your life better than you, nobody knows what you need better than you, and the government can't legislate your happiness.*

CHAPTER 6

IF I WENT from auto service management to the million-aire mortgage king, that wouldn't make much sense. Good thing that's not what happened for me, and good thing it's not what will happen for you.

Almost inevitably, the path from whatever industry you start out in to whatever industry you build your wealth on won't be a straight line. Nearly everyone makes a left turn or two along the way — but fortunately, those stops can be rich opportunities for learning your strengths, building your skills and sharpening your approach. In other words, every chapter of your life prepares you for the next step toward the person you'll someday become. Here's how that worked out for me.

One day during my second year at Cal State Long Beach, a guy named Bill walked into my Sears service department and asked us to check out a noise coming from the suspension of his Cadillac. So we could duplicate and diagnose the issue, I hopped into Bill's car with him and went for a ride. You can learn a lot about a person in small talk exchanges like this — and if you look beyond the surface of the conversation, you can learn a lot about life.

Bill said he was an engineer at The Hughes Aircraft Company (the defense contractor founded in 1932 by Howard Hughes himself). It was only natural for me to reply that I was an engineering student myself.

And just like how that young attorney got me re-thinking the idea of becoming a lawyer back in high school, Bill said something that opened my eyes about what I could look forward to if I were to graduate college and pursue an engineering career.

"You'll start at $30,000" (a decent starting salary back then), "but I've been doing this for 10 years. I'm topped out at $55,000, unless I go into management."

So far, this didn't sound so bad. Then he kept going.

"Once you go into management, you're expected to work 55 to 60 hours a week."

There it was again, just like career day at Lakewood High School. But this time — instead of a young lawyer's reality of "no job, no girlfriend, no life" before graduation and 120 caseloads at a time after — I was hearing that an engineer's lifestyle was fueled by a moderate income for the first decade, but the expectation that you'll happily progress toward a 60-hour workweek in exchange for a slightly larger income was just around the corner. And, he said, that expectation would follow you the rest of your career. Yikes.

Bill wasn't whining to a stranger; he was just stating his reality. He had climbed the corporate ladder and was gravely disappointed with what he saw at the top. I tried to act like it didn't bother me, but it certainly got me thinking. Is this what I wanted *my* life to look like? I decided to become open-minded to other options, and that's when those left turns appeared.

The first one was Amway, an organization that's either highly esteemed or highly notorious, depending on who you talk to. Personally, I was attracted to the positive attitudes and ambition I encountered there. For those who don't know: Amway is full of motivational organizations, and these organizations operate separately from the corporation that manufactures its consumable products (laundry soap, vitamins, toiletries, etc.). About once a month, you attend meetings ("functions") at a local hotel conference room to hear speakers and stay motivated. The speakers are people who have achieved some level of success with the model.

That's a neutral, nutshell-sized overview of the experience. You can meet people who found incredible success with it and people who didn't, and that will almost certainly influence the way they describe it to you.

I found very little success with it financially, and that outcome seems to be the majority one. It was a positive experience regardless; for one thing, I learned valuable lessons. One of them is this:

I am the most ambitious person I know.

I know how that sounds, but it's not just an arrogant observation about myself. It's a fact that helped me understand how a model that required me to recruit people to do what I was doing was probably not going to work out. The wholesale buying club model was not inherently bad, but people weren't ambitious enough to get on board for the full experience. This lesson showed me when it was time to move on.

But in the meantime, the organization taught me other truths about life. The most powerful one was this metaphor I heard one of the speakers use:

"By the time you've climbed the corporate ladder, you realize the ladder's leaned against the wrong wall."

That hit me like a ton of bricks. All of a sudden, the two reality checks I'd been exposed to added up:

1. What I heard from the career day lawyer who needed to impress teenagers to convince himself he hadn't thrown his life away.
2. What I heard from Bill, the engineer who said my future wasn't what I thought it was.

I immediately started to rethink what I wanted to do with my life — and while I wasn't sure what it was yet, I *was* sure of these things:

1. I wanted to do something significant.
2. Whatever it was, it probably wouldn't require an engineering degree.

Since this realization happened at an Amway function, it seemed like that was a sign that Amway would be my vehicle. I did it hard for two years: showing the business model in people's living rooms, drawing the Venn diagram circles, buying the overpriced soap. In the first year, I made no money; in the second year, my best month yielded an impressive profit of $128.

Clearly, this was not the vehicle. But unlike most people who share this experience, I have nothing bad to say about it.

To start, I loved the motivational program. The mental and emotional training you get from reading books on leadership and listening to audio tapes on success can be valuable no matter what you end up doing. This training taught me these critical lessons:

- *Some will, some won't, so what. You carry on.*
- *By serving other people, God will pay you back through people; not necessarily the **same** people.*
- *If you can control your attitude, you can control your life.*

That last one is something I still tell people today. It sounds simple, but don't discount it. Here's an example of how I used my attitude to control my life.

I've come to the realization that it takes eight hours to get through an eight hour work day. You can A) kill time or B) work it to death. If you want success, you'll choose B. For everything I've done, I've always put that kind of effort. Whether or not I get the results I want, it always opens another door or gives me a vision for the next step. As you move through my anecdotes here, you'll see examples of that.

Another thing I learned from the Amway experience was the importance of making the most of every moment. Another lesson I got from the training was this: The person *you will eventually become is based on the books you read and the people you spend time with.*

That lesson got me thinking about the people I associated with. I didn't outright tell my friends I couldn't hang out with them anymore, but examining the product of my life got me questioning which things were productive uses of my time. For instance, I started looking differently at my friends who were hardcore sports fans. I realized they were so tied up in someone else's success that they didn't bother focusing on their own. Sound like anyone you know? I bet it does.

I also started thinking about my employer — not necessarily my experience there, but what it had to offer the consumer. Sears had higher prices than the warehouse stores that were starting to enter the market, and yet people were still shopping there (for the time being). Why were their prices higher? It's because, unlike a warehouse store, Sears had to pay for:

- Well-appointed buildings with elevators, escalators, tons of lighting and powerful HVAC.
- Premium anchor store spaces at high end mall properties all over the country.
- Seasonal TV advertising, weekly print marketing materials and a giant annual catalog that was no longer profitable.

So how was it surviving in the market? I believe there were three factors:

- Sears offered a satisfaction guarantee. This was a big deal when it came to big purchases on appliances or expensive tools.
- Sears had financing options — *also* a big deal on those purchases.
- For some families, Sears was an American tradition.

However, the mid-80s was the beginning of a growing movement of American consumer awareness. People were starting to realize they didn't need the well-appointed building with brighter lights to have a pleasant buying experience. They figured out that going to the mall to get a new car battery wasn't always the most convenient option. And if they were really smart, they started to understand that the cost of printing the catalog was being passed onto them in the form of high product markups.

If it sounds like I'm making the case for the multi-level marketing (MLM) model, I'm not. In fact, I started to realize that Amway was doing the very same thing. They marked up products higher than most middle income people could afford; just like Sears, it was to cover their costs. But unlike Sears, Amway's costs weren't tied to advertising or storefronts.

Here's the truth: If Amway's products were affordable, then no one would make any money when they reached those prestigious levels. And if there's no money to be made, why would anyone bother? It makes sense on its face, but how do you explain to someone who's struggling to pay their bills that they should buy a $20 box of soap they can get for $5 somewhere else (in twice the size)?

Still, I wasn't opposed to the MLM model on principle. But I certainly wasn't seeing a return that would justify my substantial time investment. I could read the same books, learn the same lessons, and be just as success-minded without leaving my new son behind night after night to stand in someone else's living room drawing circles. I made the exit from Amway, and 35 years later there are no regrets.

The next time I was introduced to a new MLM, I dove in again — but this time, the commodity made a lot more sense to me. It happened one day in 1985, when my old friend Barry Campbell stopped by my Sears office in Riverside in the middle of the day. Barry had been a manager at Sav-on Drugs, working in Monterey Park and living in Walnut. So, I wondered, what was he doing 50 miles from home and 40 miles from work in the middle of a weekday?

"Barry!" I said. "How's Sav-On treating you?"

He was excited. "I'm not at Sav-On anymore," he said.

"Oh yeah? What are you doing now?"

He said a name I had heard before, but didn't know much about: "A.L. Williams."

I wasn't sure what A.L. Williams sold or why I should want it; all I knew was that after doing it for a year, Barry was able to quit his full time job at Sav-On. When he came to my house that night for a basic flip chart presentation, I learned the commodity was life insurance. The hook was simple: "Buy term and invest the difference."[49] I had talked to the Allstate guys at Sears about life insurance, so I had some knowledge about using it as an investment tool in addition to its primary function as a financial legacy strategy.

Barry's presentation made sense as he was speaking, and it made even more sense when I pulled out the little printout from the Allstate agent that he had given to me the week before — still being carried around in the stack of stuff in my shirt pocket. Compared to the $92 a month whole life insurance policy the Allstate guy at Sears was trying to sell me, this was a no brainer.

For $32 a month, I could get term life insurance with four times the amount of financial protection for my family in the instance of my untimely death. But as a good salesman, and knowing that sales people are easily sold, I needed to see how normal people responded to this before diving in.

After carrying the printout in my shirt pocket for a few days and thinking about what I'd seen, I asked him to let me go along on another presentation. He did arrange for me to go along with someone — but oddly, it wasn't him. As a 24-year-old, it was a little awkward to be picked up by two middle aged housewives and sit in the backseat on the way to my first shot at success. But sometimes, it's those unexpected events that end up being significant. So off I went with two older women I'd never met to watch them present the A.L. Williams life insurance opportunity.

One of the housewives was presenting to the couple we were meeting; the other one was there to learn like I was. I watched the faces of this couple as the lady who drove us conducted the world's most boring business presentation, reading the flip chart slowly, word for word, with no improvisation or changes in voice inflection whatsoever.

The couple was not engaged with her at all, but they slowly got interested as the flip chart explained why bundling life insurance and savings was a flawed concept. Eventually, the wife got up from the table. *What was happening?* She walked out of the room, came back and threw their two existing cash value life insurance policies down on the table. "Show me if that's what we have," she said. She wanted to know if the policies they currently had were not as valuable as they had been led to believe. The housewife presenter confirmed it: Their policies were the same contracts that she had been warning the couple against — the ones that were not in the best financial interests of the buyers. Instead, they were great for the financial interests of the insurance companies and agents that sold them. After seeing this, the couple was sold on A.L. Williams — and so was I.

A.L. Williams wasn't my full time job yet, but it didn't take long before I was easily making $2,000 a month part time. Lots of the books in their support program were the same ones I had been reading, and they had their own tapes too — so, there was plenty of material to keep me on the right track. When you're playing the sales game, it doesn't matter whether you're selling insurance, laundry soap, houses or cars; when you listen to people more than you talk, focus on overcoming their objections and keeping your personal attitude under control, the techniques are all the same. That's what all those books and tapes help you do.

But this time, it wasn't just the motivational material I was attracted to; it was also the product I would be selling. I'm not talking about life insurance. I was selling an intangible product: my intentions. That's important; if you're a salesperson, understand it applies to you also.

You're not just selling a product. You're selling your intentions.

While you have a product to sell, the most important thing is to sell your intentions. If you have a tangible product that people want, you don't have to sell it to them at all. You have to sell them your intentions, so that people will want to buy it from *you*. The tangible product was life insurance, but life insurance represented the necessary evil of "just in case" death protection, along with a savings vehicle that worked in the best interest of the person paying for it. The intangible product, my intention, was to help clients make the right decisions for themselves. Once they bought into my intentions being sound, they were putty in my hands.

Today, I don't sell mortgages; I sell my intentions to help my clients get the right home loan for themselves. For me, intangibles are easier to sell and more valuable than any tangible product.

When I sat down with people, I would help them see that in the event of an untimely death, the surviving spouse would need a certain amount of money to continue supporting the family. I would show them how to get as much as they needed, for as long as they needed it, and for as cheap as they could get it. Then, I'd show them how they could also use their savings from the expensive whole life insurance to invest for their future, completely separate from the insurance policy or company. But here's why I really loved doing it:

- **It made so much sense.** "Buy term, invest the difference" is a concept financial gurus (Dave Ramsey, Suze Orman and others) still promote today.
- **People understood the risk.** And more importantly, they accepted it. Life insurance is like a bet: You're betting you're going to die. The company is betting you're going to live. You spend the rest of your life trying to lose that bet. And either way, your family benefits.
- **I wasn't under any pressure to make money.** I never closed on the first appointment, and that was intentional. When people smell desperation, they run from it.

Plus, the writing was on the wall for me at my Sears job. First, because I had already sold life insurance policies to all my employees (afterhours), and the Allstate guy was starting to complain. Second, because once they made me a salaried employee, I lost the ability to get overtime pay (how backwards is it that you can make less money on a salary?). Third, because I had already exhausted all the company benefits. In those days, a Sears manager could do just about anything with the blue credit card they gave you, including furnishing your whole house (which I did).

Today, Sears is still dying the slowest, most painful death of any retailer in history — but what most people don't realize is that this death was 50 years in the making. As the company stretched itself thin with Allstate, Dean Witter and Discover Card, its retail operations were beginning to suffer and downsizing was imminent. Now that consumers were becoming more aware of their options, Sears saw their model aging out; by the mid-80s, people had lots of retailers to choose from for appliances, power tools and tires. Sears was a great American tradition, but tradition will only keep people buying from you for so long.

The company began offering some of the full-timers varying degrees of severance pay in exchange for a voluntary resignation. I was offered seven weeks, and I took it.

At the same time this was going on, I had a second baby on the way. Severance pay is a thin cushion for anyone who gets it; in my case, it was also a loudly ticking clock. But before I took it, I took two weeks' vacation; one week to help take care of two babies, and one week to look for a new job.

I landed at a Pontiac dealership as a service writer, where I got a 50% raise over what I had made at Sears, plus an assurance that it was not a conflict of interest if I sold insurance policies after-hours. I *had* to continue selling them; if I didn't, I couldn't pay my bills. You do what you have to do.

This arrangement worked out great...for all of two months.

My Sears boss, Joe, had warned me: Dealerships pay well, but new managers always bring on their own service writers. When that happens, you're out looking for a job again. Did that happen to me? Of course it did. When they brought in a slick new guy from LA, I was the last one to go.

Since I was already making $2,000 a month at A.L. Williams part time, I was sure I could double my efforts and make $4,000. So I leaned in hard, doing it full time for six months. Remember when I said I felt no pressure to make money in the beginning? Now, I was feeling *enormous* pressure to make money — and of course, it showed. When I first started, people were so eager to get on board; before I could finish my "Buy term and invest the difference" presentation, they were ready to sign up. Of course, I purposely would not close on the first appointment.

Now, their behavior was different. They started telling me things like, "We need to sleep on it." They sensed that I badly needed to close these sales, and it turned them off. But with a second mortgage on my house, a $9,000 balance on that Sears card and an overpriced freezer in the garage that came with a side of beef, it was hard to hide my desperation. Eventually, the rug was pulled out from under me. Time to go back to work at another auto dealership.

It worked out great at first. At the Nissan dealership in Corona, I was killing it at around $3,500 a month. Plus, because my aura of desperation evaporated, I started to sell insurance policies again too. But that's when I learned another lesson, and this time it was a painful one:

With every floor, comes a ceiling.

It happened when Nissan Manager Dave called me into his office. The meeting went something like this:

"Hey Ed! You had a really great month."

"Thanks, Dave!"

"When you go home tonight, I'd like you to think about what you want your new pay plan to be."

"Um...why do I want a *new* pay plan?"

Dave was telling me something I was hearing for the first time: There was a cap on how successful you were allowed to be. All of a sudden, I had gone from making nothing to making too much.

I had performed, and they didn't want to pay me for it. They weren't changing everyone's pay plan; they were only changing mine. These lessons were starting to add up, and they weren't going down smoothly anymore. Unfortunately, I let it change my attitude — and as a result, I was eventually asked to leave.

I say "unfortunately" because I should have behaved better, but it was actually a good thing. It was one more clear sign that the only employment I wanted was self-employment. I had seen the limits of working for someone else plenty of times by now. People don't think you should be able to make that much money at 25. They think you haven't earned it, even when you have. Having learned all of this the hard way, I knew it was time to be my own boss permanently.

When it came time to go back to a job, I never did. Take note, though: This isn't meant to be an MLM success story. I didn't stay with A.L. Williams permanently (if you haven't yet figured this out, A.L. Williams is the company now called Primerica Financial Services).

Instead, it's an illustration of those left turns I mentioned earlier. I'm not comparing myself to Saul on the road to Damascus, but I will say that God put these experiences in my path to help open my eyes. And the same thing can happen for you, if you *allow* it to happen.

For me, here was the result:

- Both of my MLM experiences nurtured my desire to build wealth.
- Both experiences taught me a different way of thinking that helped me build that wealth.
- I got introduced to good salespeople and good leaders, which showed me how to become a good salesman and good leader myself.
- A.L. Williams is where I first learned how to provide financial services. Even as a math whiz, I had never learned to translate that skill into understanding money — and it's hard to succeed as a mortgage lender if you don't know how money works.

Here's how powerful that was: Before A.L. Williams, I didn't even understand the concept of refinancing your house; no one had ever explained it to me. I learned it all there. Today, helping people refinance their houses is a huge part of what I do. So I feel a lot of gratitude, and you'll probably realize there are things you learned in your first jobs or ventures that opened bigger doors for you down the road.

That whole experience really opened my eyes to how life works. But the most important thing is that it led me to my wife.

56

CHAPTER 7

"You outwork, out-think, out-scheme and out-maneuver. You make no friends and trust nobody. And you make damn sure you're the smartest guy in the room whenever the subject of money comes up."[50]
- Cocktail, 1988

AFTER THAT FINAL termination at the auto dealership, I came to the conclusion that I wasn't a very good employee. That doesn't mean I was a bad worker; it meant that I worked hard, but observed and thought too much. I saw things that didn't make sense, and although no one had asked for my input or opinion — as Ron White would say, "I had the right to remain silent...I just didn't have the ability"[51]...ever!

I was better-suited for self-employment. If you feel you aren't being listened to or acknowledged by your employer, even though you work hard and you have a hunger for success, then maybe you're at the wrong employer — or, maybe self-employment is a better fit for you too. For me — since this seemed to be a regular thing with just about every employer — my best option was the latter.

And at that time, there was no other job to fall back on and no money in savings — so suffice it to say that I was pretty motivated. I also had two small kids at home (and unbeknownst to me at the time, I was less than a year or two away from raising them on my own). The day your first child is born, your license to be selfish gets revoked for a good 18–30 years. This is why I say raising kids to adulthood is the best way to acquire wisdom. Before I get excited about any presidential candidate, I always check into how old their kids are for this very reason.

Having no job was bad for me *and* my kids, but having no savings was worse. Here's why savings are important.

I'll start with an example everyone can relate to: If you have no money in savings and you need some kind of emergency auto repair — say, a flat tire or a cracked radiator — it blows your whole budget. Credit cards are helpful, but you still have to pay them back. And if you haven't disciplined yourself to save, then you probably haven't disciplined yourself to pay down your credit cards.

Here's an example for those who are a little further along: If you put all your money into an investment property and don't leave yourself some cash reserves, then you'll put yourself in a bind the moment a water heater or HVAC system goes out. You won't have the option of not fixing it; the law says your renters need a house that's inhabitable. By having the amount of repair costs in savings, you give yourself a much-needed cushion.

The point is that whatever it is that goes wrong, having savings means having money to fix it. Ideally, you want to have a minimum of three months of your budget in savings as a safety net. This is how you prepare for the unexpected — and at some point, the unexpected *will* happen, whether it's a sudden job loss, a vehicle breakdown, a costly household catastrophe or a death in the family (one where you're responsible for the burial or funeral service).

One of these things will happen to just about everyone at some point, and it's just a matter of when. Having the money in savings fixes the expense part of the problem and makes it easier to deal with it calmly, and think about options so you can get back on track without panicking (because panic usually spurs decisions that you end up regretting).

There's a scene that illustrates this from the 1997 movie *The Edge*: "Most people lost in the wilds...they die of shame...(They say), 'What did I do wrong? How could I have gotten myself into this?'

And so they sit there and they... die. Because they didn't do the one thing that would save their lives...thinking."[52]

When you're in the wild, panicking will lead you to terminal shame. Thinking will save your life.

Building Your Savings in Two Easy Steps

Building your savings shouldn't be intimidating. All you do is:

1. Decide how much you want to save.
2. Pay yourself first.

Whatever you've decided your monthly savings will be, that amount will get paid before paying your bills or paying for your fun. If you don't put your savings aside until after you've paid all your bills, then you probably look at what's left over and decide you don't have enough left to save anything this month. But if you pay yourself first, it always gets done — and saving is the most important thing to do for your future security.

How much should you save? Any number that's not zero. Put something in savings every month and it will grow. Here's how that might look if you saved as little as $25 a month and systematically invested it in a mutual fund, starting while you're a relatively young worker.

- If you start at age 25 and save this amount for 40 years at an 18% rate of return (this *is* realistic), you will have $2,114,495 when you turn 65.
- If you wait until you're 35 to do this for 30 years, you will have $352,839 — substantially less — when you turn 65.
- If you wait until you're 45 to do this for 20 years, you will only have $57,721 — and unfortunately, you'll still be 65.

And if you're already 45 but want to have the same $2,114,495 you would if you had started at age 25, you'd have to start putting in — wait for it — $915.82 a month right now. That's a hard number to hit if you haven't already disciplined yourself to save for the first 45 years of your life.

Now that you know all that, when do *you* think you should start saving?

The bottom line is this: Start saving as early as you can, be consistent, and don't touch it unless it's an emergency. Here's what an emergency is: something that leaves you no choice, such as:

- A down payment for a house, which you have no other options for obtaining (i.e. your employer doesn't let you borrow against your retirement fund).
- Your child is sick and medical bills are insurmountable without tapping into your savings.
- You lost your job today and need to make a mortgage payment tomorrow.

Here's what an emergency isn't:

- The newest iPhone upgrade.
- The next Final Fantasy or Resident Evil release.
- Your vacation (including a honeymoon).

None of those things are worth withdrawing from the savings you are using to build retirement wealth. Your mindset has to be: "This is money I'm saving forever."

Before I could save anything, I needed an income — so with no other immediate options, I did what had to be done to make a quick ascension up the ranks of A.L. Williams. That meant using the eight hours I would have been at a job to sell insurance policies aggressively (by this time, I had learned to sell aggressively without selling desperately). I pounded the pavement hard and became a regional vice president (an "RVP") in 6 months. RVP was the fifth out of nine levels in the A.L. Williams hierarchy, and the first one at which you actually started to make money you could live off of.

The "VP" part was more symbolic than anything. Looking back on it now, I see parallels between that and what some companies in my industry do today: invent a title for everyone who does anything. For instance, some mortgage lenders give every guy who has an NMLS license a name badge that says "VP of Sales." In reality, this guy's actual title is loan officer. If you're in the market for a home loan, that's something to be aware of in the event that you're dealing with a guy who introduces himself that way. It doesn't mean he's not smart, trustworthy or talented; it just means he's been given a title solely for the purpose of impressing you, and it may or may not be reflective of his actual experience.

Fortunately, there were some actual, elevated responsibilities that came with being an A.L. Williams RVP: signing authority on various forms, additional management experience — and the best part, a healthy new commission level.

In those days, the first annual income goal that got you some recognition was $50,000. The recognition came in the form of getting your name in the periodical "leader sheet" publication. My goal was to get in that sheet, and not because I wanted to see my name in print. It was to make the money that came with it.

In my first year as an RVP, I made it in the sheet. In fact, I actually made the $50,000 plus another $5,000. This was not easy, considering I was still occasionally signing up people who would bounce a payment or bail on their policy altogether. When that happened, the 70% advance on commission I received upfront would be revoked in the form of a charge back. When I was expecting a $1500 check on commission day with bills to pay and mouths to feed, being issued a check for $1.50 because some clients didn't hold up their end of the deal was like being gently tapped with a wrecking ball.

The lesson there is to choose your customers wisely. The fact was, I asked for this to happen because I was a 26 year old selling to other 26-year-olds. They were no more financially stable than me, still young enough to feel like they were going to live forever, and here I was getting them into a $50 a month term life insurance plan. In general, people are predictably undependable — and with young adults, it's even worse. Had I been selling to people 10 years older than me, I could have kept more commissions. With 30-somethings, there would be more stability, more dependability and fewer bounced checks. My apologies to any 20-somethings out there, but that's the reality (and most of you know it!).

If you're a 20-something and wondering whether it's hard to sell to someone older than you, here's your answer: not if the math makes sense. When I did sell to that 30+ bracket, all I had to say was, "Look at the math." They couldn't argue with the math, and that made my age irrelevant. So my first piece of advice would be to memorize the math. No matter what you're selling, there's some kind of math involved. I don't care if you're selling shoes, cars, real estate or food plans for a side of beef and the free freezer that comes with it — there's always math, whether it's what they can expect to save or what they can expect in ROI. In the tire business, we did this all the time to step people up to the next level of product. How many months will these shoes last compared to the ones that cost less? Using numbers shows them the value in your proposition and boosts your credibility, thereby boosting your confidence. Don't underestimate the role your own confidence plays in this.

Another helpful skill I figured out later on was becoming multilingual. If you can learn and speak the language of whoever you're talking to — whether it's a doctor, an engineer, a mechanic or a construction worker — you can sell to them. Politicians do this better than anyone. Some of them do it too well, and those are the ones who win elections (whether their ideas are good or not). As a salesperson, you're the same way. It doesn't matter what you're selling — because like a politician, you're really selling yourself.

Unfortunately, I hadn't learned any of that just yet. At this point, I still had clients who were also my peers, bouncing checks and costing me commissions. It was frustrating, but I persevered. I knew that once I crossed that $50,000 threshold, I would finally feel like I'd made it. I worked my ass off to make that amount — and when the day came, I had only one question:

Why do I still feel broke?

The answer was one word...

Overhead

In addition to the clout that comes with a pretentious title you can abbreviate, RVP was also the first A.L. Williams level that required you to run your own office. With that came space rent, phone bills, utilities...all the things I had never been required to pay for as an employee of someone else all those years. That was a bit of a wakeup call. I was happy to be a business owner, but still blindsided by these new expenses.

The truth was, I was used to deriving my primary income from a job. If you made $55,000 at a job in 1987 (the equivalent of $125,000 today), it was your money to keep after the government gets its piece. If you make that equivalent $125,000 at a job today, the same still applies: It's *your* money.

If you're an employee, you might think the owner of the company gets a lot of the profit for the work you do. Well, that's because he pays all the bills — and aren't you glad he does? Believe me, it's no picnic. That's a sidebar, but it's something you need to know if you're considering going into business for yourself. Also, it's true no matter what the business is. Space is space and lights are lights whether you're renting an office, a shop or a warehouse.

In my next career, I bought my own building because I was tired of paying rent. Now I own some commercial buildings, and other people pay *me* rent. They're living how I was back then, dealing with the reality of overhead cutting into their profit margins and probably not liking how it feels. Today, I'm okay with paying the bills — but when you're first starting out, the money doesn't taste quite as sweet as you thought it would thanks to the bitterness of overhead. Like your first sips of beer, tequila or chardonnay, the cost of doing business is an acquired taste.

After I accepted the reality of overhead, I started pondering another question:

Where did all my money go?

This time, there were two answers.

Answer #1: Taxes

When you're an independent contractor filing a 1099 and earning straight commissions, your income isn't stable. It's like being unemployed every day. You don't earn money until you go out and make it happen. So you go out and earn your commissions, and then you don't pay taxes on them until it's time to do your annual or quarterly filing. That's a double-edged sword and a lesson for anyone entering a commission-based field or an independent contractor. The more money I made, the more taxes I paid (in terms of a higher percentage). That's how our progressive income tax system works. You've probably noticed that happening to you as well.

That's why I believe in a flat tax policy. Every flat tax candidate flouts a different ideal rate of taxation, but the bottom line of the flat tax proposal is this: No matter how much money you make, you're paying taxes at the same rate as everyone else. Nobody has to pay a lot, but nobody gets to pay zero. It's fair. But what would be even *more* fair is a consumption tax, because it eliminates the probability of people lying about their income at tax time (a personal pet peeve of mine, since I look at people's tax returns every day and often have to break the news that their lies on their tax returns have impeded their ability to qualify for certain home loans). With a consumption tax system, no one would be tempted to lie on their taxes again. After all, you can't lie about what you buy. That was the idea behind the late Herman Cain's famed "9-9-9" tax proposal in the 2012 presidential election.

Unfortunately, we don't have either of those systems today, nor did we have either of them in 1987. So making $100,000 after expenses back then, which is $227,000 today, meant I only got to keep $60,000. Like a lot of you, that meant I was paper rich but cash poor. No wonder I felt it.

Answer #2: Housing

It was true then and it's more true now: California is one of the most expensive states in the country to own a home. It consistently ranks near the top of every "states with the highest home prices" list out there, barely coming in second behind Hawaii year after year. Houses cost a lot more money in California, period — but having grown up here, it was all I knew.

As I write this, the median sale price of homes in California is $524,400. In 1987, it was $142,060 ($330,368 today). This state has always been a more expensive place to own a home, but that doesn't mean you should rent for the rest of your life just because you live here.

If this sounds like a promotion for my industry, I suppose it is...but I say it because I truly believe in homeownership. Why? For one thing, you can end up paying just as much for rent. Guess what the median price of rent in California is? Right now, it's $2,775 a month. I rest my case; if you're going to pay that much to rent a house, you may as well own one and start building equity.

Devastating With Income

So those were the two reasons why earning a six-figure income for the first time didn't feel like I expected it to. Like a lot of ambitious people starting out, I thought $100,000 meant I should be living in a big house, driving a Corvette, affording nice vacations, and on the fast track to my first boat purchase. Then, by the time you pay your taxes and your mortgage, you realize that dream is further away than you thought. If you've been there yourself, you know how that feels. So what do you do then?

I fell back on a lesson from a few years before, when I was first learning to think differently. It's a little riddle that goes like this:

How do you beat a high taxation rate?

You devastate it with income.

Let that sink in, then understand that it doesn't only apply to taxes. What it means is you can overcome any financial obstacle by increasing the amount of money you make. When you have enough income because you generated a full pipeline of clients — or, happy customers that are referring you to new clients or customers — then losing one sale, customer or transaction (and thereby losing a commission) doesn't hurt so much, if at all.

Here's what that looks like for me now, but you should be able to apply it to whatever it is you do for income.

In the mortgage business, there are times when a loan doesn't fund by the end of the month. Sometimes, it's canceled and doesn't fund at all. These things could happen for a multitude of reasons, including but not limited to:

- The appraisal came in too low for the sale price.
- The client lost his job, which means no income to qualify.
- The client's credit score plummeted overnight.
- There's a cloud on the property title.
- Shit got held up in processing.
- Shit got overlooked in underwriting.
- Shit just happened.

Whatever the reason, I don't need to panic if one of my loans doesn't fund this month. Why? Because I have 25 other loans that *will* fund. A single transaction should never, ever throw the wheels off your wagon. And if you have enough business, clients, customers — and therefore, income — it won't.

So how do you increase your income? You work harder, smarter and longer to keep building: building your clientele, building your referral base, building your reputation, building your repeat business.

CHAPTER 8

"If you build it, he will come."[53]
- Field of Dreams, 1989

IT SOUNDS SO simple: Just keep building until your income exceeds the obstacles. How do you do it? Here are the essential actions you will need to commit to.

Stand Out

Stop doing the bare minimum if you truly want to excel. To make your mark (and more importantly, make money), you need to stand out from the others. Here's an anecdote that explains what standing out does *not* look like.

In the mortgage industry, we might recruit a salesperson from another field or invite someone who seems ambitious and talented to try out our business, earn an NMLS license and work as a loan officer. Once, I recruited a guy named Searle who lived down the street from me; actually, his wife recruited him for me. She saw how my wife and I were living less stressed about money than they were, so she encouraged Searle to quit his job and learn the loan business at my company...which he did. The problem was, she also wanted him to be home for lunch every day and in the door every night by 5 PM. That wasn't going to work.

Searle's wife thought he could get an entry level license for what I do, put in the bare minimum every day and make the same amount of money as me in a short time. She thought he could do it without doing anything to stand out. But you don't get paid just for showing up; you get paid for creating results. You have to be at work for a minimum of eight hours a day no matter what; you can either kill that time or work it to death. Guess which of those options leads to greater success?

Sometimes, a person who thinks he's cut out for the mortgage business will ask to meet with me. He initiates a conversation like this:

Him: "How much does a loan officer make?"

Me: "That depends on how much you do."

Him: What does the average guy do?"

Me: "The average guy quits. I'm not looking for average guys."

I can tell immediately whether he's cut out for it based on his reaction.

Every place I've ever worked, I've seen people who lived for their lunch break and worked for the weekend. You probably have too. If they don't put 100% of themselves into the work they're given in the beginning, how can they expect to go any further? If they don't do something to set themselves apart from the average person, why would they be promoted? If you're "just" a worker (or "just" anything), you'll be "just" something forever. If you want to *be* more, then you have to *do* more.

Excelling at any avenue you pursue to make money, whether working for your own business or someone else's, requires an extraordinary amount of effort. It requires you to stand out.

Provide Guidance

While writing this, I thought of a term and wondered out loud if it was already coined: "consultative selling." As it turns out, it *is* a real term and it's already perfectly defined:

Consultative selling is a sales approach that prioritizes relationships and open dialogue to identify and provide solutions to a customer's needs. It is hyper focused on the customer, rather than the product being sold.[54]

I don't just sell; I consult. One of the reasons for this is, as a mortgage lender, I have a fiduciary duty to act in my clients' best interests. How do I determine what's in their best interests? I ask them questions. God gave you one mouth and two ears for a reason: You're supposed to use them in that proportion. If you listen to people twice as much as you talk at them, you'll learn what you need to do to get them into your product.

To paraphrase Tom Hopkins, author of the classic manual *How to Master of the Art of Selling*:

"Don't be a pushy salesperson; be a pulley salesperson."[55] In other words, ask your client questions to pull out information that will help you lead them toward the right decision for them.

So, for example, I might ask a couple whether they have kids.

If they say yes, I ask how many. Are they having more (and when)?

If they say no, I ask if they plan to have any (and when)?

The objective is not to stick my nose in their marital business. The objective is to advise them based on their needs. If they're planning to start a family soon, then that small house on a busy street they're trying to finance with me might not be the right house for them later, when they have three kids under five riding around on tricycles. Now, I'm not their real estate agent; I can't advise them on what property to buy. What I *can* do is help them find the right mortgage product for the house they've set their mind on. If that's the house they want now, I can use the information I pulled out of them to help them see that they might not be in it forever.

Why would I do that? Because staying in that house for only a few years could have real financial implications, depending on what kind of mortgage they have. Say they want to have kids in the next couple of years. If that's the case, then a 30-year fixed interest rate loan might not be the best product for them as they finance this starter house. In this case, they might be better suited for an adjustable rate mortgage that has a fixed rate for five years, which is the amount of time they're likely to be in the house — or, maybe paying extra upfront to buy down the long term rate doesn't make sense for them. I'm not pushing them into a decision either way, but I can certainly explain why it could work better for them and hope to lead them to a decision that I know is better for them.

Ultimately, it's their choice — but as the professional they're consulting with who has a fiduciary duty to act in their best interests, I offer them guidance. It's an added value I provide. Which brings me to the next essential commitment as you keep building...

Add Value

If you're a fan of business jargon, then you already know the term "value add." Adding value starts with providing guidance, but it shouldn't end there. What good salespeople know, what good business people know, and what good people in general know is that a little extra service goes a long way. One of my value added services is simplifying concepts for my clients. In the insurance days, I explained the concept of keeping your premiums affordable this way:

Claims are a question mark. You *might* be in a car wreck. Your house *might* catch on fire. Your plumbing *might* have a slab leak. If one of these unfortunate events happens, you *might* have a claim. And you only need to pay a deductible *if* you have a claim — so don't worry about how much your deductible is, because you might never have a claim.

But premiums are a certainty. You're required to pay them, so you need to keep them affordable. You don't want to pay an extra $200 a month in premiums for a claim you might have once in 10 years just because it has a lower deductible. That would be like paying for a fully equipped outdoor kitchen that you'll only use for a giant party you'll only have once per decade. Most of the time, it's smarter to just choose an upgrade you'll actually use. Just like most of the time, it's smarter to choose the lower premium.

Typically, that's what they chose. But either way, I simplified a complicated concept for them and it was a valuable service. If you don't present any additional ideas to your customers, you aren't adding value. Value adds are a critical part of your sales toolkit and your reputation (notice I did not say "your brand," because I'm old school. Your reputation *is* your brand). Adding value is how you get repeat business, referrals and other exponential growth opportunities — all things you need in order to succeed long-term.

Earn Trust

In sales, you'll always find some who are in it for the game, the show, or the general excitement. I'm talking about the guys who like sexy buzzwords and live to be on YouTube, but don't enjoy helping their clients once they have them. It sounds like I'm about to call them unsuccessful, but I'm not; some of them can be *very* successful in the short-term. Those people tend to have enough ambition to tap on shoulders, hand out business cards and bring people in the door.

However, they typically don't excel at getting referrals — which doesn't help them in the long run, because any long-term business owner will tell you that referrals are their lifeblood. After almost 30 years, I'm no longer going out and trying to get business, because business is coming to me. That's the power of referrals.

People who are always out in front selling might knock transactions out one by one like dominoes, but they don't get repeat business if they never get their clients to trust them. What they don't realize is that selling yourself also means selling your intentions, not just your personality. My great personality is not going to get my clients into a house. What *will* get them into a house is carrying out my intentions to help them find them the right home loan and seeing the transaction through. That's what earns trust and inspires them to tell other people about me.

Make Time

None of this is accomplished in a matter of minutes; everything I'm describing here requires a time investment. When someone sits down in my office looking to finance their next property, I spend as much time with them as they need, no matter how much time I think I have. Because the truth is, I don't have *any* time. None of us do. We *make* time for what matters, and our clients matter. Without them, we don't have a business.

Find Clients

Seriously? Yes! It never ceases to amaze me how often people need to hear this.

Remember George from Sears, who used the idea of propositioning every girl who walked around the corner as a sales analogy? If he did this in real life, most of the women would call him a creep and kick him in the nether regions. But statistically, two out of 10 might say yes and follow him across the street to the motel. If that happened, it wouldn't be because George was lucky; it would be because he understood something important about sales.

What George meant was, you need to sell to every customer who brings their car into the shop. If they aren't literally in your shop yet, then your job is to bring them in. You do this by listening to people to find out whether you can help them. You do this everywhere you go. Did I do this at one time? Absolutely. Do I still do it? Of course. The only reason I don't do it as frequently anymore is that I no longer have to; I had my airplane at full throttle in those early years, which means now I get to scale down to cruising speed. But it was easy in those days: Because everywhere you go, people are talking about finances or houses, so this was easy to do. But guess what? Everywhere you go, people are talking about whatever it is you do too.

Don't Be a Secret Agent

Being a secret agent is when you know what you do, your spouse knows what you do, but nobody else knows what you do. Secret agents do not find clients. How can they, if they never let anyone know what they're selling?

How *do* you find clients? By listening to people in restaurant booths, on the soccer field, at neighborhood gatherings...wherever you are. Until everyone knows you, it's up to you to make *sure* people know you. It's as simple as saying you overheard them, telling them what you do, and asking if they would like your card. I would give this three-step process some catchy name, but it really doesn't need one. It's the easiest thing in the world.

If you think you'll never find those people, it's time to change your thinking. Let's say it's a yellow, early model Volkswagen Beetle (it's probably not, but let's say it is). I bet you never realized how many people drove an old, yellow VW bug until you drove one yourself. As soon as you inherited it from your dead uncle (how else would you get one?), you declared: "Okay, now I'm the VW Bug guy." You've made the decision that's who you are.

Suddenly, you start seeing VW Bugs on the freeway and in parking lots. Pretty soon, you're seeing one every couple of days. Some of them are yellow, but now you're seeing them in other colors too: blue, beige, white. Where did all these two-door German economy cars from the hippie era come from? They were there all along; you just didn't see them until you were driving one yourself. Once you did, you realized it was kind of fun; at that point, you actually started looking for them. Eventually, everyone starts calling you the VW Bug Guy and people are telling you they've always wanted to have one themselves. That's how you find clients: by deciding who you are, then looking and listening for people who can relate to you. Until you call yourself the VW Bug Guy, no one else will.

That's how you find clients: by deciding who you are, then looking and listening for people who can relate to you. Until you call yourself the car guy or the insurance guy or the real estate guy, no one else will either.

Understand Principles

There are any number of time-worn principles that can be applied to the wealth building process, but one of my favorites is the apple and the seeds. It goes like this:

How many seeds are in an apple, and how many apples are in a seed?

73

When you cut open an apple, you see it has only five seeds. But if you plant those five seeds all over and keep them watered, you're almost guaranteed to get one or more apple trees. Most likely, you'll end up with some apples this year, more apples the next year and a bonafide crop the year after that. As long as you care for it consistently, your crop will get bigger every year. So, how many apples are in a seed? A lot.

If you prefer a biblical example, there's always the Parable of the Sower and the principle of sowing and reaping. All of these point to one basic truth: If you do something, something will happen. Start doing something, and do it consistently. This is how you get results, and results are how you get paid.

CHAPTER 9

GOD WORKS IN mysterious ways. Shortly after achieving the RVP position, it became obvious that my marriage to the woman who bore my children was over. While I had been working so hard to get us to this next level of prosperity, she had been — well, let's call it "spending time" with other men in the neighborhood, and we separated shortly thereafter.

During this time, my national sales director had inherited an office space in nearby Rancho Cucamonga. It was a big footprint, 10,000 square feet. A lot of the occupants were unhappy with how their upline had been treating people, so morale was low, and his idea was for me to move in with my group to be a positive influence. With the major transitions happening in my personal life, I needed a change of scenery at work too. It was an easy decision.

Also moving into the office was a secretary and an administrative assistant. Of these two, one was let go and the other one stayed. I was glad to see it was Dawn who stayed, because she was the one who immediately caught my eye. I thought she was dazzlingly beautiful, but she was also a hard worker, friendly and smart...maybe a little *too* smart for my liking at the time, since that made asking her out more challenging (not that I don't like a challenge sometimes).

When she dropped by my wing one day with some documents, the conversation went like this:

Me: "Maybe we can get together sometime, go have a drink."

Dawn: "*How* long have you been separated from your wife?"

Me: "Um..two weeks? Three weeks? A few weeks."

It had actually been a few *days*. Being separated from a cheating spouse, I didn't feel like the traditional statute of limitations on re-entering the dating pool applied. But since I knew the truthful answer would be a bad look for me, I exaggerated. It didn't matter, because Dawn saw right through it. She smiled suspiciously as if to say, "Yeah right" and walked out of the room. Strike one.

Dawn was also separated from a cheating spouse, so I felt we had that in common. But what woman in that position wants to be pursued by some jerk at the office? It was 1988 and workplace dynamics between men and women were a lot more casual then — but regardless, I was no dummy. I decided to be less aggressive and downshifted my demeanor to friendly/kind of flirty/still professional (who knows if even *that* would be allowed today).

One of Dawn's responsibilities was printing out projections for us, and these printouts gave me an excuse to go into her office just about every day. Thanks to the printouts, I got lots of practice with my low-pressure approach. Because I used the time wisely, we became friends...but there was still no date.

Fortunately, my luck changed the day I brought Ryan and Kacie, my two toddlers, to work out of necessity (suffice it to say there were custody issues). By wandering over to her desk throughout the day to raid her candy dish, my three and two-year olds easily won Dawn over. I have them to thank for charming her on my behalf (no, I did not put them up to it! They were just kids who wanted chocolate. Luckily, it worked to my advantage.)

That day advanced our friendship, but I still kept my cool. I wasn't just after a beautiful woman; I was also attracted to Dawn for her attitude and her heart, and needed to prove I was worthy of both those things. It was a good couple of months before she agreed to a lunch date, then a little longer before an evening date — but once that happened, it was all over from there. From that time on, we were inseparable. And despite the fact that I didn't have two nickels to rub together, Dawn saw something in me that I didn't see in myself yet. The way she looked at me made me feel like I could do anything. Thanks to her, I did.

Quite often, people would call the office asking for Mike Sharpe. Today, Mike Sharpe is the number one all-time earner in the history of Primerica (over $100 million). Back then, he was my national sales director and just starting to leave behind the recruiting phase of his career with A.L. Williams. He was no longer dealing directly with newbies, so anyone hoping to speak with him would have to be referred to someone else when they called. And normally, the person on the other end of the phone was Dawn. Guess who she referred them to?

One day, there was a call from two former stockbrokers. Having come from Kidder, Peabody & Co. and PaineWebber respectively, these two were big fish; I wasn't sure I should be the one they talked to, but Dawn was. One of them, Dave, had recently recovered from a stroke at age 35; this brought him to the realization that his income was only as stable as his ability to get behind his desk, and he wanted to build something that could go on without him, should he end up leaving the world earlier than most (there's a lesson in there).

Dave had met Art Williams and admired what he had done, but thought he was a hick from down south, a guy with a Georgia high school football coach demeanor as opposed to being a polished CEO (that was *because* he was a Georgia high school football coach). His colleague Harold was similarly minded, and I could tell they both looked down their noses at me at first. But somehow, I managed to say something that made an impact on them. They opened up an A.L. Williams office in La Cañada-Flintridge.

Dave's vision was to create an office environment that was less A.L. Williams and more New York Stock Exchange. He would describe the energy of a New York City brokerage where every-one's in the middle of the floor and things are loud, intense and invigorating. For some, that atmosphere is addictive and it's what helps them produce. "If you go to Los Angeles brokerages," he'd say, "everyone's got their own little offices with the same green and brass desk lamps. It's very professional, but it's not very exciting." What I learned from this anecdote was synergy mat-ters, and I still believe that today.

Dave and Harold both saw the value of the insurance prod-ucts we carried, but they also understood they couldn't build a robust portfolio of insurance clients overnight. They started talking about other ways to hit the ground running so they could have a full-time business out the gate. They saw the natural rela-tionship between insurance investment products and mortgages. "We have all their information in front of us," they'd say. "So why wouldn't we take advantage of that?" That made sense to me. At the time, A.L. Williams was rolling out a product called SMART Loans (SMART was an acronym for Save Money and Reduce Taxes). These were 16.9% second mortgages that helped home-owners pay off their credit cards, get a tax deduction and reduce their monthly payments. I loved the product and thought it was an amazing idea.

But Dave and Harold saw the potential for us to do more. They'd ask questions like, "If we can do that for someone with a second mortgage at 16.9%, why wouldn't we get them a new *first* mort-gage at 10% and do a cash out refinance? Instead of leaving their first mortgage as-is and strapping on a second one at a higher rate, we could take their 12% mortgage *and* all their high interest credit card debt and put them into a better product." This benefited us too, because instead of doing a $20,000 loan, we could do a $120,000 one — a much bigger transaction. Now that mortgages are my lifeblood, it amazes me today that I had no knowledge of these concepts back then. I didn't even know what a refinance was yet. But I was game for whatever they were proposing, and I watched carefully to learn how to do what they were doing.

For those who are aware that an NMLS license is required for originating mortgage loans, keep in mind that the NMLS system did not exist back then. NMLS was created in 2008[57] by the Conference of State Bank Supervisors (CSBS) and the American Association of Residential Mortgage Regulators (AARMR) as one of many government responses to the crash that year. At the time when Dave, Harold and other enterprising finance whizzes like them were entering the mortgage business, all you needed was a real estate license in order to lawfully originate mortgages.

While Dave and Harold taught the rest of the organization how to do home loans outside of the A.L. Williams model, I was still teaching people "buy term and invest the difference" within it — but regardless, I now had my foot in the mortgage business. Eventually, the Rancho Cucamonga location closed; I went back to my previous Riverside office space and drove to La Cañada frequently to learn all I could from Dave and Harold. Dawn was working there too, so that gave me even more incentive to be there as often as possible. They took me under their wing, and I still got to work near the woman I loved. Best of both worlds.

Dave and Harold continued to embrace the idea of creating New York synergy in their L.A. office. It was one room, with countertop desks around the perimeter and one countertop going straight up the middle. Dave ran the show from that center counter, taking calls on speaker phone all day long (in fact, he had two phones in front of him: one for the call he was on now, and one for the calls that would come in *during* that call). Could everyone hear him and whoever he was talking to? Yes. Did it get a little loud sometimes? Of course. But it wasn't impossible to transact business that way; if anything, it motivated everyone to work harder. Dave wanted everyone to hear what he was doing; maybe that was connected to his ego in part, but it made for an excellent training ground. He wanted us to learn from him, but he didn't have time to sit by each of us side-by-side. This is how he accomplished his sales goals while still mentoring his team. They were never mutually exclusive.

Dave taught me to use the phone in other ways, too. He'd facetiously invite me to come along on jaunts to various real estate agencies (as anyone in mortgage sales knows, building relationships with real estate agents is a critical way to build business.

That's because most people, especially first-time homebuyers, call a real estate agent before they call a mortgage lender).

Dave would say, "So you want to go to that Century 21 office down the road? You get in your car; I'll stay here on my phone. We'll see who gets there first." His point was that prospecting by phone will almost certainly help you cover more ground than wasting time driving around. He showed us how to be effective with our time while learning the mortgage industry. The things I learned from Dave are things I still incorporate into my craft today; so now, they're *my* techniques. I teach them to everyone on my sales team.

At some point, I realized that the mortgage business was a lot more appealing to me than the insurance business. In insurance, I was spending 90% of my time trying to build an organization (although this might have something to do with the MLM model of the corporation) and only 10% of my time on personal production, which is how most people earn a living for their families. All it took was about one year of working under Dave's wing to figure out that mortgages were what I wanted to do long-term. And it was a good thing I had learned a lot by then, because it wasn't long after that when Dave and Harold asked me to leave.

Just like that? More or less.

Long story short, I had clients who had questions and I didn't have all the answers yet. With no FICO scores until 1989 and the practice of using them in the loan approval process not going mainstream until the early 90s, underwriters made decisions about lending based on less concrete markers than they do today (in fact, most of us were confused by FICO scores when they were first introduced). So before the FICO, loan approval was largely at the underwriters' discretion; they had a lot of power, and it was incumbent on the applicant to convince them of his or her creditworthiness. If I had a client who was deemed unworthy, I had to be able to tell him why. To most clients, "Because you had a late payment on your Visa card five years ago" was not an acceptable answer, and I understood that. When a client had a credit report that looked like Swiss cheese, it was my job to present that person as a survivor rather than a dirtbag.

One of those clients was Randy, my arm wrestling buddy who later joined me in the loan business and is still a close friend today. But in those days, Randy was my client — and when there was any kind of roadblock to his approval, he grinded on me hard: "So because I have this ding on my credit from years ago, now I'm a dirtbag?!"

As closely as I had watched Dave and Harold work their magic, I still didn't always know how to respond to questions like this. I had to be able to answer people and explain to them what they needed to do to move forward.

So while my ass was being grinded by my clients, I'd grind the asses of the loan processors who were throwing up these obstacles. When they'd say, "We need an explanation for (insert negative credit incident here)," I'd respond by asking them what I should say to my clients when they would (inevitably) ask me why that explanation was needed.

After a string of these confrontations, Dave finally sat me down. "Your clients are grinders, and now you're a grinder. You grind on everybody all the time, and you're stressing out our staff."

Well, you don't learn unless you ask questions. But Dave and Harold, who had previously been supportive of my enthusiasm to learn, didn't seem to think I was just asking questions anymore. I got their point, but I refused to quit. So they asked me to leave.

Fortunately, I had a good amount of business under my belt and a woman who made me feel like Superman. Dawn looked me right in the eye and said, "I know you can do this on your own." That was the first time I learned the true meaning of the age-old idiom, "Behind every great man is a great woman." Before that, I just thought it was a nice thing people said to wives and girlfriends. That was before I had an example of it in my own life.

Out of all of these anecdotes from this chapter of my career, here are a few takeaways.

Consider your surroundings. Truth be told, I was working out of a mortgage office that doubled as an insurance agency under the umbrella of an MLM corporation. Dave and Harold made it an exciting atmosphere, but they had also hired a bunch of their relatives to come be loan processors (people who pre-underwrite the files before sending them to actual underwriters). These were smart people, but they had no previous industry experience — and here was this guy relentlessly pressuring them to produce a detailed reason for every decision they made. I'm sure I was in some of their nightmares.

But it probably got some of them to reconsider whether this was the industry for them (or better yet, decide to learn more about the industry so they could improve). In any case, I probably could have shown them more grace had I considered my surroundings — and, that probably would have spared me the experience of hearing my new mentor telling me to hit the road.

Stay curious. Even if I overreacted, there's still nothing wrong with having that childlike curiosity. You *should* want to know why things are the way they are. If you don't know *why* it is, how can you really understand it?

The comedian Gallagher used to tell a story about how his baby daughter taught him to see the world through new eyes. He'd say, "Babies...look at the world with new eyes and you begin to see things, too, through their eyes. I had a problem with her with toilet training and I don't blame her a bit. 'Cause first I showed her you can't hit your cup on the coffee table. Then I showed her you can't eat on the couch. Then here was this chair you could shit in."[58]

He'd go on to talk about how literally his child saw things through these eyes. She didn't call a restaurant a restaurant; she called it a "dinner store," because a store was the place where you bought things and a restaurant was the place where you bought dinner. Her foot didn't fall asleep; it "sparkled," because that's an accurate description of how your foot falling asleep feels.

The point is, children are still learning the basics of life; you and I are adults, but we're still learning the basics of whatever it is we're trying to learn. Often, the most literal answer to people's questions is the best one. "Because I said so" is a bad answer from a parent, and it's a bad answer from whoever you're dealing with. It's also a bad answer from you. Don't be afraid to ask people why, like a child would — and when someone else is asking *you* why like a child would, be prepared to answer them also. This is part of treating people how you would like to be treated.

Take ownership immediately. When A.L. Williams recruits came in for a Tuesday night presentation or a Saturday morning training, it seemed like they mostly did this because they enjoyed the ritual of attending a meeting and hearing about finances. It was probably exciting for them, and maybe it motivated them to do *something*; however, "something" wasn't always building an A.L. Williams business.

When they had someone they wanted to present the opportunity to, they were still asking me to do it. Part of that may have been their lack of confidence in the opportunity itself, but the rest was almost certainly their lack of confidence in themselves to do the presentation. And why did they lack that necessary confidence? Because they weren't taking ownership of their own new businesses by mastering the presentation, understanding the numbers behind it, and anticipating people's questions (which would have required them to learn the answers).

Now, am I saying everyone who wants to try something new should quit their full-time job and risk their livelihood in order to master the new venture? No, no, and no. I'm saying to start somewhere that's willing to give you a salary while you learn, and make sure they're the right people to teach you. But don't rely on them to do the legwork for you. Watch them, learn from them, and then get out there and start duplicating what they've taught you.

While you're doing this, don't be afraid to fail. When you fail, fail forward. By the time you've closed six sales, you'll have a lot more confidence in what you're doing. You're going to screw some of them up – but if you're going to screw up anyway, you may as well learn while you're doing it.

Today, I don't bring people into my business to work part-time, especially if they're coming from some entirely different industry. It's not about me being their "all or nothing" overlord; it's about bringing on people who can give it their full-time effort. If they don't have the ability to do that, that's okay. It doesn't mean they aren't cut out for success *somewhere*. It just means they aren't cut out for success in my industry at this moment in time.

Calculate risks. The time when I entered the business was a squirrelier time in the mortgage industry, with very little fraud control compared to what we have today. At my next stop after leaving Dave and Harold's office, I saw a lot of things happen that are not allowed today (and yes, I know that's a good thing). If you can imagine it, I probably saw it.

Maybe you've seen some things in your industry too — and if you're like me, it probably scared the hell out of you when you saw people get caught (when one person gets caught doing something unethical, it's easy for the entire company to get implicated). So the lesson here is to calculate the risks happening around you.

When I saw certain things happening around me and those things were quickly becoming the industry norm, I realized that staying in that environment wasn't worth risking my license on. Whether you call it karma or something else, what you try to get away with will come back to you in some way and your associate's lack of integrity can rub off on you like tar on the beach. Calculate these risks carefully.

Those lessons can carry you through your career in any industry, even a blue collar one. Whatever you want to do, you can learn from my experiences. You can learn from *anyone's* experiences.

CHAPTER 10

"There comes a point in every match where a fight has to start."[59]
- Against the Ropes, 2004

SO FAR, I'VE only scratched the surface when it comes to all the unethical (and now, illegal) activity I witnessed in those early mortgage years. If you've seen movies like *The Big Short* or *The Wolf of Wall Street*, you already have ideas about the kinds of things people did to pull in commissions before they were being closely watched by the government.

I wouldn't blame you for being curious, and it's probably important to explain the lengths some people would go to. After all, these are the reasons we now have regulators. So without going into excruciating detail, here are a few things I saw happen routinely, with or without clients' knowledge, to get their loans approved and funded:

- Altering their W-2 forms, sometimes with the help of a tax attorney or accountant.
- Falsifying entire tax returns, using the name of a firm rather than a tax preparer.
- Copying their signatures in jaw-droppingly creative ways (one of them involves holding a form they've already signed against a sunlit window — need I say more?).
- Creating fake paystubs from scratch for jobs the clients didn't have.

Obviously, this stuff is nothing to brag about. Like everything in this book, it's about you learning from my experiences. And in this part of the book, it's also about establishing what your values are so you can have a successful career built on honesty and integrity.

Ask yourself:

- How far would you go to close a sale...what's your stopping point?
- Are you willing to sell your soul for a commission check?
- Can you live with the consequences of getting caught?
- Do you even know what those consequences are?

In reality, this doesn't only apply to sales occupations. There's a point in *every* career where you have to figure out what you stand for. But all I can speak to directly is what it looks like in my own industry. So to illustrate that, here's a scenario that might happen in my field.

Regulators like the Department of Real Estate, HUD and Fannie Mae routinely perform quality control checks of previously funded home loans; that's a large part of their job. If, during one of those QCs, they encounter a past transaction that appears to be a red flag — for example, it's only been a year and the buyer has already fallen behind on payments and defaulted on the loan — then at that point, the regulator will delve into the original file to see if further investigation is needed.

If anything looks fishy (a strong possibility in this scenario), then they may choose to open a fraud investigation. A fraud investigation doesn't just mean they silently examine the file without contacting the original players. It means they hold live, in-person meetings where everyone who was originally involved is required to sit down and answer for whatever the hell happened. It doesn't matter how ethically everyone is behaving now; all that matters is what they did when that transaction took place.

In these meetings, they may put the entire cast of characters in a room together: the agents, the lender, any investors...and yes, even the clients. It's like being forced to attend a class reunion with people you were never even friends with. You did business together once, a year ago, two years ago or five years ago, and now you're all being held together on a desert island — and we're not talking about a pretty, tranquil island like *The Blue Lagoon* or

Castaway. We're talking about a place where natives straight out of National Geographic force you to dance on hot coals before impaling you with their spears and roasting you on a spit in the sand. That's what it's like to be caught up in a fraud investigation.

Even if everybody manages to come out with their licenses intact, there are likely to be some aggressive measures to deal with. For instance, the lender might be given an ultimatum: *Buy back this $500,000 loan, or you don't get to sell loans to this investor any-more...or to Fannie Mae...or to whoever.*

If you're that lender, it's going to cost more than you can afford to lose. If you're lucky enough to get the best case scenario, you might skate by with a slap on the hand when all is said and done. But regardless, you'll still pay in the form of a damaged reputa-tion — and that's the highest price there is.

Reputation Above Everything

Hopefully, all of this makes one thing clear: It's never worth it to have dishonest dealings as the skeletons in your proverbial closet. But if you already have some, then you may find out that the skel-etons don't stay closeted for very long.

No matter how big your industry is, it's still a small world. Word can spread like wildfire when someone gets in trouble; this is especially true if they get in trouble with the government, but it can happen even in smaller matters: false advertising, bad deal-ings with the public, even poor customer service.

If you're doing shady business, your competitors will find out and use that knowledge against you. With social media and online reputation platforms, that's now easier to do than ever. But, let's say you're wondering why your reputation is the most important thing. Let's say you're not into business ethics, or you're one of those types that's addicted to the thrill of the hunt at all costs. If that's you, then you may wonder: "Do I really need to care about my reputation *that* much?"

The answer is yes — because as long as your reputation is solid, you can always make more money. But if your reputation is damaged, you can't...at least not without changing industries or relocating. And who wants to be a traveling salesman? Nobody! That's why there aren't very many of them anymore.

So whatever consequences come, it's just not worth the money that dubious transaction brought in. And believe it or not, you aren't even the one who gets hurt the most. That honor goes to your clients, who just wanted whatever your service is. In my industry, they're people who just wanted a house.

Now, sometimes the clients are not so innocent themselves. They may know they're getting into a loan they can't afford. But that doesn't mean what their fiduciaries did was right. It's our job to make sure they understand the pros, cons and possibilities of consequences down the road.

Not Just for Business

This mindset of drawing the line on how far you will go isn't just a business ethos. It needs to be a *life* ethos. At the time of this writing, there are government-backed relief programs created to assist people, including business owners, to offset the economic impacts of COVID-19. Even people who normally try to do what's right (in business *and* their personal lives) have taken advantage of programs they didn't necessarily need to. Right now, millions are taking advantage of the inflated unemployment benefits that are disincentivizing people to work.

When the government offered a forgivable loan program clearly designed to help people who really need it, the Paycheck Protection Program (PPP), millions of business owners took advantage of it whether they needed it or not. I had two businesses that didn't do anything in 2019 or 2020, but not for reasons related to COVID. Regardless, I could have applied for a PPP loan and made off with a whole bunch of cash. All it would take is to say I'd keep paying my employees for the next four months — and the government would've sent me four months' worth of payroll, even though I wasn't doing business. I didn't, but some business owners in similar boats did. All they had to do was sign and the government handed them money.

Was that ethical? It wasn't illegal. But somewhere down the road, someone 's going to have to answer for that. Whether it's when they get an IRS audit, run for office, or die and face the man upstairs, those people will have to pay the pied piper. My guess is that the government will eventually audit those who took the money.

There was a version of this happening during the mortgage melt-down. People were upside down on their loans, so the banks were doing short sales left and right. Some of those upside down homeowners saw an unethical opportunity and jumped on it: Sell their houses to family members so the bank would write off half their loan.

It worked like this: People were finding themselves with $400,000 of debt on properties that were now worth $200,000. Whether or not they were in trouble, they would be advised by a real estate agent to let their payments fall behind and short sell their houses. They would follow this advice by claiming they couldn't make the payments, even when that wasn't always the case. What *was* always the case is that they were upside down on the loan because home values had plummeted.

Based on these peoples' hardships (real or fabricated), the banks would be willing to sell their houses for 50% of the amount owed. So, agents and investors were approaching these homeowners and offering to buy their homes at short sale for half their value. Some of the homeowners took it, and that was fine. Others made this highly unethical choice:

- Intentionally lapse on their payments.
- Ask an uncle or cousin to come in with an offer.
- Lie about the relationship.
- Sell the house to that relative.

They would then rent the house back from the family member so they could continue living there, all while walking away from half their debt. They'd hang on for a little bit until their credit gets better and then refinance the loan, using a deed as an instrument to put their name back on the title.

Now, a decade later, what banks *should* be doing is performing audits and pulling titles on all those short sales. In cases where the original owner is back on the title (indicating they committed the scam I just described), the banks could recover the trillions of dollars lost to short sales while the market is up again.

This isn't some revenge fantasy of mine. This is something that could very well happen at some point. After all, there's no statute of limitations on fraud. It's just one example of why ethics aren't just for business. Ethics should be practiced in every area of our lives.

It reminds me of a quote from the great football coach Vince Lombardi, although I became acquainted with it from the 1989 martial arts movie *Best of the Best*: "Winning is not a sometime thing; it's an all the time thing. You don't win once in a while; you don't do things right once in a while; you do them right all of the time. Winning is a habit. Unfortunately, so is losing."[60]

Ethics aren't just a business thing. Ethics are a life thing.

Working With What You Have

None of this is to say that you shouldn't try to work with what you're given. One area where I may try to do that is appraisals. In real estate, a technical definition of an appraisal is *the highest amount a buyer will pay, and the lowest amount a seller will accept, on any given day.* On face value, that sounds like the amount could be any figure both parties agree to. But that's not the case.

No matter what the offer amount is, the appraiser has to have data on the property to substantiate it. Without that data, the appraised value isn't supported — and the lender can't lend based on an unsupported value. That means if a buyer offers more than a property is worth (in an attempt to be the "winning bidder" with a stronger offer) — say, they offer $500,000 on a property that's only worth $475,000 — then it doesn't matter if the seller is willing to accept it. Unless the appraiser has the data to prove the property is worth $500,000, a lender can't lend that amount. The buyer *could* pay the $25,000 difference if they wanted to — but because the bank is putting out their money based on the borrower's qualifications and the value of the col-lateral, they need an accurate value on which to base the total risk that is being taken on that loan. In the 80s and 90s, many loans went into default, and many banks found out they could not resell the properties for what the represented the values were when they leant on them. That turned into the savings and loan meltdown (better known as the S&L crisis).

Of course, we can still attempt to *find out* if it can be done. Sometimes, we can rebut the original appraisal or request a new one. I tell appraisers in these situations, "If the value's there, get it." Sometimes, it is. When we're able to save a deal by working with what we have, that's a great thing.

But if the value isn't there, then there's nothing that the appraiser or I can do about it. As the lender, I'm not about to lose my license to push one deal through. If the buyer doesn't get that house, they can always find another one.

The point is, this is just one transaction. As the appraiser, the real estate agent and the mortgage lender, we'll all (hopefully) have the opportunity to work on thousands of transactions like it throughout our respective careers. None of us should put our licenses at risk over one deal. You shouldn't either.

Often, clients have no idea how big our stakes are in these situa-tions. They think we work our magic, cash our commission checks and move on. Not so. We have a lot at stake, and we need to conduct business accordingly. Nothing is worth risking your live-lihood. There's a risk of that in every career.

Next Chapter, New Opportunities

Believe it or not, all the unethical things I described at the beginning of this chapter were happening long before the sub-prime mortgage days. What I saw go down was enough to scare me straight out of this environment of short-term greed into a place where I could build long-term business, long-term respect, and long-term wealth. We'll call that a place of "long-term greed," although really it's not about greed at all. It's about integrity. Through the connections I made at that next place, I experienced my first shot at steady and stable growth. Here's how that happened.

For the past few years, I had been commuting heavily; the kids and I had settled in Riverside County, but work was still in L.A. County. After Dave and Harold let me go, the next company was located in San Bernardino County, which meant work was a *little* closer (but not close enough). Then when I left that place behind, someone told me about a company called American Builders Mortgage. Lo and behold, it was in Riverside County. Finally, no more commuting! I took my loans over there; at that time, they were primarily refinance loans.

Thanks to my large network of investor clients from the A.L. Williams days, I was having a lot of success with refis. But as you may recognize from the name, American Builders Mortgage didn't focus on refis; their objective was to focus on targeting builders, who were plentiful at that time thanks to the early 90s tract home boom.

As you may recall, there was building going on everywhere (not just in California, but it sure seemed like we were the epicenter of it). Every weekend, there were floods of people walking into housing tracts in search of their next home. From that emerged a new subset of the industry, and I was interested in seeing how it worked. But with most of my clientele being homeowners who just needed to refinance the houses they already had, the guys at this company weren't sure how I was going to fit into their puzzle.

"We don't do refinances," they'd say. "They never close."

"Really?" I'd say. "Mine close."

They explained the way they viewed the refinance market: Interest rates aren't always stable. Appraisals don't always come in. Deals don't always close.

That made sense, but here's how I saw it: I had a catalog of customers who already knew and trusted me. They didn't want a brand new house; they just needed a lower payment on the house they were already living in. That's how my refinances closed. This strategy worked for several months, maybe even a year.

But I was destined to learn the lesson they were trying to teach me. When interest rates ticked up from 6.75% to 7.25%, it no longer made sense for about a third of my refi clients to refi. In a matter of days, I got one call after another: "I think we're going to hold off," or "I don't think we're going to move forward right now." These were people who paid attention, and that half a percent increase scared them.

Great...*now* what? Somehow, I had managed to get this far in the mortgage business without making friends with any real estate agents. It looked like it was finally time for me to change that.

The problem was, I didn't know any real estate agents except for the one who had sold me *my* first house. The last time she'd heard from me, I was married to my first wife and working at Sears. Who knew if she'd even remember me? Fortunately, she *did* remember me; that meant she was a good agent! I told her I'm in the business now and looking to meet some other good agents like her.

She had one for me to meet, a guy named Bill working at an office called Home Life Discount Brokers. "He's been in the business for a year and a half and hasn't closed one deal," she said. Hmm, I thought. Thanks, but that's not exactly the type of agent I had in mind. I was grateful for her help, so I stopped short of asking: "I'm sure Bill's a nice guy, but how is *this* the guy who's going to help me find clients?"

But I had nothing to lose by calling Bill, and right away, he explained what the problem was. "I haven't been able to get anything done," he said, "because we're supposed to give all our leads to the in-house brokerage." As it turned out, said brokerage was overly cautious and underly competent.

When Bill and I met up the first time, he handed me a list of 28 leads. "These are all the leads I've given them in the past 30 days," he said. "They haven't given me a greenlight on any of them." These weren't prospects Bill hunted down; these were people who had called the office or walked in, and the loan officers onsite completely blew them off because their credit wasn't perfect or they had just started a new job. In other words, they weren't willing to work with those clients who required a little effort. I promised Bill I wouldn't make that same mistake; he could trust his leads to me. 30 days later, I had given him six greenlights, which meant he now had six of them under contract to purchase homes.

This was still before FICO scores were the normal way to prequalify and credit was more subjective, but it could still be done today. What the in-house guys at Bill's office were doing was looking for the low-hanging fruit and rejecting everything else. Here's what I did differently from them: Instead of looking at a client's credit, yelling "Blech!" and never calling them again, I did what I had been doing since my days working for Dave and Harold: I asked questions. "What happened here...what happened there?" It was the only way I could help them. Credit challenges aren't necessarily a stop sign; they're just a speed bump you have to help someone get over. The past doesn't always equal the future; I considered it my job to present them as having *been through* financial challenges, as opposed to *currently having* financial challenges.

By that time, I'd been through plenty of financial challenges myself; they didn't make me, as my buddy Randy would say, a "dirtbag." And I didn't think these clients' challenges made them dirtbags either. As I looked at their credit profiles, I'd notice patterns of late payments at specific times, in specific years. And nine times out of ten, the answers to "What happened?" for them were things I had been through too: job losses, divorces, custody battles. Through that, I developed a talent for putting their stories together in credit explanation letters. These letters are no longer the norm, but they were then — and nobody wrote them better than me. The elements were always the same:

- What happened to us.
- Why it was beyond our control.
- How we fixed it.
- Why it's not going to happen again.

Then, you end every letter with a grateful request for approval. Not everyone did this, but they should have. For my clients, it was the difference between getting a new house or continuing to rent an apartment.

After one month, Bill had six properties in escrow. Now, everybody at Home Life Discount Brokers was looking at him and asking, "What changed for this guy?" What changed was that he finally knew a loan officer who gave a damn about turning his leads into loans, and that guy was me. They didn't argue about him not giving the leads to the in-house guys, because he finally had some deals on the board and that meant they were making money too. Pretty soon, I was getting calls from other agents at Home Life Discount Builders too. Bill was finally in the game, I was *back* in the game and clients were becoming homeowners. The only people who lost were the loan officers who overlooked these opportunities.

Like I said earlier in the book, every opportunity you move on leads to more opportunities later. That's what happened in this new partnership with Bill. On the other end of every transaction we did together, there was another real estate agent with his own clients too.

One of them was another Bill; unlike the first Bill, *this* Bill was already a mover and a shaker. He was a New York guy with a New York accent and a New York attitude, a big player who was in all the magazines...the type of real estate agent every loan officer wanted to do business with. Because I had been planting seeds all over the place, those seeds had germinated by the time I finally got to meet him at some social engagement. By that time, Bill had heard from other people about what I was able to get done for them. He decided to give me some of his most challenging clients – all the stuff the other guys were turning down. Every time we'd meet, I'd say, "If you've got anyone you need me to handle, send them my way." And he would.

The lesson: *Always, always ask for business every time you meet.*

Bill wasn't the only one this happened with. This would occur again and again over time, as I continued to market to every agent on the other end of a transaction. If I knew an agent doing a home buying seminar, I'd ask if they'd like to have a lender there to support them and help them get people prequalified. I'd pre-qualify 10 to 12 people from a single event and they'd be out looking for houses by the weekend.

I realized that agents spend thousands of dollars in advertising — then they gave their business to lenders who could close deals, period. We controlled the transactions, because we held the money needed for anyone to perform. The lesson there is to identify all the targets; all clients are targets, but not all targets are clients. Some targets are the other professionals who you'll work with to give each other referrals. Prove they can rely on you, work well with them, and help each other make money. This can happen in any networking situation, no matter your industry. Some of these professionals won't just stay targets; some of them will become friends, and those friendships will become your assets. Put that into practice, and watch your career start to flourish.

CHAPTER 11

"A-B-C. A, always; B, be; C, closing. Always be closing! Always be closing!"[61]
- Glengarry Glen Ross, 1992

IN THIS CASE, I have to alter the movie quote a bit. For the lessons learned here, it's actually A-B-M: Always be marketing.

You knew the marketing chapter was coming. Maybe you think you know enough about the subject (it seems like everybody does these days), but don't brush past this too quickly. There's more to marketing than what you're learning at sales rallies and business schools. Here's the background on the marketing principles that always worked best for me: low-tech, simple and effective.

As I said before, things grew quickly once I learned to maximize my new connections with real estate agents. While I had been doing consumer direct marketing to clients in search of a home loan, I was now making an effort to market to the agents who spend thousands of dollars to attract new buyers and then give them to us. That was a starting point, but I didn't end there.

In addition to real estate agents, there are other professionals attached to every transaction. You have:

- An appraiser
- A title company
- Credit repair services
- Escrow offices
- Other vendors

And of course, those companies are made of people. Whenever I needed to call one of these companies for something involving one of my transactions, I took the time to market to the people on the other end of the line. Most of them weren't even aware they were being marketed to. Does that mean I gave them a sales pitch? Not at all.

3 C's of Reputation Marketing

Yes, I would tell them to let me know if I could help them with any clients other than the ones we were discussing. But even if I didn't say that, I was still marketing to them; I was marketing myself. I did that by always being:

- Conscious of the way I presented myself to them
- Careful with my words and tone of voice
- Cognizant of their time constraints and workloads

Call that the 3 C's of Reputation Marketing if you like. Basically, I was acutely aware of everything that would contribute to their impression of me — because as we just learned in the previous chapter, your reputation needs to come before everything else.

Real Reputation Marketing

I know the term "reputation marketing" means something different than what I'm describing here, but I'm talking about something more powerful than paying someone to get your bad reviews buried. I'm talking about acting in a way that reduces your risk of getting the bad reviews in the first place. Real reputation marketing requires you to understand that the people you deal with hold your reputation in their hands every time you conduct business with them. Here's a rule of thumb to remember:

If you make a good impression, they might tell 10 people about you: friends, family, co-workers. If you make a bad impression, they'll probably tell 100 people about you: friends, family, co-workers, people they run into at the store, total strangers and pretty much everyone who passes by.

That's why, whether you feel like it or not, it's always better to make a good impression.

Marketing isn't just about being slick, salesy and savvy with technology. It's also about these timeless concepts of courtesy and professionalism. Utilizing them reveals your confidence and maturity, and those are things people are attracted to.

Being Long-Term Greedy

My friend Mike happens to be one of the top Remax agents in the country. He's one of the agents I go back with the furthest, and we joke about how he used to call me "The Greedy Bastard." The thing is, he didn't mean it as an insult. As the character Gordon Gekko says in the movie Wall Street:

"Greed, for lack of a better word, is good. Greed is right. Greed works. Greed for life, for money, for love, for knowledge has marked the upward surge of mankind."[62]

Mike meant that I was motivated by *good* greed like Gordon Gekko describes — the kind that's long-term, with gains that trickle down to the people under you (I know certain politicians have told you that "trickle down economics has been tried and failed,"[63] but that's a lie).

Think of the lasting impact you could have with a long-term approach that helps other people succeed too, compared to short-term greed that's based on instant gratification feeding your own ego. That kind of greed helps no one.

Making a good impression is part of that long-term thinking; you're not doing it because it's the marketing trend of the moment. You're doing it because it's effective marketing that will work just as well 30 years from now as it does today. It does for me.

Cameras Then, Cameras Now

At this point, it might sound like I'm saying you shouldn't embrace digital marketing. That's not what I'm saying at all. In fact, I think today's technology makes the classic marketing strategies more important than ever. Think of it this way: We've always had cameras on us, both then and now. But here's the difference: Back then, all the cameras had on them were lenses (also known as your eyes). There was no place to store your "photos" and "videos" (also known as your interactions with people). If you wanted to share those things, you actually had to edit your videos, have your photos developed, and call a meeting with your intended audience (or, use them to create some kind of print or video ad for TV or radio broadcast).

That metaphor doesn't only apply to business. Think about how you used to do that in your personal life. Some of you may be too young to remember this — but prior to social media, sharing your photos with family and friends required you to call them up and invite them over. When I was growing up, that's what families did. Mom or Dad would announce, "Let's have everybody over for dinner tomorrow night and show them the photos of our vacation." Then, Mom had to cook dinner for 20 people and Dad had to figure out how to hook up a giant projector in the living room. It actually required work!

But today, we have *real* videos and no shortage of places to share them. People can film us and post it on Facebook or Twitter. They can write about their interactions with us on platforms like Yelp. In both our personal and business lives, our actions are being recorded, stored and shared.

Before this, you had the freedom to flip someone off, tell someone where to stick it or go make a fool of yourself at the bar; if someone shared it, it was just "hearsay" as opposed to a video. But as you are likely aware, you don't have that freedom today; someone is bound to be filming, and five minutes later it's posted on social media.

If you're in business and still acting like you have the freedom to make bad impressions on people, then let me be the first to say that you are bad at marketing. Sorry, but it's true. It doesn't matter how motivational you sound or how great your YouTube ads are. With all the tools to monitor your behavior now, there's no way to separate your personal behavior from your professional brand. Your reputation *is* your brand.

3 S's of Reputation Marketing

Reputation marketing is so important that it gets two lists. Here are my 3 S's of Reputation Marketing:

1. Someone is always watching. You can't go anywhere without someone holding up a phone to capture their surroundings, and most of the time they're filming rather than clicking snapshots. It doesn't matter what their intentions are; all that matters is whatever they catch you doing. And even if no one is filming, *someone* is watching your moves. You need to be conscious of that.

2. Someone always knows someone else. Just look at your Facebook friends; for almost everyone you know, there's at least one mutual friend attached. When you meet someone professionally (or personally, for that matter), there's a good chance they already know something about you because they've been told by someone else. *What* they know about you all depends on the reputation you've built.

3. So, Always Be Marketing. A-B-M means you make that good impression every time you have someone on the phone, in your office or at an impromptu meeting. By being courteous, professional and helpful, you're marketing to them. It's more powerful than you realize.

Everyone Starts Somewhere

What if you're brand new to your industry? It doesn't matter, because you can start these from day one. The same applies if you're brand new to your location. My goal is to practice these principles so consistently that if I was dropped into a remote desert town where I know literally no one, I could still close 10 deals in 90 days. I would be able to do this because of how well I know my business — but even if I was brand new to the business, I could do it because I've learned to:

- Use my ears and mouth in the proportion in which God put them on my head.
- Reject the urge to be a secret agent, even if I'm having a bad day.
- Practice reputation marketing everywhere I go.

101

- Do things the right way over and over, no matter who the client is.

Here's what that last one means: If you always do things a certain way, you don't have to remember what you told somebody before — because you know the way you always do things.

It's like the advice lawyers give to their clients before testifying in court: If you always tell the truth, If you always tell the truth, you don't have to have a great memory.

As long as I practice these principles consistently, I should be able to meet my goal no matter where I am. And so should you.

The Value of Partnership

By putting all this into practice, I was able to pick up leads from all over the place. Eventually, so many agents were spreading my name around that I couldn't keep up. I had more business than I could handle, but not enough time for my kids (still a single dad... Dawn and I hadn't totally locked things down just yet).

That led to another new partnership, which led to eventually owning my own company within a couple of years. But when it started, I was still working at American Builders Mortgage. One of my most valuable contacts was Jim, who didn't have a license for anything remotely related to real estate — so, it was ironic that this would turn out to be my biggest partnership yet.

Jim was a recruiter for ITT Technical Institute, which has since closed down but was at one time one of the largest for-profit educational centers in the country (remember those daytime TV commercials?). He was basically a salesman for student loans that financed ITT educations, and he was good at what he did. So good, in fact, that people would sometimes feel comfortable sharing unrelated information with him — for example, that they were looking to refinance their homes.

Jim started feeding me these refinance leads, and yes, I gave him kickbacks (that was allowed then). Something I learned from studying a mogul like Art Williams was that as the pie got bigger, he would take a smaller piece in order to "sweeten the deal" for people he recruited. As the piece got smaller, the pie got bigger. The concept made sense to me, I needed the help, and Jim was able to line up transactions for me so well that it didn't make sense to ask anyone but him.

After a few months of dividing things up that way, I was ready for a bigger partnership. Jim's part-time help was great, but I still wasn't seeing my kids nearly enough. Jim's kids were grown and he was happy to work longer hours, so I saw an opportunity.

"Come on full time," I told him. "We'll split all the purchase deals 50/50, but I'll keep my refi deals and you'll keep yours."

It was a match made in mortgage industry heaven. With him as the worker and me as the thinker, we quickly built a reputation as "Ed and Jim kicking ass out there." All he wanted was to go on a short vacation every three months, which was fine with me. All I wanted was to have a little breathing room in the evenings and on weekends, and that's what he signed up to deliver. Sometimes, people who remember those days say to me, "I remember when it was you and Jim in a smoke-filled room, and neither one of you smoked!"

Don't Count the Cost

Joining forces with Jim taught me the valuable lesson that two guys can accomplish at least three times what one guy can do on his own, in the same amount of time, as long as you're both working like machines. Of course, I can't say the division of labor was always equitable. Were there times I split my commission with Jim on a loan he had nothing to do with? Yes. And were there times I wondered why I was doing it? Yes. But that worked both ways, because there were times when he did that for me as well. The lesson there is, don't count the cost transaction by transaction.

Sometimes, putting a ton of time and effort into one deal only to give away half my commission was painful. But I lived by what the classic guide *Success! The Glen Bland Method* advised:

Get in the habit of doing more than you are paid for. One day you will be paid for more than you do. Service—success—then money! Lasting success is a gradual process.

If you honor your obligations and serve others, you aren't putting those people in debt to you; you're putting God in debt to you, and God always makes it right somewhere down the road. When you help people, God pays you back through other people helping you — not necessarily the same ones.

That's what happened for me every time I honored my obligation to Jim. Sometimes it went my way and sometimes it went his, and that's the nature of any partnership. If you do what's right and uphold your agreements with your business partners, the integrity you act with will come back to you. Likewise, *not* acting with integrity will come back to you as well.

But what if your agreement isn't working out? Then you adjust the agreement. You don't decide not to honor an agreement just because you don't like it. That would be like ignoring a law you don't like, or making up your own rules about what laws you should abide by based on how you're feeling. It might be trendy right now, but it's not acting with integrity. And you can see how well that's working out for the people who are doing it. As I'm writing this in 2020, there are streets that are literally on fire in some of America's once-great cities. However you feel about the issues leading up to it, it's hard to deny at this point that the people causing the chaos aren't acting with integrity.

Shortsighted Marketing = Unsustainable Business

In any case, the choice to partner with Jim was an easy one when I saw what the loan officers around me were being required to do. American Builders Mortgage was making the other guys stay evenings to do telemarketing; they had to work every night from 6:00 to 9:00 PM. The only reason I wasn't required to was because I was generating enough business on my own, and much of that was thanks to the leads brought in by Jim.

There's nothing wrong with telemarketing on its face, but the way it used to work in my industry was too shortsighted for me to get on board. These guys would get on the phone, call up home-owners unsolicited and tell them that thanks to the low interest rates, "Now is the perfect time to refinance!" Obviously, everyone needs to supplement with some temporary marketing solutions from time to time — but who wants to do this every day? If you keep marketing like that, you never get to stop marketing. If you do things my way by marketing to centers of influence, then the referrals keep coming back. You'll be able to reduce your marketing budget and spend more time closing your sales.

There's a very good reason why you shouldn't want to make aggressive direct sales pitches your only form of marketing. What happens when the interest rates go up, and it's no longer "the perfect time" to refinance? (Or, think of an equivalent for that in your industry.) What happens is that business goes away, and that's what I mean by shortsighted marketing. For the telemarketing loan officers, these deals were all they had. When rates went up, they had to figure out how to do something else, and it was the very thing I had been doing all along: real reputation marketing.

My friend Mike at Remax would tell me, "As soon as the interest rates go up, all these loan officers start coming in to hit up our agents for business." He would ask these guys what they were doing before the rates started climbing, and they never had good answers. Then he'd tell them, "Ed's been here with us the whole time, so he's the one we're giving business to." Mike knew my reputation and my long-term thinking, and that meant I was the only kind of greedy bastard he could trust.

On a side note, short-term greed is the reason there are so many fly-by-night mortgage companies. Every time the interest rate drops, dozens of new shops will pop up overnight, only to disappear in a year or two. Over three decades, I've seen it happen with hundreds of them. Why don't they make it? Because they're just as shortsighted as the telemarketing loan officers I knew back then. They have unlicensed lackeys dialing for dollars; if any of the calls is a genuine lead, it gets transferred to the only licensed guy in the office and he typically cares very little about his reputation. These guys are only motivated by short-term greed, which means they don't feel like making connections with agents or builders is worth their time. They don't care about real reputation marketing — and so, they're really not companies. They're just shops, and they're unsustainable.

Like everything in this book, you can find a lesson in that no matter what business you're in. Whatever short-term successes are in your industry, don't get so hung up on knocking those out that you blow off your opportunities to aim higher. Find out what long-term success looks like in your field, and then start planting seeds wherever you can to get there. Short-term gains feel great for a minute, and then they're gone. Long-term gains feel great *and* pay you back in dividends, and that's why they're called long-term. They're what you need to build a sustainable business.

Strange Negotiations

At some point, Jim and I became such a big deal that other companies were pursuing us to move over to them. One of them was a branch run by two guys, Norm and Al, who had been on the periphery of American Builders Mortgage for a while. Their company (with a similarly generic name) offered us an 80% commission, plus a portion of branch profits.

At that time, we were getting 60% commission with an extra 5% for every month we had 10 or more loans. So moving somewhere offering 80% seemed like an easy decision, but we had become pretty well known with American Builders Mortgage and I wasn't sure it was a good idea to give that up just yet. Having read the book *The Art of the Deal*, I thought I could negotiate with the owner of the company to get more out of him and not have to move. "I'll stay if you just raise us to 65% commission," I said, "and we still keep our extra 5% if we hit 10 in a month."

"Mmmmm," he said. "No."

No? Really? Someone was offering me a 20% raise to leave this company, and here I was only asking for a 5% raise in order to stay. What was this guy's problem? "Go ahead," he said. "Go work for them."

There's no way he really wanted us to go. I figured his ego told him I was just playing hardball. Well, his ego was wrong. Jim and I were ready to go work for Norm and Al — but meanwhile, I still had six loans to finish up at American Builders Mortgage. The owner gave me the go-ahead to work with the processor to get them done, and I assumed that meant he intended to pay me at the end. As it turns out, he didn't. And that's when I learned this lesson: You can't get a good deal from a bad guy.

One of those loans was for a powerful gang member who had some notoriety for the book he published on his time in the Crips (where he had earned the nickname "Monster" for disfiguring a robbery victim so badly that the police labeled him as such). But believe it or not, Monster wasn't the bad guy in my scenario here. As far as I was concerned, he was just a guy who wanted to buy a house for his wife using his book royalties. I was happy to do the loan; the only problem was, Monster was serving five years in Pelican Bay State Prison.

Actually, even *that* wasn't a problem until the underwriter decided to make it hard on me. Upon initial review, she denied his loan application on the grounds that his income appeared unstable. I saw why she might think that, being that he was behind bars for the foreseeable future. But, not only did Monster have his book royalties; they were also working on a movie deal. My loan processor had my back; she took it upon herself to send the file to HUD for review. Technically, she argued, this guy was not unemployed; he was self-employed. And that's the way HUD saw it too. They said that as a literary author, he was generating income and his approval process could be like any other business owner's. Upon receiving HUD's letter, the underwriter was pissed at me for going over her head. So, she did exactly what a mature professional should *not* do in this circumstance; she decided to punish me by making the transaction as hard to complete as humanly possible. The only way this loan would be approved, she said, is if I held a face-to-face interview with Monster — a man who, at various times, has made the LAPD's list of top 10 most wanted gang members — where he would sign the documents in person.

And to do that, I had to travel 800 miles north to the maximum security prison where he lived.

At least I didn't pick a boring industry.

So, I sent a letter to Pelican Bay. There was a background check, a month-long approval process and the stipulation that my meeting could not be during regular visitor hours (only "lawyer hours"). Alrighty then. One month later, I was on a flight to San Francisco.

But it still wasn't that simple. From San Francisco, I would hop on a puddle jumper over to Eureka. There, I would shuttle to a nearby rental car establishment. To rent the car Jim had reserved for me, I would present the rental car clerk with Jim's credit card and a handwritten note from him giving permission for me to use it along with a photocopy of his ID (can you believe this was allowed then? It was!).

You might wonder: What was a guy who was finally making good money doing without a credit card? The answer is complicated, but it came down to me being gun shy. Having gone through a post-divorce period of feeling like everything I touched turned to shit, I was strictly cash-and-carry for a long time. That eventually changed, but I wasn't there just yet; also, paying off your past life is a common procrastination when you're busy trying to build a new one. Of course, a situation like this moved me closer to realizing I needed to.

After a perilous journey that took me on two planes and a shuttle just to reach my rental car, I drove an hour and a half through the redwood forests until I reached the outskirts of Crescent City, where Pelican Bay State Prison sits on 275 acres just before the Oregon border. From there, I was led on foot through the most powerful metal detectors I've ever been exposed to (the only ones that have ever picked up on the metal that went in my leg after a bike accident). I was taken into a building and an officer asked me for the documents. Through a slot in the door, he handed Monster the docs and a Bic pen without the cap or sheath on it (because those things can become deadly shanks if someone really wants it to). Then, finally, he let Monster sit down on the other side of the glass from me. I took a deep breath and began to explain what he was signing, just like I would with any other client.

Another thing I would do if this was any other client would be to engage in some light personal conversation. Of course, a guy like that doesn't always keep it light. Monster said a few things that day. He started off by apologizing for his appearance ("I'm normally darker, but I haven't seen any direct sunlight in a long time"). But the line that stuck with me was this:

"I've brought humans into this world, and I've taken them out of this world."

Other than that, he seemed like a nice guy who appreciated me helping out his wife.

They notarized the docs right there at the prison, and I was out of there. For one day, I got the thrill of being a lawyer without all the hassles I heard about on high school career day — and it was all thanks to Monster who wanted to buy a house for his wife and kids, the pain in the ass underwriter who tried to stop it from happening, and my partner Jim who helped me get where I needed to go.

Some time later, Monster's wife called to let me know he was actually getting out. I dropped by the house (which wasn't far from mine) to say hi and congratulate him on re-entering society. Once again, it was a brief but positive visit — and with a guy like that, I wouldn't want it any other way.

Getting a Good Deal

Monster's loan was one of the final six I had to finish up before leaving American Builders Mortgage. When the last loan closed, Jim and I were ready to head to Norm and Al's company; after all, the owner had told us we should. Of course, we had commission checks to cash first. I drove to Orange County to pick up my check in person and deposited it at my bank like any other payment, having no reason to believe it wouldn't clear.

Our official separation from the company happened one week later — and, as if by magic, that was the day I received a letter from the bank saying he had put a stop payment on the check. Then, he failed to pay me commission on the other five loans as well. When I called him, the conversation went something like this:

Me: "What the hell?!"

Him: "I don't have to pay you. You left."

Me: "We'll see what the labor board says about that."

Him: "Go for it."

Not surprisingly, the labor board said the law was clearly in my favor — but the company owner made sure the whole shitshow was strung out for months, with him failing to show up to the hearings until it reached California's Superior Court.

At that point, a judge with more power than anyone previously involved told him he was required to pay me. With this thing dragging out so long, I thought he might be using the time to come up with a better argument than, "Well, my attorney says I don't have to pay." But that was all he had. Pathetic.

Eventually, I was awarded a $45,000 Superior Court judgement. So I finally got paid, right? Nope. The day the judgement was issued in writing, that snake sold American Builders Mortgage to another company. He slithered away with no intention of paying me, and I doubt I was the only one.

I called the company he sold to; I wanted to get paid. My conversation with that company's owner went like this:

Me: "I have a judgement against American Builders Mortgage. You bought the company."

Him: "I didn't buy American Builders Mortgage."

Me: "I'm told you did."

Him: "We bought some of American Builders Mortgage's assets. We didn't take over their liabilities."

I never saw that $45,000. And that's how I learned that you can't get a good deal from a bad guy.

In this case, the guy was so bad that he had been running the company from Boron Federal Prison for the first year I was there. I didn't find that out until later; I thought his daughter was the owner at the time, but it turned out she was just the face of the business until he got out. When he did, he started showing up and became the boss again. I hoped that whatever white collar crime had landed him in prison was a one-off — but the problem is, bad people don't typically do one-offs. Bad guys are just bad guys. If they're capable of screwing somebody else, there's a good chance they'll screw you too if you give them the opportunity.

Unfortunately, the experience at Norm and Al's company was only a little bit better. Those guys weren't screwing us, but one of them was screwing the broker by lying about the number of loans we were funding. When Jim and I saw that happening, we knew the writing was on the wall; time to find yet another place to hang our licenses before the branch closed (which, of course, it soon did).

This time, it was an Orange County company that agreed to open an office for us. It was owned by a woman who, we were told, was a millionaire who would give us all the support we needed: great commissions, great infrastructure, even great equipment. We happily negotiated an arrangement there, ready to start over yet again. And things *were* great...for one whole month.

Technically, the first red flag was the cheaply furnished office. That should have sent us running in the other direction right off the bat, but it didn't. The next red flag surfaced immediately after we began bringing in business. We were qualifying new clients, putting new loans in the pipeline and doing our thing...business as usual. Then, said millionaire mysteriously started leaving bills on our desks and the desks of our loan officers (implying, of course, that we were responsible for paying them). These were bills for credit reports, which don't cost much but add up quickly, especially for someone newly licensed. Plus, what happened to having all the support we would need?

So once again, I found myself in an uncomfortable conversation with a company owner I was supposed to be answering to.

Me: "Whoa whoa whoa, what is this?"

Her: "This is the cost of doing business."

Me: "Yes...*your* cost of doing business. Credit reports are part of the overhead, and this is your company. We produce the business; you pay the overhead."

She would not concede, so Jim and I started eating costs like that to keep the peace and keep her from passing them on to our loan officers. We were paying company costs for a company that wasn't even ours. Then, more red flags emerged. Like we had everywhere else, we generated 10 to 15 loans a month easily; but here, we had to sit on them because there was only one processor to handle them all (the one we had brought with us). One last time, I went back to the millionaire.

Me: "We need another processor."

Her: "You guys don't do enough business to justify another processor."

We sure as hell did. But thinking back to those days with Dave and Harold, I caught myself: "You're a grinder...you grind on everyone..."

"You know," I said calmly, "If the loans get out faster, they'll come in faster."

"Oh no," she replied just as calmly. "That's not how it works."

It was, but I didn't have time to explain to her anymore. Jim and I were tired of being nickeled and dimed, with someone who was just looking at us as a paycheck calling all the shots. We wanted to call our own shots. And that's exactly what we did.

CHAPTER 12

"That was all foreplay; let's go for the real thing."[64]
- Other People's Money, 1991

JIM AND I agreed we needed to start our own company, but we knew it would take at least six to nine months to become FHA approved brokers and build something profitable. Unfortunately, I didn't have six to nine months; I had young kids who needed to eat every day, starting today. And if I didn't have time, Jim didn't have time.

How do you start a business in that situation? One way is to find an existing business to buy, one that has all the credentials you need; then, work hard to make it your own.

Since we had plenty of connections in the industry, it didn't take long before we were introduced to someone with a company to sell. His name was Bob, the owner of a little mom-and-pop mortgage shop called Wholesale Capital Corporation (WCC). I found out Bob had chosen his company name based on the specific meaning of each word:

- "Wholesale" means you're getting things cheaper than retail. It sounds like you're getting a good deal.
- "Capital" is synonymous with money. So, "Wholesale Capital" = "Cheap Money." Bob also saw it as an opportunity to put an image of the U.S. Capitol on his business card...which is a very different kind of capital. I'm not sure if he knew that.

- "Corporation" meant the business was already incorporated, which was a big plus for us.

Bob wanted us to keep the name, which we were fine with; however, the company had only closed a total of 14 loans in the last fiscal year. For those who don't know the mortgage industry, that's not great volume. But on the bright side for us, it meant Bob could set a relatively low asking price. Someone had already offered $15,000, and that was a little too low for him. Jim and I offered $25,000, and Bob accepted.

For that amount, we would get this set of pros and cons:

- Pro: The corporation already had an FHA approval.
- Pro: Three old computers (in 1995, no one knew what a computer's lifespan was).
- Con: A bunch of corporate books that weren't kept up properly.
- Con: A copy machine that broke before we closed escrow.

As the cons revealed themselves, we decided that none of them were dealbreakers; only the pro mattered, and that was the FHA approved brokerage. As long as we had that, we could make the company into whatever we wanted. We did see *one* problem, though, and it was a big one...

Jim and I didn't have $25,000.

That's a pretty big barrier to most people, but we were not about to throw up our hands and go back to some company where our hands were constantly tied. The lesson there is:

Don't be most people.

So, how did we buy the business? We got creative.

Bob wanted to retire, but he had to stick around until he had finished closing all the loans in his pipeline. While he did that, we moved in and started doing our loans with him as our broker. This meant he received all the service release premiums on our FHA and VA loans (service release premiums always go to the broker). If you're wondering what any of this has to do with us buying the business, hang in there!

We proposed to Bob that the service release premiums on our loans would go into a joint bank account with all our names on it. Once the balance on the account reached $25,000, Bob would consider that payment in full. We'd finish signing the papers and Wholesale Capital Corporation would be ours.

The Amazon Example

Was that like buying Bob's company with Bob's money? The answer is no, and Bob agreed. The fact was, Bob only had those premiums because of us. Here's a story that illustrates this concept on a larger scale.

In 2019, Amazon proposed a corporate facility in Queens that would have employed 25,000 to 40,000 New Yorkers. In exchange, the state was willing to give the company around $3 billion in tax breaks and other financial incentives. The deal was good for New Yorkers and good for Amazon. But after a very public fight, the company backed out. This was largely thanks to the protests of the highly vocal, deeply vapid Congresswoman Alexandria Ocasio-Cortez (D-NY), known to most as "AOC."

AOC's primary gripe was giving Amazon the tax breaks; she claimed that money could be better used to fix New York City's crumbling subways. But what AOC failed to acknowledge (or maybe didn't even understand) was that without Amazon, New York City wouldn't have that money anyways. It would only be there *because* of Amazon.

After months of trolling from the congresswoman and her minions on Twitter, Amazon withdrew its plans. Even New York's Democrat governor, Andrew Cuomo (who has plenty of far left ideas of his own), called it "a lost economic opportunity" that cost the state up to 40,000 jobs. And the subways *still* didn't get fixed. Brilliant!

Lucky for us, Bob was smarter than a 30-year-old bartender in Congress. He understood that had we gone to work for him, the service release premiums would have been his money — and without us, he wouldn't have them in the first place. With that, we negotiated the deal. It was good for us and good for him, just like the deal above would have been good for Amazon and good for New York City.

Why do you need all these details? Because maybe, like Jim and me, you want to acquire a business but don't have the funds to do it. Negotiating a creative deal was how we were able to get what we wanted, and you can do it too.

Signing it Over

It only took a few months for our service release premiums to add up to $25,000. Jim and I had an attorney review Bob's corporate books and prepared to sign the final documents for the sale. But now, at the eleventh hour, guess who *didn't* want to sign them? You guessed it.

All of a sudden, Bob had a serious case of seller's remorse. Three months prior, this same guy was ready to sell his company to us so he could retire. His wife was certainly ready; she stood over the table, handled the papers and showed Bob every place he needed to sign. Poor Phyllis was ready to get the hell out of there and go enjoy life with her husband, and now he was paralyzed with fear about the whole thing. He actually snapped at her: "Dammit Phyllis, why are you in such a hurry?!"

Where did this sudden regret come from? I think it was Bob's realization that thanks to these two guys Ed and Jim, he now had a humming company — so why would he walk away from it now? But unfortunately for him, *Bob* didn't have a humming company; *we* had a humming company. If we had never entered the picture, Bob would still be closing 14 loans per year.

After a lot of hemming and hawing with all of us standing around waiting for him to knock this shit off, Bob threw his hands in the air and started signing. Jim and I breathed a collective sigh of relief. Finally, we were business owners.

As he and Phyllis turned to walk away, I heard Bob say something he may not have meant to say out loud: "Oh well, I wasn't doing anything with it anyway."

That was certainly true. A couple of lessons for the Bobs of the world:

First, see the value in your raw materials.

Before you decide to sell an asset, take stock of what you have and consider whether investing in some improvements will make it more valuable. If Bob had seen what we saw in his materials, he could have made some improvements and had a more profitable sale (or, he may have decided not to sell at all). Either way, he would have been more satisfied with the outcome.

Next, be realistic about what you have.

We had the business; we just didn't have a company. Bob had a company; he just didn't have any business. Bob had a Ferrari; he just didn't have any racing fuel. We had limitless gallons of racing fuel, just no Ferrari to put it in. To make anything happen, one of us needed to trade.

Is that enough metaphors to make my point? Here's one more.

If you're selling a house that's a piece of crap, price it accordingly and understand that you can't buy it back for the same asking price once an investor puts $25,000 of renovations into it. It's not the same house anymore. You sold him a piece of crap and he turned it into a masterpiece.

That's what happened to Bob; the business we turned WCC into wasn't the same business we bought. Bob knew it, but he didn't admit it until he was forced to be honest with himself. He literally said it out loud: *"I wasn't doing anything with it anyway."*

We *were* doing something with it. And we never looked back.

CHAPTER 13

"To the next step."[65]
- American Pie, 1999

NOW, JIM AND I had a company; all we needed was a staff. Knowing that every tick on the clock was equal to money in (or out of) our pockets, we quickly assembled a small dream team by:

- Making our old loan opener a loan processor.
- Retaining Bob's loan processor.
- Stealing an underwriter from a competitor and making her head processor.
- And hiring two new loan openers who happened to be our wives.

Remember what my breaking point at the last company was: that conversation where the owner didn't understand my simple proposal of, "If the loans get out faster, they'll come in faster." Surprise, surprise...I was right:

- In month 1, we funded four loans.
- In month 2, we funded 14 loans.
- In month 3, we funded 24 loans.
- In month 4, we funded 42 loans.

If you get sales out faster, then sales will come in faster.

The next step was to move our office closer to home. Just because we bought a business located in San Bernardino, that didn't mean we had to stay there. We closed escrow on the sale of the corporation in March 1996; by June 1, we were moving into our new digs in Moreno Valley.

We still weren't a direct lender yet; we were just brokers, which made us kind of like middlemen. Being middlemen made it hard for us to have the kind of control we wanted over our transactions. For instance, we wanted our own in-house underwriter. Access to your own underwriter meant that if you were dealing with a challenge, you would have the ability to go to that person and ask directly: "How can I make this work?" But only direct lenders have their own underwriters. So to get what we wanted, we would have to get creative again.

Relying on our industry connections once more, we actually found a direct lender who liked our ambition and understood what we were trying to do. After all these years, I don't remember their actual name; it probably had some combination of "National," "Home" and "Mortgage" in it, as many direct lenders did at the time (unfortunately, the industry was severely lacking in creative business names back then).

This company proposed a deal: If we submitted all our loans to them, they would pay an underwriter to work for them, but work out of our office. We liked it, of course.

After about a year, an old friend from one of the previous companies, Danny, contacted us around the same time. His company was interested in doing the same thing, and they *were* local — so, we negotiated the same arrangement with them.

It was a perfect hybrid: They wanted our business, and we wanted their service. Because we brought in *enough* business, they were willing to negotiate with our terms.

That brings us to another lesson: *If you have enough of what they want, people will go out of their way for you.*

And, conversely...

If you don't have enough of what they want, no one will go out of their way for you.

Relationships matter — but as we all know, money talks. Even though we had relationships there, Danny's company wouldn't have done anything special for us if we were only doing Bob-level loan volume of 14 loans per year. That amounts to one or two loans a month max. We were doing 40 to 60 loans per month, so that made us worth their time and effort.

Even if they didn't want to move their people into our office, they would have had to add on payroll anyway just to take on the extra business we brought in. Since we *were* the ones bringing in the business, they were willing to put an underwriting, funding and doc drawing department right in our office. It's another example of structuring a deal that was good for us and good for the other party. One more time, the lesson is:

Don't be most people. Get what you want by negotiating something that works for everyone.

Now, we were working as a fully functional direct lender before we could officially obtain that status. It felt great, but I knew that making it official would feel even better.

At that time, the threshold at which one could become a direct lender was $1,000,000 net worth. That would enable you to have your own warehouse line (a big line of credit used for funding mortgages) and be approved to sell as a correspondent lender (this meant closing the loans in your name, funding them to your warehouse line and then selling them to Fannie Mae, Freddie Mac or another mortgage company).

My goal was to become a direct lender as quickly as possible. What did I need first? $1,000,000 net worth. And what was the fastest way to reach $1,000,000 net worth? Buying properties.

A Mammoth Proposal

I started skiing in 1993. Some hobbies you try once or twice and decide they aren't your thing. But with skiing, I had the opposite experience. I never really skied before age 32 — but once I did, I took to it like a duck to water. In California, there's almost no better place to ski than Mammoth Mountain. I knew one person who had a place in Mammoth: Ray, who owned a company that we would refer Title 1 loans to before we were licensed to do them. For every Title 1 loan I sent his way, Ray would give Dawn and me a weekend stay in his Mammoth condo. That was our first real exposure to the area.

Eventually, Ray asked if we wanted to buy his place. At the time, the answer was no; I thought Big Bear was a better option for us, being only an hour from home (as opposed to five hours from home, which was the drive time to Mammoth). Unfortunately, it didn't take long to figure out that ski-worthy conditions were not always a guarantee in Big Bear. But in Mammoth, they are. There's more than enough snow every year. That got me looking at the area more closely.

Sometime in 1996, I read in Ski Magazine that Intrawest Corp. (now Intrawest Resorts Holding) was planning to buy a huge stake in the Mammoth Mountain Ski Area from Dave McCoy, the skier and businessman responsible for transforming the remote mountain peak into a world-class ski destination way back in 1942. Intrawest owned a bunch of high-class ski resorts, and Mammoth would be their next conquest. Soon, it seemed like everyone in Mammoth was preparing for this promising future. And at the end of one of those weekend stays, that's when the idea hit me like a lightning bolt:

- I could pick up cheap properties in Mammoth.
- As Intrawest began improving the area, the values would go up.
- And that would be the fastest way to get to $1,000,000 net worth.

Paul Oster, a titan of Mammoth real estate, wrote an article in the Mammoth Times entitled "Location Location Location" that got me even more excited — and the next thing I knew, I was meeting with him to look at properties.

"What you really want to do is get near the north village," Paul said. "It's good for skiing and everything else." The first property Paul found for us was Crestview 44, a one bedroom/loft and three bath condo priced at $91,000. The price was right, but I saw why. We spent one weekend there, during which we slept on the foldout couch (because that's how gross the beds were). At the end of the weekend, Dawn had two reactions:

1. "Ick" (or perhaps it was "blech").
2. "Can we get out of this?"

I called Paul to tell him this wasn't really what we had in mind.

"It's not just what you see here," he said. "You need to see what else is in the building."

He took us around to some other units — and then, I saw it. These other units were 100% better than what we had just stayed in, and we could make Crestview 44 look just like them. So we decided to buy it, renovate it and rent it out. That way, we could use it and make money off it when we weren't there.

The problem, I discovered, is that resort rentals rarely give you positive cash flow. People only rent them for one, two or three nights; then, you have to pay the cleaning crew to get it ready for the next guest. There's a separate cleaning fee every time they come in. In this case, it amounted to 36% of what we just made by renting it out. If I rented it out for $200 a night, I lost $72 on each guest stay.

When it comes to a resort rental, the bottom line is this:

- If you *don't* have it rented out every day, you won't collect a net big enough to cover your mortgage payment.
- If you *do* have it rented out every day, you'll never get to enjoy it yourself.

That's not necessarily a lose-lose, just something to be aware of.

There are other drawbacks associated with using a property management company in a resort area, especially if it's a place where big events take place. One year, when the Gravity Games event was held in Mammoth, the property managers informed us that renters would be in our home the weekend we planned to use it (in fact, they were going to be in it for the entire month of January). I really wanted to use it in January, but the idea of making money instead won out.

So we missed out on access to our mountain property in the peak of ski season in exchange for making a profit. By the end of January, I was feeling great about all the money I was making by letting these tenants use my property instead of me. I thought it might be enough to cover two or three months of mortgage payments. But on the day I got the check, I saw that it was only half of what I was expecting.

Obviously, I asked the property manager what the hell happened.

"Where's the rest of my money?" I said.

"They're with the Gravity Games," she said, "so we gave them a 50% discount." *Really*?!

So now, I didn't have access to my condo *and* I didn't make nearly the amount of money I thought I would? Also, why did no one *ask* me if I was okay with giving a half-off discount? The property managers gave a discount because of what the Gravity Games meant to the city — but the city didn't pay my mortgage, and the city didn't pay my HOA dues, the city didn't make my down payment and the city didn't invest in the renovations. This wasn't the city's place; it was *my* place.

How much was the check? With these people staying in my unit for next to nothing, it was barely enough to cover my mortgage payment for one month. I had thought I would be able to cover several.

So here's the lesson:

If something seems too easy, there's probably a reason.

And if someone acts like they can help you make a lot of money, there's probably a big chunk of money in it for them. It might even be more than what you'll make. You'll have to decide if that's worth your time and investment.

I understand things are a little different today, with vacation rental models through services like Airbnb and VRBO. Just be aware: If you're looking to make money off vacation rentals, research all the pros and cons of whatever model is facilitating it.

Figuring Out the Formula

Eventually, we acknowledged that building a $1,000,000 net worth was going to require a lot more than buying a single condo. So we started the pattern of buy, renovate, and rent out until the appreciation was there — at which time we had our net worth and could consider whether to sell or continue to rent out. Today, that's a strategy that real estate investors call "buy and hold." And that's what we did — we bought and held, all over the north village of Mammoth Lakes.

And when I say "we," I'm not just referring to myself and Dawn. Wholesale Capital Corporation, my business, was making the mortgage payments and collecting the rents. I was managing the projects. This is how we were able to use these investments to inject net worth into the business, moving us closer to our goal of becoming a direct lender.

We started with Crestview 44. We had bought it for $91,000 and put $45,000 into the renovations. The next step was renting it out while the market cycled back up, then selling it for $294,000. During this time, we bought three more properties for our buy and hold strategy, working our way through the condos of Mammoth.

- We bought Mountainback 50 for $130,000 and put a renter in it right away.
- We bought Crestview 40 for $140,000 and put a renter in it right away.
- We bought Viewpoint 106 for $161,000 and put a renter in it right away.

We held these properties for three years. Since I had deeded the properties to my company, my company was collecting the rents and making the payments. Within a very short time, this gave us the $1,000,000 net worth we needed to become a direct lender. We didn't have that cash on hand, but as the value of the properties was increasing, the company was building in net worth because equity was being assigned to the company. We got our warehouse lines, our FHA approval, our HUD mortgagee status and then, finally, we officially became a direct lender on October 15, 1998. Goal achieved.

When we saw there was enough appreciation to sell:

- We sold Mountainback 50 for $294,000.
- We sold Crestview 40 for $280,000.
- We sold Viewpoint 106 for $325,000.

And on and on we went, continuing to do that throughout Mammoth and a couple of homes in the Inland Empire. That's how the buy and hold strategy worked for me.

Now, back to the story of the company.

Getting Screwed

After officially becoming a direct lender, we had to inform our tenants (Danny's company) that we were no longer going to broker to them. After all, a direct lender doesn't broker to anyone...hence the name *"direct lender."* But people will find any excuse not to pay you, and this company was no exception. Once again, I had someone telling me they didn't plan to pay me for the work I had done because of some perceived slight. We even went the extra mile to get a few loans they were concerned about refinanced, but that didn't matter. They would not pay us for the six loans we brokered to them right before going direct.

I wasn't about to let them get away with it. This wasn't just about me not getting paid personally; this was about the six loan officers who brought in the business and worked on the loans not getting paid. As the president of WCC, I had responsibilities to other people who trusted me enough to work for me. So WCC paid the loan officers for their loans, and the company took the loss.

Unlike the previous times I was told we wouldn't be getting paid, I wasn't notified in a face-to-face dialogue. This time, it was on an answering machine message. Danny called one morning while everyone was still asleep (probably to avoid confrontation) and left me a 6:00 a.m. voicemail:

"Hey man, just wanna let you know that the company isn't going to pay you. Don't bother having your lawyer send letters...just go ahead and file a lawsuit...you'll probably lose...at least I hope you do, because then I'll get that money."

What a dick.

We sued the company, which we won. We sued Danny personally, which we lost. The judge made us pay Danny's legal fees, and the

$50,000 we got from the company barely covered that plus our own attorney fees. So the lesson there is:

The only people who win in lawsuits are the lawyers.

It also reminds me of a line from the 1996 movie *Primal Fear*: "If you want justice, go to a whorehouse. If you wanna get fucked, go to court."[66]

Getting Screwed Again

Our company continued to grow and we added on more staff: more underwriters, more doc drawers, more funders and a secondary marketing guy to do loan locks. We even got a little revenge against Danny's company by hiring some people away from them. If mortgage isn't your business and the job titles bore you, just think of the equivalents in your industry. When you make your first million and start really branching out, what positions will you be filling? Start thinking about them now; use them as motivation.

With the staff growing so quickly, some of them would start asking if we'd consider hiring their family or friends. Sometimes this works out and sometimes it doesn't. A woman named Elaine, who had helped us get our warehouse lines and FHA approval, told us about her boyfriend Gene. She wanted him to be our secondary marketing guy.

Meanwhile, my loan officer Will wanted us to hire his friend Scott to be our first information technology specialist (although with this being the late 90s, we were still just calling the position "computer guy." No one was saying "IT" yet). I hired Scott and asked him to create a program that could track our rate sheets. The sheet would show which companies we were selling our loans to on the secondary market based on applicable rates: Source One, Countrywide, Principal Financial. When reviewing these sheets every week, I kept noticing loan after loan being sold to Principal Financial no matter what the rate was. That was suspicious, so I approached Gene.

Every time, his strategy was to talk over my head: "This is not just a numbers thing," he'd say. "It's a gut feeling. You have to really analyze where it makes sense to sell each of these loans." I didn't buy that for very long, and my suspicions were soon confirmed: Someone at Principal Financial was Gene's golf buddy. He was funneling them business to further his personal relationship. Without going into points and percentages and mortgage minutiae, suffice it to say that this greatly affected how much we would make from each sale on the secondary market. Over the course of the 18 months this was going on, Gene ended up costing our company $600,000.

Here's the lesson I learned from that:

If someone is acting like something involving money is over your head, there's probably a reason. You need to:

- *Take a pause.*
- *Use common sense.*
- *Look at the numbers.*

Chances are, you'll figure out you're being screwed.

And of course, the other lesson learned is that hiring the personal connections of employees is a crapshoot. It might work; it might not. Unfortunately, there's no math to help figure that out. When it comes to hiring decisions, sometimes it's best to go with your gut. I should have done that when I first had suspicions about Gene.

At least hiring Scott worked out.

CHAPTER 14

NOW IT WAS 2000, a time when most professionals were either caught up in the dot com bubble or breathing a sigh of relief that Y2K didn't happen. As a nation, it was also the last year that we shared some kind of collective innocence before the events of September 11, 2001 took that away.

It was pretty exciting to enter the 21st century as a direct lender. By this time, *everyone* had an IT guy. But in our industry, the next big thing I was told we needed was Fannie Mae approval.

The idea behind this was to make ourselves look bigger with the prestigious title of Fannie Mae Seller/Servicer. Everyone was saying that if we had that, we would be on a faster track to going nationwide. However, I didn't necessarily *want* to go nationwide. I was doing just fine being solely licensed to do loans in the once-great state of California (it wasn't quite that bad here yet).

Here's a quick primer on Fannie Mae:

- It's part of the secondary market, where loans are bought and sold.
- People invest in Fannie Mae bonds, and those bonds are made of mortgages.
- Those mortgages are guaranteed and "backed by the full faith and credit of the U.S. government." The

government backs these loans because they are loans for hard, tangible assets (real estate).

That guarantee looks great on a lender's resume.

Looking back, I realize there's a fascinating parallel here. Remember why kids go to college before they know what kind of career they want?

- Because they think it's what they're supposed to do.
- Because everyone tells them it's the "natural next step."
- And because it looks great on a résumé.

With a great résumé and $5, you can buy a cup of coffee at Starbucks. But it won't have whipped cream, nor will it have any toppings. I don't know a single kid who likes coffee without those things anymore.

A lot of kids learn that the hard way. They graduate, don't know what career direction they want, then apply for jobs that have nothing to do with their major. This amounts to a wasted degree. And if you're the parent, that amounts to your wasted investment.

So where's the parallel? It's right here.

I decided to move forward on becoming a Fannie Mae Seller/ Servicer. As a company, we worked to attain the approval, including paying all the required fees. After all...

- Isn't this what we were supposed to do?
- Everyone said this was the "natural next step."
- And it looked great on a résumé.

Then, we never sold Fannie Mae a single loan. It turned out we did much better selling to banks and other servicers. But hey...we had a title to put on our résumé.

Exactly like a college degree.

Branching Out, Falling Hard

By this time, lots of people were wanting to come work for us. I liked hiring my friends, as long as they were interested in learning the business and motivated to succeed. My target was someone who had good people skills and a good work ethic. The mortgage part was something I could teach them as we went along. Someone who fit that bill was my friend Randy. He was smart, he was energetic and his big personality was a great fit for the mortgage business.

Randy did great working out of our office. So when the time came that he asked to open his own branch — closer to his home in the High Desert community, where the real estate market was exploding in the early 2000s — I thought it sounded like a great idea. In fact, it sounded like such a great idea that we agreed to give him 25% of the branch profits on top of his regular commission. There was no reason to believe Randy wouldn't make it worth our while; as a salesperson, he had been kicking ass for quite a while.

As the owner of the company, I still had to pay all the standard overhead for Randy's new branch: office space, equipment, alarm services...and of course, a staff. Randy seemed cut out to manage them at first; after all, he had learned from me.

Unfortunately, it was thanks to Randy that I learned this lesson for the first time:

Not every good salesperson will make a good manager.

Randy knew how to sell, and I thought I had taught him how to manage (if he was paying attention). But once it was up to him to take what he had learned and duplicate it on his own, he just...couldn't.

Like I said, salespeople wake up every day unemployed. And every day, 1/30th of your next house payment, electric bill, car payment and grocery budget is used up. So if you can't go out there and do what it takes to ring the cash register every day, you're moving backwards. Randy moved backwards quickly. He was our first guy to branch out and expand our company, and he was about to fall hard. That was bad for both of us.

Synergy in a Sales Context

People hear a term like "synergy" used in business and dismiss it as a buzzword. But let's think about what it means. Its definition is "elements that work together to create a total effect." In a sales environment, those elements are people, and those people are often competing with each other.

When a bunch of salespeople are in the same workspace, everyone's working to do better that month than the next guy. Everyone wants their name to be at the top of the chart at the next meeting. Everyone wants to get pats on the back and shout-outs in emails, all those little dopamine hits we seek out that become our incentives to do better. That's synergy in a sales context: one guy competing with a bunch of other guys, all of you working as little elements together and amounting to a total effect that moves you forward.

Some people can leave that synergy behind and go create their own. They can duplicate what they've learned and inspire synergy as a leader of other salespeople. Unfortunately, Randy was not one of those people. When he was in my corporate office, he would be the one who had to close 11 loans as soon as he heard someone else had closed 10. Once he didn't have anyone to compete with, that drive started to diminish. And while some people would at least be motivated by the bills piling up on the desk for all that aforementioned overhead, Randy wasn't — because he knew I was the one paying those bills, not him.

On top of all this, he was in deep denial about what was happening.

Shiny Objects

For the first couple of years, Randy had a profitable run. He was hiring loan officers and producing. But eventually, he got distracted by glossy-painted, chrome-plated classic cars (as men of a certain age and personality type often do). I was hearing stories from his team — and in fact, he would even tell me himself — that every Tuesday at 5:30 p.m., Randy had to leave for "cruise night" at whatever local 1950s-themed diner was hosting his car club. It didn't matter whether clients were coming in the door or not.

Managing his staff and finding new clients to serve were not Randy's priorities anymore. His priorities were, in this order:

- Get to the diner parking lot by 6 p.m.
- Crank up the oldies radio station.
- Stroke and shine his Corvette.
- Talk to all the people oohing and aahing.

Although I'm sure he used some of that as a marketing opportunity to meet people and pass out cards, it wasn't showing in his volume.

A New Deal

At some point, we determined that Randy needed to close six loans a month just to break even. Otherwise, it was not feasible for the company to continue paying for his office space and expenses. When it was time to renew his lease, I proposed a new deal to him.

Me: "I'll renew the lease if you sign on it with me. I'll give you 50% of the branch profits, plus your commission. But if your branch goes negative, then you'll write me a check for half the loss."

Him: "That's not fair."

Me: "What do you mean it's not fair?"

Him: "Well, I don't have any control."

Me: "You have control over how hard you work."

Him: "I don't have any control over the bills."

At this point, I had to level with him.

"Randy...when it comes to your branch, you have *all* the control. I don't pay any bills that you don't rack up. I don't hire people unless you ask me to hire them. I don't buy a new copier unless you tell me you need one. We don't buy new computers unless you need them for the people you ask me to hire. I don't come up with new ways to spend money on your branch; *you* do. Most importantly, I don't have any control over how hard you or anybody at your office works — and recently, it appears that's not very hard."

I thought I knew what the outcome would be. I figured he would sign on the dotted line, go negative once in the first month, honor the agreement by writing me a check for half, and be motivated to never go negative again.

But that's not what happened.

What did happen was another mistake: Randy, along with one of the guys he had brought in, decided *now* was the time to go open their own company. They couldn't succeed at running a small branch of *my* company — but somehow, they planned to succeed at starting their own (to be fair, I knew they would do fine at the "starting it" part. That part is usually the most fun. It was the "running it" part that wouldn't be successful).

"It's not personal," Randy told me. "It's just business."

Oh good grief. I love movie quotes, but only when they make sense for the situation. And this one didn't.

"No," I told him. "I understand the personal part. You want to be masters of your own universe, and I'm okay with that. But the business part doesn't make any sense. We are not making any money *now*. You think I'm making a bunch of money off you, and I'm not. I'm showing you the books; I'm not hiding anything. You think you're going to make more money working at the same rate you are now, with all the costs of opening up an office of your own?"

He didn't have much to say to that, which tells me A) he was surprised by the revelation that I wasn't hiding anything from him, and B) he really hadn't thought this through at all.

So I just kept talking, hoping something I said would resonate. "You're telling me you're ready to go drop $65,000 on furniture, signs, licenses and all that stuff? I know you're not. If you want to do that, just take over the office space; I'll sell you the furniture for $25,000 just to cover what I put into it." To help him transition as smoothly as possible, I even said he could keep operating as one of my branches until he was sure he was ready to flip the switch. I was being a lot more generous than most people are in the mortgage industry, but that's what friends do.

This was a very good deal. I had heard Randy's desire to start his own company (which, technically, would be my competitor), and was giving him everything he could possibly need to hit the ground running. If he really wanted a successful new business of his own, he would take it...right?

Wrong. I couldn't believe what came out of his mouth next:

"But it's used furniture."

Was he shitting me?

"Randy, it was used by *you*!"

What was his problem? It was pride, which is a poison pill until you swallow it (and he was clearly refusing to do that). Rather than taking over the lease on the office he was already occupying and giving me $25,000 for the furniture he had already been using (only half of what I had put into it), Randy and his partner spent $65,000 to open up a new office in the same neighborhood, plus additional one-man branches for anyone they could recruit. But without him or anyone else working hard enough, he was running it into the ground.

Because all of this was "just business," Randy and I stayed friends the whole time — which, unfortunately, meant I still had to watch his downward spiral. When we got together, I'd try to reason with him; my hope was that he'd come back to work for me, in my corporate office, where he'd been so successful. After all, that's what gave him the confidence to branch out on his own in the first place.

Every time, he refused to admit things just didn't work out; meanwhile, his wife would be inside telling my wife the truth about how bad things were. But apparently, Randy didn't know that. Because a short time later, when we sat together on a harbor cruise at a friend's wedding, he actually had the nerve to casually announce this to me: "I'm retired."

Retired? Um, no.

Randy's company had failed and he was no longer working. But that's not the same as being retired, especially when you're living off Social Security in a trailer while your wife still hustles to bring home a paycheck by cutting hair. He could *call* himself retired, but I knew it was not in the way he (or anyone) wanted retirement to be. Also, I knew my friend had too much life left in him to go on like this.

The lesson of Randy's story is this: *Your pride will make you broke.*

"Randy," I said. "You're not retired. You were making money working for us. Come back. You have the talent; you have the knowledge. All you need is some motivation, and you know you can get it with us." After a long night of coaxing him on a Hornblower boat wedding cruise, Randy was convinced to come back to us. But not before he gave me every excuse in the book for why he didn't make it as a business owner:

- "I just don't like having to kiss agents' asses."
- "I just don't like having to take out the trash."
- "I just don't want to dust and vacuum, and we could never afford a janitor."
- "I just don't want to deal with alarm companies."

Okay, fine. If he had been honest about all of that early on, he could have saved himself a lot of money, time and grief. And if he had worked hard enough to do one extra loan a year, he could have hired a janitor.

But Randy couldn't motivate himself to do it. He had to be around other people who energized him. That's what happened when he came back to work on my team. He put in a good five years, and then he *actually* retired...with dignity.

Some salespeople can live by the mantra, "Me motivates me." Typically, those are the ones who also make good managers. The ones who can't are not necessarily bad salespeople; often, they just need to be in a competitive environment with other sales-people to stay motivated. They need the synergy.

What to Do If That's You

If that's you, it's okay. Just be honest with yourself about it and find a place where you can stay employed. There are great sales jobs out there where you can make a lot of money off commis-sions; sometimes, you can still earn a wage on top of it. In my industry, the law now says your employer has to pay you a min-imum draw on top of commission.

But if you don't do anything — well, then you don't *make* anything. And unless you have some very generous relatives willing to support you indefinitely, not making anything is not an option.

One More Lesson

Randy's branch was my first one, and it was a failed experiment we both learned from. The next branch we opened, in the Temecula valley (Southern California's wine country), eventually became successful. But when we first opened it up, the woman running it turned out to be a bit of a swindler. She was a real estate agent simultaneously licensed to originate loans (this is legal as long as it's disclosed). The problem was, she used our resources to run her real estate business and made the mortgage origination a secondary priority (if that). Meanwhile, she was using our office space and equipment to sell homes, an endeavor which only benefited her. Basically, that amounts to theft.

Once I got suspicious, I sent someone out there to be the eyes and ears and report back to me. If you're planning on branching out, this is a necessary thing from time to time and you shouldn't feel guilty about it. You're investing in new branches, and you need to make sure the people running them are doing it properly. You are your brand, and these people are representing you.

I found out what she was up to, fired her and learned one more lesson for this chapter:

Before you invest in someone, make sure they're capable and willing to produce a return.

Fortunately, that branch got on track with the team that took it over. And in the coming years, we opened some very successful branches. But what I found even more success with was real estate investing. As I say on my talk radio show every week (The Main Event, which airs on Salem Media Group stations in Southern California and in podcast on iTunes, Soundcloud and my website EdHoffman.net), there are some fantastic opportunities in real estate. If you're ready to learn more about those opportunities, I'm ready to tell you.

CHAPTER 15

*"You wanna play the game? Learn to play it right...
the best game in the world. I'll teach you."*[68]
- Other People's Money, 1991

EVERYBODY THINKS THAT the best way to support yourself in retirement is to "live off the interest" of your investments. I used to think that too.

But what if your investments haven't earned enough interest for you to live off by the time you retire? A lot of people find themselves in that position. Back when I did real estate investment presentations, here's something I started out with:

To have $50,000 a year in retirement income...

Based on a 5% return on the investment...

You need $1,000,000 in investment assets.

This is assuming you want to live off the interest only, never touching the principal.

Do *you* have $1 million in assets? If the answer is no, then you need to protect yourself from the fallacy that you'll be able to "live off the interest" in retirement. Here's how I did that.

A Strategic Bet

After seeing the returns on my Mammoth properties, I was feeling pretty confident as an investor — and yet, I still held onto the idea that my best long-term vehicle was mutual funds. By 2002, I was stashing away anywhere from $10,000 to $20,000 a month in them.

Based on the formula you see above, you'll need $1,000,000 in investment assets to yield $50,000 a year in retirement income. By pouring so much into mutual funds, I thought I could get to $1,000,000 in just a few years — and then, repeat the process until I had my goal amount for retirement. So in one moment of exceptional confidence, I proposed a bet to a guy named Jeff at the office.

Me: "I bet you I can put $1 million into mutual funds in three years."

Jeff: "I'll bet you $10,000 bucks you can't do that."

Me: "Watch me."

Jeff: "If you make enough money to put $1 million in mutual funds in the next three years, that means I'm gonna make a ton of money too. So I won't mind paying you $10,000 — but since I still don't think it's realistic, I intend to collect if you lose."

Challenge accepted.

At the rate I was going, all I had to do was maintain a deposit of $28,000 a month into my mutual funds for the next three years in order to win the bet. I'm not sure why Jeff thought I couldn't do it — and, there was something I knew that he didn't: The stock market had just taken a dump, largely in response to the accounting scandals of major corporations like Enron and WorldCom. By October 2002, the Dow had fallen to 7,268 points (which is a big drop even today, but back then it was even more significant — around 50% of the value of the Dow Jones Industrial Average).

When we made the bet and Jeff said he "intended to collect," I had an intention of my own: It was to get halfway there before the stock market would come back up, increasing the value of my shares and essentially handing me the other half. I thought I had everything figured out, and I thought my mutual fund investments were the key to a comfortable retirement. I was wrong.

A Thought-Provoking Prophecy

Later that winter, Dawn and I went to dinner with Paul, the Mammoth real estate agent who helped me buy all those vacation rentals. As we were eating, drinking and being merry with him, the conversation naturally turned to our investments and individual quests.

A few drinks containing Myers's rum into the evening, I told Paul about the bet. I guess I expected him to be impressed; what I didn't expect was a reading recommendation.

"You ever heard of a book called *Rich Dad's Prophecy*?" he asked.

It didn't sound familiar. "Mmm, no."

He continued. "Have you ever read *Rich Dad, Poor Dad*?"

"No." By that point, I thought I had read just about everything.

"I just bought a copy for everyone in my office," he said. "You should read it."

It wasn't long before I came home one night to find the book waiting for me on the couch. Dawn knew that if Paul thought the book was important — important enough to give to all his employees — then it was important enough for me to read too.

I had no idea what a big deal the *Rich Dad* books by Robert Kiyosaki were at the time. *Rich Dad's Prophecy* was the most current installment. Its premise was that the biggest stock market crash in our lifetime would occur in 2016, when the first wave of baby boomers (born in 1946) would turn 70. By law, that's the age at which they would have to start withdrawing from their 401(k)s, IRAs and other retirement funds (and of course, begin paying taxes on them).

As those 70-year-olds (around 2 million people) would pull that money out of the market en masse, the natural result would be for the stock market to plummet. That would make the younger boomers (who were lined up behind them to retire next) see the stock market take a drop, go into panic mode and begin to pull their funds out, too. Whether they moved it to bonds, bank accounts or under the mattress, they would get their money out of the market to protect it. Furthermore, a new batch of these boomers would turn 70 every year for the next 18 years.

According to the book's prediction, the end result would be 71 million Americans pulling money out through 2031, plunging the market further and further down. That would mean there would be opportunities to grab up low-priced investments, which would then increase in value as the market climbed back up, eventually peaking again. This is how, in theory, one could profit from a major stock market crash.

I asked around about it, getting the opinions of people who were more knowledgeable than me on the subject (always a good idea). Most of them said they didn't see any reason to fundamentally disagree with the prediction.

Today, we know Kiyosaki's prophecy wasn't entirely accurate for 2016 (whether it happens a few years late remains to be seen). But at the time, it certainly got me thinking about my habit of stashing away so much in mutual funds. Maybe putting $20,000 a month into these funds wasn't as smart as I thought. Maybe they weren't the long-term, super-safe, end-all-be-all vehicle for wealth building. Eventually, I lost the bet with Jeff. But the good news is, it was by choice — because I found something that worked much better.

Introduction to Passive Income

Kiyosaki and his *Rich Dad* book series have been credited with bringing the concept of passive income into the mainstream. Passive income is generated without the aggressive, day-to-day maintenance of a job or traditional business. It doesn't mean there's no work involved; creating it requires you to take a risk by investing time and money in the beginning. But if you use the right vehicle, your investment essentially maintains itself over time.

Kiyosaki is also known for peppering his books with anecdotes to illustrate financial lessons; one story in *Rich Dad's Prophecy* was particularly inspiring to me as I learned more about the concept of passive income. It was about an investment he and three friends made in a large apartment complex. They acted as partners and split the costs four ways, from the down payment to the renovations of the vacant units. Along the way, they filled the vacancies. Naturally, the value went up substantially.

One year later, they were able to refinance the property and pull out their entire original investment. For the sake of simplicity, let's say the total investment between the four partners was $1 million; that means they each pulled out $250,000. That's an arbitrary figure, but I do recall reading that each partner's net, after all the expenses were paid, was $120,000 a year in positive cash flow. Think of that: Everyone netting six figures a year without any active participation in the upkeep or management of the property. That's an illustration of generating passive income.

When I started investing in real estate, I didn't see it as a retirement strategy. Remember, I only bought up vacation properties in Mammoth to build the net worth of my company and meet the goal of becoming a direct lender. Technically, I was still sold on the vision that some of you have today:

- Get a good job or build a successful business.
- Invest in your 401(k) or in mutual funds.
- Hopefully, have enough to live off the interest when it comes time to retire.

There's nothing wrong with doing that, but most of us are going to need more if we plan to live more than a few years past 65. Here's another scenario to illustrate.

Let's say your kids are raised, your house is paid off and you're relatively debt free. Rather than needing $50,000 a year in supplemental retirement income, you'll only need $36,000. As you get closer to retirement age, you'll typically move your funds out of aggressive, high return investments and into something with more stability/less risk. You can expect a much lower rate of return (maybe 3%), but without the volatility. So here's the formula:

> To have $36,000 a year in retirement income...
>
> Based on a 3% return on the investment...
>
> You need $1,200,000 in investment assets.
>
> Once again: This is assuming you want to live off the interest only, never touching the principal.

The point is, retirement requires more money than you realize.

Let's look at the original concept of retirement accounts. When the government enacted the Employee Retirement Income Security Act of 1974 (ERISA), the idea behind 401(k) and IRA accounts was:

- Put money away in a retirement account.
- Defer the taxes until you retire and start withdrawing from the accounts.
- Reduce your liability as you get closer to retirement (by paying off your house and your kids being grown), which means you'll naturally need less money to live and be in a lower tax bracket.

But what if you don't *want* to be in a lower tax bracket when you retire? What if you want to live off more than $2,000–$3,000 a month? What if you want to replace the 40 hours a week you spent at work for the last 40 years with travel and enjoying life?

If that's the case, then you need to create additional retirement income.

But the point is, most of us need a lot more than $36,000 to get through the year — and *that's* why we need passive income. To create it, you might choose to take one of these actions:

- **Invest in your retirement account more aggressively.** For the entire 40 years you build your retirement account, you can continue to maximize your contributions and choose more aggressive investments to get a higher rate of return on your money. But for most of those 40 years, you'll still have living expenses and debts to pay — so realistically, how many years can you afford to do that? And, what if you need to access your funds early because you're putting so much into your investments that you don't have enough to cover an emergency or live comfortably? You'll have to sell some of your assets off, which means paying a capital gains tax.

- **Have a business that continues to pay you after retirement.** Maybe you've spent these 40 years building a thriving business that someone else takes over when you retire, with a provision in place for you to continue getting paid. That's great — but what happens when they figure out they don't need you anymore? Many times, they find a legal way to stop paying you.
- **Own a piece of property that generates income.** With the right real estate investments, you can make that $1,200,000 long before retirement. If you need to access any of your profits early, you can do that by refinancing one of your properties. By doing a 1031 Exchange, you can avoid paying a capital gains tax and continue to invest in *more* properties to build up even more assets. As you may have guessed, this is the method I suggest to generate passive income for retirement. We'll talk more about the 1031 Exchange as we go along; for right now, just know that it's an IRS-approved strategy to help you defer paying taxes as you build your investment portfolio.

My Bright Idea

Right away, I set out to duplicate Kiyosaki's apartment complex investment; this included the part about partnering with like-minded friends. To generate the capital needed for a down payment on a building, I thought I would need to team up with at least two people. The down payment would be in the neighborhood of $6 million, which required each of us to put up $2 million. Jim (now my longtime business partner) and Dan (my appraiser) were on board, since they were both fairly experienced. Dan had

15 or 20 long-term rentals, Jim had one or two, and I had none. So of course, it made perfect sense that I would be the one to devise the plan!

"Here's the plan," I said. "We each buy 20 properties. We hold them for five years, or until each one has $100,000 in equity. That's $2 million in equity each, which gives us $6 million for the down payment on an $18 million apartment complex. Then, we can finance the balance with a $12 million loan. If we're renting out 300 units for $1,200 a month, that's $360,000 a month in gross income."

Was I factoring in costs? You bet. I accounted for all the overhead I could think of, deducting:

- $90,000 for 25% unit vacancies, leaving us with $270,000.
- $80,000 for the mortgage payment/PITI, leaving us with $190,000.
- $40,000 for utilities, repairs, management and incidentals, leaving us with $150,000.

Then, divide that $150,000 between the three of us. That gave us each $50,000 — *per month, in passive income.* Multiply that by 12 months, and we each had $600,000 a year in positive cash flow. Not bad.

From Three Partners to None

However, it didn't take long before I realized that my prospective partners weren't investing in the kinds of properties that would get us to the goal. Here's what I mean.

Over time, I developed some parameters for investing in single family homes. I learned that the assets should be:

No less than three bedroom, two bath properties. Most families with kids need at least three places to sleep and two places to use the restroom. And if a couple is just starting out, they may want room to grow. You can always find a renter for a three bedroom, two bath home — and when it's time to sell it, you can always find a buyer.

No more than 2,000 square feet. It's difficult to find renters for houses over 2,000 square feet; that's because people who can afford to rent them are more inclined to buy them. And because they're priced higher, you have a harder time getting the rent to cover your mortgage payment.

My partners weren't convinced of these things, and it was clear their investments weren't going to get us there. Seeing their lackluster properties that were well outside of my optimal parameters, I decided to try to get there on my own. It's like what a friend of mine used to tell me: "Partnerships only work in odd numbers, and three is too many. So that only leaves one."

Since we hadn't made the plan official yet, I was free to do this. I would just need to aim for a smaller apartment complex and adjust the numbers accordingly.

So now, my plan was to:

- Buy 20 properties.
- Hold them for five years or until there was $100,000 equity in each.
- That gave me a $2 million down payment for a $6 million property with 100 units.
- Renting out 100 units for $1,200 a month, that's $120,000 a month.

To recalculate my positive cash flow/passive income, had to adjust the overhead costs again:

- $30,000 for 25% unit vacancies, leaving me with $90,000.
- $27,000 for the mortgage payment/PITI, leaving me with $63,000.
- $13,000 for utilities, repairs, management and incidentals, leaving me with $50,000.

And this time, there was no one to split it with (other than my wife) — so I had the same amount of monthly positive cash flow, $50,000. Multiplied by 12 months, it still amounted to $600,000 a year in totally passive income.

The First Step

The first step was to find houses that were local to our primary home in Riverside County. In fact, homes that were on my route to work would be ideal. Jan, one of our closest agent friends, started telling me about houses around town I might be interested in. The first one sounded...how should I say it...*sketchy*.

"This guy is renting to his grandson and a bunch of other kids," Jan said. "They're doing drugs and not paying rent. He can't get them to voluntarily vacate, so he's moving forward with eviction."

Like I said, *sketchy*. But then, Jan said these magic words: "If you buy it as-is, he'll probably take a lowball offer from you."

Alrighty then. After the eviction was done, Jan gave me the lockbox code and I told her I'd check it out after work.

When I got there, the kids had been locked out. So I never saw them, but I saw the remnants of them: Probably while high on shrooms or acid, they had made the porch an art project by gluing colored rocks all over the concrete.

It was a full-blown art installation, with the rocks forming a mosaic that continued all the way into the house; they had pulled up the carpet to accomplish this. And where I didn't see rocks, I saw that every inch of this hippie crash pad was a mess of clothes and cats. Lots of cats. As I walked down the hall, I felt the glowing green eyes of felines staring at me the whole way; there were at least two or three of them in each room.

So the kids were gone, but the cats and clothes stayed. And I was supposed to buy this house *as-is*? In my mind, I tried to focus on the magic words: "lowball offer, lowball offer." Maybe the seller would throw in that giant jar of leafy green substance I saw in the kitchen (that's a joke, but I assure you it was there). There was a lot more stuff in there too, and I didn't dare touch any of it. Everything around me just looked...slimy.

Well, I had to start somewhere. So I took the plunge and negotiated a deal with Jan to buy the house as-is for $85,000; because this didn't appear to be a livable property, I used a private money loan rather than traditional financing (more on that later, since

I'll be teaching you how you can do that too). The escrow closed in June 2003. And while I didn't get the jar of weed, I did get the upright piano that was in the living room. To this day, Dawn and I don't know how to play it. But we keep it as a memento of our first local investment.

A Simple Strategy

I put about $45,000 in renovations into the house; within 30 days, all traces of its very recent past as a psychedelic cat brothel covered in rocks had been removed. Now, it was financeable — so five weeks after closing, I was able to refinance for $153,850 with a regular 30-year fixed rate mortgage. After all the renovations I had put into it, it appraised at $205,000 and I was able to pull cash out with the refi. The refi closed in July. This is part of the strategy: keeping things on a tight timeline.

Next, I listed it for rent. People started calling, and I made sure they would drive by to check out the neighborhood before they applied or consented to a credit check (always do this!).

The first applicant was motivated and qualified, which means I got a renter in the house by August 1.

The first month's rent was $1,250, plus a $2,000 security deposit. On September 1, they made the second month's rent. Now, I had collected a total of $4,500 before the first mortgage payment of $1,075 was due. This meant I would always be one month ahead.

"So this is successful real estate investing," I told myself. "I'm not making tons of money yet, but now I own two properties!" That alone was pretty cool.

The Next Opportunity

It wasn't long before the second opportunity came along; just like the first one, this one was thanks to a melodrama involving young adults. This couple had just broken off their engagement. Barely in their 20s, these kids had bought a 1,000 square foot starter home; a few months into it, they decided they weren't meant for each other after all. On top of calling off a wedding, they needed to sell their house. Since I was the lender on their purchase, they called to ask for my advice — and that's when I found out they were two months behind on their payments. They had just bought the house in April, and it had only been four months.

I wasn't sure what they were really looking for, so I explained their options (which were limited).

"Well," I said, "you could rent it out. Or do you just want to get rid of it? I could buy it from you, but I won't be able to finance it because there's no equity yet."

Not surprisingly, they seemed to like the "I could buy it from you" option the best. Of course, I had to come up with a way around the fact that it wasn't financeable.

"I'll tell you what," I said. "You deed the property to me. I'll pay you for what you put into it, bring the payments current, stick a renter in there, and keep making the payments on your mortgage to keep your credit clean. When it appreciates, I'll refinance it and pay your loan off. By the time either of you is ready to buy again, the late payments will be off your credit and this will be a clean mortgage."

Of course, they liked that idea. And so, they deeded me the house in August 2003.

Sometimes, you can do a good deed and make money at the same time. Nothing wrong with that. And it was a *very* good deed, because this house wasn't in a very desirable neighborhood.

Once again, I did the renovations (fortunately, they were minimal this time; no rock art or cats to get rid of). I listed it for rent, took calls from people, told them where the house was and waited. But this time, I waited a lot longer to get calls back.

Finally, a couple called who was ready to move in. They admitted their credit was in the toilet, but they had enough to pay me for the whole year in advance after selling their house. That was good enough for me. So now, I had two properties where I was ahead on the payments; in the case of the second one, I was ahead by $13,000 because they paid for the year upfront. Was it huge cash flow? Not yet. But it would be once they appreciated enough to sell. And remember, my target timeline was five years.

So now, six months from the date I first decided to invest in real estate, I owned two properties. By the time my first renter had been in the house one month, I already had a second property. Was I lucky? No. I was conscious, with my eyes open, and the opportunities appeared. Remember the VW Bug Guy example? Once I bought my (metaphorical) yellow VW Beetle, I started to see how many others there were on the road.

The lesson here is this: *Recognize opportunities when they're in front of you.*

The VW Beetles were houses, and I started to see how many there were in my community.

In every community, there are homeowners stuck with properties they want to get out of. They don't always have a lot of equity right away, but they will eventually. Some might say this is taking advantage of people, but keep in mind: Lots of people don't have any other option. As long as it's a win-win, there's nothing wrong with helping someone offload a house they can't afford while preserving their credit. You can help someone out *and* make money.

CHAPTER 16

"I love money more than the things it can buy...
but what I love more than money is other people's money."[69]
- Other People's Money, 1991

LET'S SAY YOU follow my advice and get your first couple of properties the same way I did. Your monthly mortgage payments are covered, and you understand that you'll only have minimal cash flow on these properties for the next few years as the market cycles back up.

You've only financed two, and Fannie Mae allows you to finance up to 10 properties at once. If I were teaching this in a seminar (and I have), this would be the point at which some poor guy would raise his hand and say, "So I see how I get the first two. How do I get eight or nine more?"

Here's what I tell that guy: *Don't worry about it.*

To do this well, you need to focus on acquiring one asset at a time. When you feel good about where the last one is — the renovations are done, you've got your renters moved in and their rent is covering your payments — *then*, you can take a deep, cleansing breath and start looking for the next property. Remember, you're looking hard for opportunities that are a bit out of the box — not just looking for any old house for sale. And that takes time.

Fortunately, finding them is easier than ever today. Back when I was doing this, the only tool for online searches was the Multiple Listing Service (MLS), and I was only able to look at the MLS because I had a broker's license. If you were a regular Joe Schmo who wanted to invest in a house, you had to call up an agent, tell him or her what you were looking for and wait for him or her to find it. But now, every real estate aggregator is fed by the MLS: Zillow, Redfin, Realtor.com...and they're available to everyone.

How to Search for Properties

In addition to the previous parameters of three bedroom/two bath homes no larger than 2,000 square feet, you can refine your search even more to find the right properties to start out with.

To do that, you'll first need to understand the four classes of properties and four classes of neighborhoods. These four classes are the same for any area of the country; simply use the information to identify the classes in your target area. Once you understand these, you'll know what class of property and neighborhood to look for in your search.

Classes of Properties

Class A - Less than 10 years old, turnkey and in excellent condition.
Class B - Less than 20 years old, in good shape with only minor repairs needed.
Class C - Less than 30 years old, with some deferred maintenance.
Class D - More than 30 years old, with a lot of deferred maintenance, functional obsolescence and management challenges (in short, everything else on the market.

Classes of Neighborhoods

Class A - The "nice" part of town, with few renters and evident pride of ownership.
Class B - Blue collar/working class, with more renters and closer proximity to thriving retail areas.
Class C - Older and/or more neglected areas of the city with lots of renters. Close to retail areas that are neglected and no longer thriving.
Class D - The most neglected area of the city, with high vacancy rates and signs of crime or residential neglect (bars on windows, junk cars parked on the streets and front yards, etc.).

What do you want to look for? Ideally, you want to start out with B or C properties in an A or B neighborhood. If you've already started looking at listings, then you know those can be hard to find. That's why it's important to take your time and focus on choosing strategically.

Here are other tips for looking at listings:

- **Look locally.** For long-term rentals, don't go too far outside the town you live in. This makes your properties much easier to manage, especially once you have several in your portfolio. As a general strategy to keep things simple, I started out by choosing properties that were on my route to work. That was about a three-mile radius from home. You may choose to widen your parameters a little more, but take it from someone who's been there: The closer they are, the easier your life is.

- **Look for new listings.** To be more specific, look for new listings or price changes. If the price of a property has dropped in the last 24 hours, the seller may be more willing to take a lowball offer. On that note...

- **Look for lowballs.** "Lowball" is not a dirty word; making lower offers is how lots of successful investors start out. And even if a listing doesn't say the seller will accept a lowball offer, sometimes it pays off to use one as a starting point. If the seller counters, you can make your next offer a little higher based on what you think it will take to complete the renovations. If there are no competitive offers, you may have a good chance of getting accepted.

- **Look for the listing language.** The way things are written in the listing will reveal the seller's motivations. Does it say they won't consider any offers for 10 days? They might, if they get the right offer. Does it say they'll be taking offers "sight unseen" for the first week? It might be a matter of not wanting to disturb the renters, which means they're *good* renters (and you can write an offer that allows these good renters to stay in the house, which means they'll be *your* good renters). Bottom line: When agents say in the listing that they will or won't do something, there's a reason. Figuring out that reason can help you get what you want.

In addition to knowing what to look for, you need to focus on buying only one property at a time. We covered this a little, but there's a reason why I give people this advice. I once got myself in a very tricky position, and hopefully you can learn from my mistake. Here's what happened.

I saw a house on a decent street (a C neighborhood) and made an offer. The next day, I made an offer on a second house on an even nicer street (a B neighborhood). The third day, an agent friend told me about a third house, and it was on a street that beat out the first two (an A neighborhood). At the time, each one seemed too good to pass up. So now, I had three offers out there. You guessed it; they were all accepted. Now what?

Getting Creative Again

I wanted to move forward on all three purchases, but doing it was going to require a lot of money upfront. When three properties are set to close escrow in the next 30 days and the rules don't allow you to get your money back with a cash-out refinance for at least six months...well, you're in a pickle.

Think about this:

- 20% is the standard down payment for non-owner occupied properties.
- 20% down on a $200,000 home is $40,000.
- Closing costs are around $6,000.
- Basic renovations of carpet, paint and appliances plus more involved repairs average $15,000.
- For just one of these homes, that's $61,000 out of pocket.

And I was trying to do that with not one property, but three. Withdrawing from my previous mutual fund investments to cover this until I could refinance was not part of the plan — so once again, it was time to get creative.

The answer for me at the time was a private money loan, also known as a hard money loan, with the terms set for a cash-out purchase. Here's how a loan like that works, along with my method for new investors who don't have a lot of cash to pay out of pocket costs. I call it the money for nothing method.

The Money for Nothing Method

Throughout this section, terms you may want to become familiar with will appear in bold text. Pay attention!

A **hard money loan**, sometimes called a **private money loan** or **"other people's money" (OPM)**, is only available from a **hard money lender** (sometimes called the **investor** or **private money lender**) who trusts you, or trusts the mortgage lender you work with. Unlike a conventional loan, the only hard money rules are the rules the investor makes. They make those rules based on the value of the property, rather than your credit or other traditional lending markers.

To pay the upfront costs normally associated with buying, renovating and refinancing a home as an investment, some hard money lenders could fund you for a cash-out purchase that covers all three, using a **purchase-money mortgage** secured by a **deed of trust**. That's the idea behind my money for nothing method.

Instead of getting a loan based on the purchase price of the home today, your loan would be based on the **inflated appraised value** (the amount it's expected to appraise at once you've put your renovations in). In some circles, this value is called **"after rehab value" (ARV)**. The idea is to cover all or most of the upfront costs so you pay as little out of pocket as possible. Ideally, you would pay zero.

That's important to note: "Money for nothing" means that paying nothing out of pocket is your *goal*. It does not always work out that way, for reasons such as:

- Some hard money lenders (understandably) would like you to have some skin in the game.
- The appraisal doesn't come in quite as high as you thought it would.

- The costs of rehabbing the property exceed your initial estimates.
- Some other unforeseen reason (that's just the way real estate is).

But ultimately, money for nothing is the goal. If you end up with some out of pocket costs, you can call it "money for a little something instead of a lot of something" (catchy, right?).

Quite simply, a money for nothing loan is when you use a hard money loan to:

- Buy a B or C property.
- Renovate it to increase the value.
- Refinance it based on the new value.
- Complete the transaction with little-to-no cash out of pocket.

If you manage to complete the transaction having paid nothing out of pocket, then your rate of return will be infinity. Let that sink in: Whether your monthly return is $1 or $1,000, your rate of return is *infinity*.

That's because of this formula: *Any number (your annual return on investment) divided by zero (your amount out of pocket) is infinity.*

Even though a money for nothing property investment will generate a reduced monthly cash flow due to the higher loan amount, that's offset by the amount you paid out of pocket to buy the property in the first place — which, ideally, is zero. Even if the amount you paid out of pocket *isn't* zero, it will still be an amount that's more favorable to a new investor — and that allows you to buy more properties with the cash you have to invest.

Making Your Money Back Faster

This type of loan will put you on the fast track to doing a **rate-and-term refinance**, which is how you'll make your money back and earn a return on investment. Here's why you'll need a rate-and-term refinance.

To invest using a conventional loan, the way to make your money back is with a **cash out refinance**. The problem is, you would need to wait a full six months (lenders call that a "**seasoning period**") before a cash out refinance would be allowed. This is based on Fannie Mae's rule that the price you paid for the house is considered the home's "value" for the first six months in relation to doing a cash out refinance.

But when you refinance the loan used for the purchase of the property and *not* taking cash out, there's no longer a seasoning period required. You can do a rate-and-term refinance in a matter of weeks (or however quickly you can complete the renovations) using the ARV and stop paying the hard money rate right away. Refinancing from a 10-12% rate to a 4-6% rate (or whatever the A-paper rates are) right away makes a big difference.

To illustrate, here's a money for nothing loan example with real numbers.

Money for Nothing Loan Example

Let's say you want to invest in a home that's listed for $110,000, with the goal of making the ARV of the home $165,000 after renovations (this is nowhere near current prices in my home state of California. If that's where you are, hang in there; I have an example for you later on).

To purchase, renovate and refinance this home with the money for nothing method, you would need a loan of 75% of the $165,000, which is $123,750. That's because Fannie Mae allows for up to a 75% **loan-to-value ratio (LTV)**. That means the loan can be up to 75% of the current appraised value of the property.

In this scenario, $123,750 is your **maximum refinance loan amount**.

However, you may find that the hard money lender will only advance you the amount of the purchase price and closing costs. He's asking you to have skin in the game by putting up *some* of your money — in this case, the $10,000 in renovation costs. He will draw up a loan for $120,000, but he'll only advance you $100,000 upfront. That means you need to put in $10,000 of your own money, plus closing costs. The closing statement on the purchase will show that he gave you a $120,000 loan, minus the $20,000 being held back for the renovation.

Now, you go forward with the renovation, which will convert that $110,000 house to a $165,000 house — after which time, the hard money lender will advance the balance of the funds to you. This protects the hard money lender by ensuring that he never has more money out of his pocket than the value of the property.

It may even be possible to have the renovation costs delayed, if you can find a contractor willing to do a basic rehab (carpet, paint, repairs and appliances) on a 30-day contract in which he gets paid at the end. When you make the right connections, you'll find that these resources are out there.

Let's get back to the loan. Here's a breakdown of the numbers in this example:

Purchase price of property	$110,000
Closing costs (escrow, title and recording fees)	$ 2,000
Renovation costs	$ 15,000
Hard money costs (points and interest)	+$ 6,000
Subtotal	$133,000

But we're not done yet; that subtotal is not the total amount of your loan. Remember, you're getting a loan based on the value after renovation. So far, you know that you need $133,000 before the refinance; in this scenario, the refinance (which will be a conventional, non-owner occupied, conforming loan) will cost you $4,500 in additional fees: escrow, title, appraisal, processing, underwriting, etc.

Initial project cost	$133,000
Refinance cost (fees + impounds)	+ $4,500
Total project cost	$137,500

Now, to calculate your net cash outlay. This is the amount you paid out of pocket once the entire project is finished, from the initial purchase to turning the property into an entirely different product.

Total project cost	$137,500
Refi loan amount	- $123,750
Net cash outlay	$ 13,750

Next, we want to know how much your monthly positive cash flow will be. Ideally, you get a renter into your property before the first mortgage payment is due. To figure out your positive cash flow, just subtract your monthly mortgage payment from the amount you collect from your tenants.

Monthly rent collected	$1,500
Monthly mortgage payment	$840
Monthly positive cash flow	$660

You are now making a net profit of **$7,920 a year!**

Finally, let's calculate your rate of return. In this example, you had to pay some small upfront costs. That means your rate of return is not infinity, but it will still be pretty damn good. To figure out your cash-on-cash return, use this formula: *Your annual net profit ÷ your cash out of pocket = your annual, cash-on-cash rate of return.*

Net profit	$ 7,920
Cash out of pocket	÷ $13,750
Annual, cash-on-cash rate of return	57.6%

This means you have recovered 57.6% of your investment in the first year. Not bad for your first investment, right? Especially considering what the banks are paying when you try to invest with them. In my lifetime, the highest savings account interest I've ever seen at a bank is 7.25%. And that was back when I was riding my bike five miles to deposit my paper route money at Home Savings. Your first real estate investment can earn eight times what the highest rate would be if you let your money sit in a high interest bank account.

I promised all the Californians there would be a scenario for our market. With these examples, let's add in a new factor: your offer. In a high priced market like California, your offer can and should be based on how much of a return you hope to earn. So, we'll add the listed price to our figures and talk about how making lower offers can help boost your return on investment.

Here we go.

Money for Nothing in the California Market

Remember, your first investment will be a B or C property. In the inland market of Southern California, it's common to see those listed around the $300,000 price point. So let's say the listed price of the property you're considering is $300,000.

As a new investor who's done your homework, you know you can turn this $300,000 house into a $360,000 house after renovations. However, you also know that by the time you put $25,000 into the renovations and finish paying all your fees, you won't end up with much of a return. Does that mean you pass the property up? No, it means you make the seller a lower offer.

If you offer less, you'll have a better return. How much better? Let's look at the numbers.

Example #1

Asking price		$300,000
Projected ARV		$360,000
Maximum refinance loan amount (75% of ARV)		$270,000
Negotiated purchase price		$275,000
Closing costs (escrow, title and recording fees)		$ 2,000
Renovation costs		$ 25,000
Hard money costs (points and interest)		+ $12,000
Subtotal		$314,000
Initial project cost	$314,000	
Refinance cost (fees + impounds)	+ $ 10,100	
Total project cost	$324,100	
Total project cost	$324,100	
Refi loan amount	- $270,000	
Net cash outlay	$ 54,100	
Monthly rent collected	$1,900	
Monthly mortgage payment	-$1,564	
Monthly positive cash flow	$336	
You are now making a net profit of **$4,032 a year!**		
Net profit	$ 4,032	
Cash out of pocket	÷ $54,100	
Annual, cash-on-cash rate of return	7%	

If you're not happy with that return or the amount of net cash outlay, then you need to make a lower offer. The idea is to know what rate of return you want and how much cash you can afford to pay out of pocket, and then reverse engineer your offer accordingly. Here's an example where you negotiate the price $25,000 lower, down to $250,000.

Example #2

Asking price		$300,000
Projected ARV		$360,000
Maximum refinance loan amount (75% of ARV)		$270,000
Negotiated purchase price		$250,000
Closing costs (escrow, title and recording fees)		$ 2,000
Renovation costs		$ 25,000
Hard money costs (points and interest)		+ $12,000
Subtotal		$289,000
Initial project cost	$289,000	
Refinance cost (fees + impounds)	+ $ 10,100	
Total project cost	$299,100	
Total project cost	$299,100	
Refi loan amount	- $270,000	
Net cash outlay	$ 29,100	
Monthly rent collected	$1,900	
Monthly mortgage payment	-$1,538	
Monthly positive cash flow	$362	
You are now making a net profit of **$4,344 a year!**		
Net profit	$ 4,344	
Cash out of pocket	÷ $29,100	
Annual, cash-on-cash rate of return	15%	

That example doubled your rate of return, but what if you want to triple it? You could negotiate an even lower price of $240,000.

Example #3

Asking price		$300,000
Projected ARV		$360,000
Maximum refinance loan amount (75% of ARV)		$270,000
Negotiated purchase price		$240,000
Closing costs (escrow, title and recording fees)		$ 2,000
Renovation costs		$ 25,000
Hard money costs (points and interest)		+ $12,000
Subtotal		$279,000
Initial project cost	$279,000	
Refinance cost (fees + impounds)	+ $ 10,100	
Total project cost	$289,100	
Total project cost	$289,100	
Refi loan amount	- $270,000	
Net cash outlay	$ 19,100	
Monthly rent collected	$1,900	
Monthly mortgage payment	-$1,527	
Monthly positive cash flow	$373	
Cash-on-cash rate of return	23%	

Whatever market you're in, the concept applies: Decide your rate of return and make an offer that will create that outcome. You can plug any numbers into this formula.

Revisit the Goal

Let's wrap this chapter up with a summary of the key points.

Your goal is to:

- Acquire the assets (properties).
- Rent them out while they appreciate so that renters will cover the payments.
- Once appreciated, sell off and buy one larger asset that will generate significantly higher, lifelong passive income.

The most effective way to find properties is to:

- Look locally.
- Look for new listings/price changes.
- Look for lowball opportunities.

If you're a new investor with little-to-no cash for out of pocket costs, you can use the money for nothing method:

- Find a hard money lender.
- Get a cash-out, purchase-money mortgage secured by a deed of trust.
- Invest with a goal of paying zero out of pocket and an infinite rate of return.

This is the simplest way to get started.

CHAPTER 17

"These are gamblers ready to risk what they can't afford for what they can't have, you're selling the world's rarest commodity: certainty, in an uncertain world."[70]
- Two for the Money, 2005

A New Type of Asset

AS YOU BEGIN to near your goal number of residential properties, one thing that might change is the large asset you invest your profits in. That's what happened for me. The apartment complex, it turned out, was not meant to be. Along the way, I found an opportunity that was a better fit for my goals.

Before we get to that, let's take a look at the events shaping my decisions. As you embark on your own journey, you'll find that the events in the background can play a big role in the decisions you'll make as well (and they should).

We're still in 2003, and I continued to repeat the pattern we've talked about until I was up to seven rental houses. My appreciation was going up and the interest rates were going down. I was making offers all the time, because I saw what was happening: Prices were climbing to new, sometimes unbelievable heights. This was no time to fall asleep at the wheel. It got to the point where Dawn was saying, "*Another* house?" And my answer was always, "Yes!" There was an invisible clock ticking, and I could hear it. At that time, *everyone* who had anything to do with real estate or financing could hear it.

I bought another seven houses in 2004 — but as prices still soared into 2005, the math wasn't necessarily making sense anymore because as home values went up in accordance with a diminishing supply, market rents weren't necessarily going up. So, I slowed it down to four purchases that year. Now I'm up to 18, just two properties shy away from my goal of 20. Because easy financing was the driving force behind this market activity and I'm a mortgage lender myself, I was warning my loan officers and anyone else who would listen what the writing on the wall was. I knew the banks did not have an appetite for infinite risk. If you know anything about the 2008-09 financial collapse, you know how that part of the story ends.

But in 2005, we weren't quite there yet; new opportunities were still being explored. I was open to hearing about them, whether or not they ended up being for me. Here's one example.

An Out-of-the-Box Strategy

Someone invited me to a seminar that hyped the idea of selling all your California properties ASAP, doing a 1031 Exchange to avoid the capital gains taxes, and shifting your investments into states where the markets weren't quite as inflated or volatile: Arizona, Nevada, Texas, Oregon or Washington.

The proposal was based on a prediction that the California market would collapse and drop by 20% over the next five years (a very solid prediction that turned out to be a massive understatement during the financial collapse) — so you needed to sell now, while prices were still at the top. Once that drop happened, you could come back to California. But in the meantime, you would park your money in a less volatile market like one of these states. Texas, in particular, piqued my interest; people don't invest as speculatively there. Unlike California, it's not the place people go to get rich quick. So the idea was intriguing, kind of like what stock traders do.

It made a ton of sense to me, and I share it with you because it illustrates the kind of out-of-the-box thinking needed to make it in real estate investing. Plus, it also crystallized my faith in market cycles, which turned out to pay off later. However, I didn't end up going to Texas (or anywhere). I was too close to my goal, and no one seemed to be able to answer the question of how long it would take to actually sell a property in Texas. And that's when I realized that even though someone may have a perfectly good concept, there can still be a better way. I don't blindly take anyone's advice without checking it out myself.

Fortunately, it wasn't long before I found it. Yes, it was better than moving my money out of state — but also, based on what was happening in the market, time was of the essence for me to retain all the equity I had built up over the past few years. If I continued to wait and the bubble suddenly burst, it would take at least eight years to regain all that equity based on what the market was doing. And as we all know now, that bubble burst was coming quickly.

The lesson: *Sometimes, the market dictates that you have to find your opportunity on a dime and seize it.*

I no longer had time to find an apartment building. That's when a different opportunity presented itself, and I was smart enough to seize it.

From Residential to Commercial

I was still thinking about the ideas presented at the seminar, but pretty soon, one phone call changed everything. It was from a guy named Al, who had been a client a couple of times in the past. Al owned a commercial building not far from my office. Actually, it was five commercial buildings, on four lots, with 31,600 square feet of office space — all of it rented out. He wanted to refinance the property to lower the payment. When I asked Al about the cash flow, he told me the property generated a little over $50,000 a month in rental income. *Wow*, I thought. *$50,000 a month.* Then I asked him what he thought the property was worth. "Well," he said, "I had it in escrow last year to sell it for $5,250,000. It fell out of escrow because the buyer didn't qualify."

"Wait a minute," I said. "Are you looking to sell this fairly soon?" I was asking because of the fees and pre-payment penalties associated with commercial loans. I needed to figure out how quickly the refinance would pay for itself if he were to sell it in the next two or three years. If the refi didn't pay for itself before he intended to sell, it wouldn't make sense for him to do the refi within the next few years because of those fees and penalties. Some lenders would just move forward with the refinance whether it made sense for the client or not. But that's not me.

And in addition to that, I knew Al was too sophisticated to do something that didn't make sense for him. If it didn't make sense for him to refinance, *he* would tell *me* — so to make sure I held all the cards, I needed to be the one to tell him first. When you're dealing with a client who knows what they're doing, make sure they know that *you* know what *you're* doing, too. And of course, there's the matter of having integrity. I always think about how I would advise my brother, sister, mom or dad.

So what was Al's answer? By now, you've probably forgotten the question: "Are you looking to sell?"

Al replied, "Not right away." He had been investing in mobile home parks, and his plan was to continue doing that — selling his properties and 1031 Exchanging them into mobile home parks in other states to avoid capital gains. But he wasn't sure he wanted to do that with this one at this moment in time. It would be a big decision: Pay the taxes on a $5,250,000 sale, or quickly figure out where to invest the profits to avoid capital gains. He had already been flying all over the place in search of mobile home parks to invest his other profits in. I didn't blame him for wanting to take a rest.

That phone call with Al was on a Friday — and as I worked on quotes and formulas for him over the weekend, all I could think about was that figure: $50,000 a month. For my 18 rental houses, my gross rents were probably 40% of that and I only netted around $1,000 a month (but I did realize I had earned a boatload of equity that needed to be preserved). And with the residential market nearing the point of pricing insanity, this commercial property might be the closest thing to an apartment complex income I could get. Plus, it was right in my neighborhood; I didn't have to fly anywhere to go see it.

At that time, I was on a swimming exercise regimen. When you're swimming laps, all you can hear is your thoughts. So as I swam laps that weekend, I thought about what it might take to buy Al's property. Maybe he could be convinced.

What was the point? Although I'm proud of my long-term greed, that wasn't the only motive. The fact was, I didn't need to snatch up two more houses to reach the magic number of 20 and buy an apartment building in a rapidly inflating market; what I *did* need to do was sell as many of my 18 houses as necessary, 1031 Exchange them to avoid capital gains taxes, and use all the equity I'd been earning over the last few years to buy the asset that would generate lifelong passive income. I hoped it would be Al's commercial property.

By the time I had swum somewhere between 50 and 80 laps, I had convinced myself. Now, I just had to convince Al.

The Better Half

But just like Dawn is my better half, Al's wife Marilyn was his. I managed to have a conversation with her. "We'll have six months to close escrow," I told her, "maybe even a year. This doesn't have to happen overnight."

Marilyn was a good listener, and she was pretty sure she could get Al to listen too. "You and Dawn come have dinner with us and let's talk about it," she said. "Al has enough money; he can pay the taxes. I'll convince him to sell."

Convincing Dawn was the next hurdle to clear, and I understood why. First, we had only owned residential real estate up to that point. Second, this was a total shift from the original goal. Third, this was a $5,000,000 investment. For all those reasons, I wouldn't have blamed her for thinking I was crazy.

Over the years, I used math to sell everything from tires and batteries to insurance policies and home loans. Now, I would use it to make the biggest sale of my life (after convincing her to marry me). I reminded Dawn that we had 18 houses, for which we collected 18 rent checks and made 18 mortgage payments. With this commercial property, we would collect *larger* rent checks, make only *one* mortgage payment, and bring in *a lot* more money. Like it always had, the math made sense. Dawn was starting to get comfortable with it.

Over the course of the dinner with Al and Marilyn, *everyone* got comfortable with it. And then we drew up the contract.

The Final Stretch

But before I could give Al any money for *his* property, I had to sell off mine. Because of the Internal Revenue Service rules of a 1031 Exchange, I only had six months to get my residential properties sold and close escrow on his. That's the window of time the IRS gives you: Identify your new property within 45 days of selling the first property, and close the sale on the new property within 180 days. Otherwise, no tax shelter for you. And I had to do that with more than a dozen properties.

Only a dozen? At first, I figured it would take 12 properties to give me enough capital for the down payment. But because some of my tenants left the homes in worse condition than they found them, I ended up having to put more money into rehabs — so to cover those costs, I would need to sell three more. This ended up taking not just more money, but more time. All of these bumps in the road were unanticipated, which is why I'm sharing it with you. Remember: *Experience is the best teacher, especially when it's someone else's experience.*

There was also one more thing I didn't expect: for my tenants to turn down the opportunity to buy the homes they were already living in. Not knowing for sure which properties I wanted to keep vs. sell, I mailed a letter to each tenant, figuring they would help me decide. I thought most (if not all) of them would jump at the chance to buy a house they were already renting, and not one of them did. In fact, a lot of them moved out sooner than I needed them to. At one point, I had 13 empty properties.

Lesson: *You can't assume anything.*

So as you can imagine, this was a huge mistake. I should have made the decision for each property myself (after all, I was the owner), and then mailed letters out as each decision was made.

Most people can't afford 13 mortgage payments. So to avoid getting yourself into a situation like this (where you would likely end up sabotaging your credit in the process and fail to qualify for the loan you're trying to get next), here's another lesson:

Don't do what I did. Do your best to sell your properties one at a time.

If I had to do this over, I would have gone to each tenant one by one with the news that I was selling and the offer to sell them the house. For those who said no, I could have coordinated agreements to sell the house while they were still there, so they wouldn't move out and leave me with an unrented house for months while scrambling to find a buyer. The promise to give their security deposits back in full (or even refund a portion of the final month's rent) would have been the incentive.

But unfortunately, that's not what I did. So for three months, I had to make 13 mortgage payments on houses I did not live in. I had to sell these properties fast, *and* do whatever I could to delay the start of the clock on that six month timeline before capital gains kicked in.

Thankfully, someone was willing to help me kick off the whole chain of events. Jim, still my partner at the time, offered to be my first buyer. He had a renter who needed a place, and my house on Coldspring would fill that need. So we'll call that House #1.

I proposed a strategy; by this time, Jim was used to my big ideas. "Jim," I said, "go ahead and move your renter into House #1 now. You can pay me the rent until the house becomes yours. I need to hold off on closing escrow until the escrow on House #2 closes — whatever house that ends up being." That meant the clock wouldn't start until the end of the second sale, and my first two sales would close at the same time.

This was a necessary strategy; six months is a tight window to close sales on 12 to 15 properties *and* buy a new one, so I needed any help I could get. Al didn't think I would be able to pull it off, but I did.

But before we go any further, let's talk about 1031 Exchanges.

What is a 1031 Exchange?

The IRS defines a 1031 Exchange as "gain deferred in a like-kind exchange" under Internal Revenue Code (IRC) Section 1031. It allows you to sell an investment property and defer paying taxes on the gains by investing in another property within a specific timeframe.

The 1031 Exchange is a great tool for investors, but it does come with some rules. Let's talk about those.

The Like-Kind Property Rule

A 1031 Exchange is only possible when you are exchanging "like-kind" property. This rule:

- *Does not* mean you're required to exchange a condo for a condo, a house for a house or a commercial building for a commercial building.
- *Does* mean you're required to exchange investment real estate for investment real estate.

Because of the like-kind property rule, personal residences (also known as owner-occupied properties) do not qualify for a 1031 Exchange.

In other words:

- You *can't* sell an investment property, then buy a house to live in and use a 1031 Exchange.
- You *can* sell an investment property, buy another investment property and use a 1031 Exchange — provided that you follow the replacement property rule.

Let's look at that rule next.

The Replacement Property Rule

Another rule of the 1031 Exchange concerns how much you need to spend on the replacement property. The replacement property rule requires you to spend at least as much on the replacement property as you receive for the original property — and, the amount of debt you end up with has to equal or exceed the amount of debt you had on the original properties. In other words, a 1031 Exchange does not allow you to get rid of debt.

For example:

- If you sell your original property for $1 million, you'll need to spend *at least* $1 million on the replacement property.
- You *can* spend more than $1 million, but not less.
- If you owed $500,000 on that original property, you need to end up with at least $500,000 in debt on the replacement property (or properties). You are allowed to buy multiple properties, and you can arrange your new debt on some or all of the properties.

In my case, that meant I had to make sure that the sum of the sale prices on the properties I sold did not exceed the price of the replacement property I was purchasing (the commercial building, which was priced at $5 million). As for having "the same amount of debt or more," it meant the total amount of the loans being paid off couldn't exceed the debt I would have on the commercial building ($3.35 million, which was the amount I financed after the down payment).

Here's how useful the 1031 Exchange can be: When I bought these houses for $100,000, I spent $30,000 on improvements for each one. I sold them for $330,000, giving me $200,000 gains on each one. Paying capital gains taxes on each one would have eaten up about 38% of my profit.

But by doing the 1031 Exchange, I was able to defer those taxes until I eventually sell my replacement property (the commercial building). And if I never sell it, then I don't have to pay them at all.

Defer, Defer, Die

The ultimate strategy when doing a 1031 Exchange is to defer taxes until you die. Once you do, then your heirs may benefit from what's called the "stepped-up basis" loophole. The stepped-up basis is the fair market value of the property at the time of your death. Upon your death, all of the built-in gain disappears, and the property value on the date you purchased it "rolls up" to the property value on the date of your death. That value will now pass through your estate to your heirs. At least, that's the law as of this writing.

This loophole relieves your heirs of any tax burden on the gain you deferred with a 1031 Exchange when you were alive. In my case: If I die and my wife sells my commercial property, the stepped-up basis allows my wife to avoid paying capital gains. In your case, your heirs can avoid capital gains on an investment property they sell after your death, as long as you did a proper 1031 Exchange while you were living.

What Happens During a 1031 Exchange

In a 1031 Exchange, you never touch the money on the sale of your original property. Instead, that money will be held by an intermediary; we call this person or entity a 1031 Exchange accommodator. Usually, your accommodator should be a CPA. No matter what, it cannot be your real estate agent, your relative or someone else who has an interest in the transaction.

While you work on identifying what your replacement property will be, the accommodator holds the funds in a trust account. The timeline on identifying your replacement property is 45 days, and you have 180 days from the date of the original property sale to close escrow on the purchase. Right before your escrow closes, your accommodator will transfer the funds for the down payment on your replacement property. This is the most common type of 1031 Exchange, called a delayed exchange.

By doing a delayed exchange, you can put the whole chunk of cash you just made from the sale of your original property into the replacement property, and not have to pay taxes on the gains until some faraway day when you sell the replacement property. If you never sell it, then you'll never have to pay the taxes at all and your heirs can take advantage of the stepped-up basis loophole.

There is also a reverse exchange, which is another way of structuring your 1031 Exchange if you are able to buy the replacement property before selling your original one. In my case, I had to do a reverse exchange for the properties I wasn't able to sell by the time the down payment was needed.

How it Ended Up

In the end, I sold 15 of my 18 rental properties to generate the $1,642,000 I needed for a down payment and closing costs. And in July 2007, I became the owner of a commercial property.

The problem was, I still had three properties to sell before my 180 days was up. This required me to come up with additional cash, which meant taking a bridge loan (a short-term, temporary, private money loan) on the final three properties and doing a reverse 1031 Exchange. This means that instead of selling them and letting the accommodator hold the funds, I transferred the titles of the properties to the accommodator and he signed a deed of trust. This documented a debt to me for the equity that would go toward paying off the bridge loan.

That year, I went from $12,000 in annual positive cash flow from my rental properties to $200,000 in annual positive cash flow from the commercial building I now owned. This was it: passive income.

Recapping the Steps

This isn't my "look at me" story. It's meant to educate and inspire. To recap, all I did was:

- Get into real estate investing by taking advantage of a unique opportunity.
- Buy one house at a time (usually).
- Let my renters make my payments for me.
- Be patient and watch the equity build in my properties.
- And watch the markets until I had the right passive income vehicle to exchange into.

When you look at it that way, these are all things that just about anyone with brains and ambition can do if they apply themselves and keep their eyes open. Maybe you're one of them.

One of my new commercial tenants was a guy who had previously tried to buy the property, but didn't quite have the capital. "Everyone's talking about you, Ed," he told me. "They're saying you're either the smartest guy in town or the luckiest." At that point, I felt like both. I was lucky enough that the opportunity presented itself, and I was smart enough to recognize it.

CHAPTER 18

"If at first you don't succeed, lower your standards."[71]
- Tommy Boy, 1995

WHEN YOU HAVE decades of experience in the mortgage business, people like to ask you what caused the collapse of the housing market in 2007-08. It's complicated, and that's the reason people are still asking about it more than a decade later. Here are the major contributing factors I usually include in my answer. Some of them are people, some of them are products, some of them are pieces of legislation and some of them are even presidents of the United States. As we get further along, you might gain some new perspective on what took place — especially when you see how early its origins were.

Contributing Factors to the Crisis

The Community Reinvestment Act (CRA). The CRA was a law first enacted in 1977 by Jimmy Carter. In the beginning, it was an attempt to eliminate the discriminatory housing practice of "redlining" (an example is lenders refusing to fund home loans in minority communities). That objective was noble — but unfortunately, the law evolved over the years as more politicians stretched and expanded it. The president who first used the CRA to loosen credit restrictions far beyond the original intent of the law was (surprise surprise!) Bill Clinton.

President Bill Clinton. Under the Clinton administration, Congress rewrote parts of the CRA to give banks higher ratings for home loans made in "credit-deprived" areas (AKA areas in which the residents don't pay their bills on time, which means they aren't responsible enough to handle a house payment). This rewarded banks for throwing out their underwriting standards and imposed consequences if they didn't (more on that when we talk about the member of Congress largely responsible for that rewrite). Clinton also repealed FDR's Glass-Steagall Act of 1933, the law that separated commercial banking from investment banking. That repeal enabled the banks to become so large that they were "too big to fail."

Chris Dodd and Barney Frank. Obviously, a president doesn't do the rewriting of legislation personally. It was Senator Chris Dodd (D-CT), who was Chairman of the Senate Committee on Housing, Banking and Urban Affairs, along with Congressman Barney Frank (D-MA), Chairman of the House Financial Services Committee, who did the actual revision of the CRA. In so doing, they lowered the mortgage buying standards at Fannie Mae and Freddie Mac.

Fannie Mae and Freddie Mac. To get an accurate overview of the events leading to the collapse, it's important to understand Fannie Mae and Freddie Mac.

- Fannie Mae was founded as the Federal National Mortgage Association in 1938 by Congress under President Franklin D. Roosevelt. This created the secondary mortgage market, where mortgages are bought and sold so that banks can make more money and lend to more people. It remained a government entity until 1968, when the government privatized it and opened it up to shareholders. Now, it is funded entirely with private capital (in other words, a fund people can buy shares in. The fund is made up entirely of mortgages, and therefore was considered to be "safe").
- Freddie Mac was founded as the Federal Home Loan Mortgage Corporation in 1970. Although it was also created as a government-sponsored entity (GSE), Congress chartered Freddie Mac to be a private corporation from its onset.

Because Fannie and Freddie had a government-sponsored monopoly over the secondary mortgage market (as well as the government's guarantee that they would always remain solvent), both played a role in the market collapse. But as you just read, it was Dodd and Frank's revision of the CRA that forced Fannie and Freddie to lower their buying standards.

As early as 2001, the George W. Bush administration wanted to limit the risks that came with Fannie and Freddie becoming so large and overleveraged[72]. According to Bush's White House Deputy Chief of Staff Karl Rove, the administration wanted to raise Fannie and Freddie's capital requirements and limit the size of their portfolios. "Why should government regulate banks, credit unions and savings and loans, but not GSEs?," Rove wrote in a 2009 Wall Street Journal op-ed. "Mr. Bush wanted the GSEs to be treated just like their private-sector competitors. But the GSEs fought back. They didn't want to see the Bush reforms enacted, because that would level the playing field for their competitors." The sad conclusion, Rove wrote, is that, "Congress finally did pass the Bush reforms, but in 2008 after Fannie and Freddie collapsed."[73]

Alt-A loans. Most of Dodd and Frank's work on the CRA was connected to this idea: *If people couldn't afford to buy a house, the government would just make it easier to qualify by manipulating requirements.* That was the start of Alt-A loans, which were somewhere in between a traditional mortgage and a subprime loan. While they weren't quite subprime loans, Alt-A loans paved the way for the subprime products that people associate with the crash.

Alt-A loans were designed for borrowers who were just outside Fannie Mae, Freddie Mac and FHA guidelines, whether it was because of a slightly higher debt-to-income ratio, a slightly lower credit score or slightly less documented income than the normal parameters dictated. In exchange for easier qualifying, the borrower got slightly worse terms (i.e. a slightly higher interest rate).

To qualify for an A-paper loan, you would need to check all the boxes in what I call the I.C.E. Theory:

Income—If your income is strong, you check one box.

Credit—If your credit is strong, you check another box.

Equity—If you have enough equity in your downpayment (or in the value of your house, in the case of a refinance), you check a third box.

By checking all three boxes, you would qualify for an A-paper loan.

But if you were unable to check all those boxes, it might look like one of these scenarios:

- You can't prove all your income because you work under the table, but you do have a down payment and your credit is good.
- You don't have a down payment, but you have enough documented income and your credit is good.
- You have a down payment and enough documented income, but you have some minor credit issues.

If you were in one of these scenarios, you would qualify for an Alt-A loan.

Alt-A loans weren't dictated by the government, but government pressure to make home loans more accessible led to the normality of Alt-A lending. The pioneers of Alt-A lending were:

- **Greenpoint Mortgage.** Greenpoint moved aggressively into Alt-A lending in 1995.[74] Another Alt-A lender, Headlands Mortgage, merged with Greenpoint and the company was eventually bought in 2006 for $13.2 billion.[75] The new owner, Capital One, shut it down one year later as the beginning of the crash led to $1 billion in losses.
- **IndyMac.** Founded in 1985 as an offshoot of Countrywide, IndyMac was "different" because it used its customers' bank deposits to fund its loans.[76] This worked as long as home prices kept rising — but once the bubble burst, a wave of defaults ensued. With close to $1 billion in uninsured customer deposits, the bank was seized by the federal government in 2008.

- **Countrywide.** Without Countrywide, there would be no IndyMac. Angelo Mozilo made it the number one mortgage company in America before he became the poster boy for the mortgage crisis. The only way Countrywide avoided federal seizure was a 2008 sell-off to Bank of America.

Before these companies met their fate, Alt-A loans appeared to be good for the market. But once these loans became more commonplace, the boys in Washington D.C. decided to take things to the next level. This evolved into allowing "stated income" loans. Stated income meant borrowers had only minimal documentation requirements to prove their income, assets and expenses. And when I say "boys in D.C," I have one very special boy in mind. Once again, his name is...

Barney Frank. When it comes to his role in this fiasco, he truly deserves more than one paragraph. For much of his 32 years in "service," Barney Frank was the #1 advocate in Congress for using the power of the federal government to force banks to lower their underwriting standards. For at least some of that time, pressure from left-leaning activist groups like ACORN played a role[77] — but in 2003, as concerns about the unsustainable, artificial inflation of the market were growing, it was Frank who famously said, "I want to roll the dice a little bit more in this situation toward subsidized housing."

Like I said, Clinton didn't rewrite the rules himself. In 1992, Frank introduced a bill that imposed new requirements on Fannie Mae and Freddie Mac. The bill became law, effective in January 1993 as the Housing and Community Development Act. It required Fannie and Freddie to make 30% of their mortgage purchases "affordable housing" loans (also known as *high risk* loans, whether they were Alt-A or subprime). The quota was raised to 40% in 1996 and 42% in 1997. By 2000, HUD ordered the quota to be raised to 50%. The pressure continued under the Bush administration, growing to 55% by 2007 and 56% when the crisis erupted in 2008.[78]

Prior to 1992, Fannie and Freddie were only supposed to buy prime mortgages; now, they had to buy loans that were in serious danger of defaulting. Furthermore, the banks who sold loans to Fannie Mae on the secondary market were also being pressured *by* Fannie Mae. In order to make sure these quotas were met, Fannie had to pressure banks to originate risky loans. At one point, banks were told that if they wanted to continue to sell loans to Fannie Mae, they needed to fund at least 38% of their portfolios in these high risk products.[79] Otherwise, they were in danger of losing the ability to sell to Fannie Mae — which, of course, would force them out of the mortgage business.

That's a vivid illustration of what the unintended consequences of government interference look like. The banks got all the blame, but many of them were reacting to forces on Capitol Hill, where Barney Frank thought he was being a hero by pushing for higher homeownership rates. He didn't care what it took, because he didn't have to execute it.

Furthermore, Frank had a partner in this endeavor. At the time he worked to develop the Housing and Community Development Act and push it into law, the congressman was involved in a domestic partnership with Herb Moses — a barely-out-of-grad-school economist who quickly landed a prestigious position at Fannie Mae thanks to Frank's influence[80] (both went on record acknowledging that's how Moses got the job). *But that's not a conflict of interest, right?* Moses worked at Fannie Mae, which Frank was overseeing, from 1991 to 1998. He left Fannie Mae soon after he and Frank ended their relationship, a fact that was used as an attempt to wash away the idea that this was a problem. *After all, how could it possibly be a problem that the congressman responsible for overseeing Fannie Mae got his boyfriend an important job **at** Fannie Mae?* And if this connection was not a conflict of interest, why would the Associated Press call Frank and Moses "Washington D.C.'s most influential gay couple"?[81]

As the bubble continued to swell, Barney Frank made it clear he was unaware of the damage his actions would eventually cause. One example is this speech on the floor of the House of Representatives:

"Those who argue now that housing prices are now at the point of a bubble seem to me to be missing a very important point...we are talking here about an entity, homeownership....This is not the dotcom situation... Homes that are occupied may see ebb and flow of price at a certain percentage level, but you're not going to see the collapse that you see when people talk about a bubble."
- Rep. Barney Frank, 2005[82]

Unfortunately, no one wanted to hold Frank accountable in any meaningful way. He stayed chairman of the committee until 2011 and retired from Congress in 2013.

In September 2008 (the month that Lehman Brothers became insolvent, Merrill Lynch was sold to Bank of America and the Federal Reserve stepped in to prevent the collapse of AIG), Barney Frank had the nerve to say this: "The private sector got us into this mess. The government has to get us out of it."[83] Way to take responsibility. This attitude led to the most dominant piece of the crisis: subprime loans.

Subprime loans. Some people summarize the crash by calling it "the subprime housing crisis." This isn't entirely inaccurate, but subprime loans were a product of their environment. Over time, the Department of Housing and Urban Development (HUD) lowered minimum down payments from 20% to 10% to 5% to 3.5%. By 2000, many borrowers were qualifying for 100% financing — a downpayment of zero. Fannie and Freddie were forced to participate as well; in response to Barney Frank's relentless push for "affordability" (which really meant "easy access to credit"), they drastically reduced their credit documentation requirements. All of this created an environment in which subprime loans could thrive. For the banks, going from Alt-A to subprime didn't seem like that big of a leap. While Alt-A meant *low*-documentation loans, subprime allowed for *no*-documentation loans. The people who Gordon Gekko refers to as the "N.I.N.J.A. Generation" in *Wall Street 2* — "No income, no job, no assets"[84] — were the people subprime loans were designed for.

With subprime loans, the federal government had forced the mortgage industry to tell borrowers:

- **You don't need any equity.** At the height of subprime, zero down payments were nearing the majority. The National Association of Realtors reported that 43% of loans originated in 2005 were no money down purchases.[85] With almost half of mortgage borrowers buying homes with no skin in the game, it was a recipe for default.
- **You can state your income.** Because stated income was now the norm, people were just filling in numbers. Gee, what could possibly go wrong?
- **And, we've lowered the credit score requirements.** It was very possible to originate a no money down loan for a borrower with a 580 credit score. Often, this was done with an 80/20 loan (two separate loans where the second mortgage has a higher interest rate than the first). Under these conditions, things were so loose that people were qualifying for a lot more house than they could afford. The idea was that by the time their fixed rate mortgage became a (much higher) adjustable rate mortgage, they'd have a raise at work, a better credit score and more equity in their homes. But as we now know, many of them didn't.

Until their new rate kicked in, most people didn't seem to care. The buyers didn't care; they just wanted a house. The sellers didn't care; they just wanted to cash in their equity and buy their *next* house. And if people didn't care, builders didn't care. They kept building and prices kept going up in accordance with the demand. Every five houses, they built a phase of another five houses...and kept pushing the price up with every phase.

Hedge funds and banks started bundling the loans into mortgage-backed securities and selling them off in tranches: packages of 1,000+ mortgages sold on the secondary market all over the world. Standard & Poors and Moody's were giving them AAA credit ratings, because they were being paid by the people who asked for the ratings. People who bought mutual funds, stocks and Fannie Mae bonds thought they were safe. After all, aren't securities backed by mortgages safe? In a normal market, maybe — but these ones weren't, and this was not a normal market. When the market fell, everybody got screwed.

As prices got out of control in 2008, people who bought with a three-year fixed interest rate in 2005 needed to refinance; otherwise, they'd be hit by an adjustable rate they couldn't afford. But unfortunately, a lot of people didn't (or couldn't) refinance. Now that banks were starting to back off some of the products, this prevented people from getting into a new loan — and if they already refinanced once to pull out equity for cars and boats, they had no leverage. Many of them just refinanced into another subprime. People who couldn't afford their house when they got it were about to experience a huge jump in payments, and they were in no better position now to afford it. Prices were plateauing, so they didn't have the extra equity to make up for their shortage of income or lackluster credit.

This is where the term "self-destructing loans" originated. They were destined to fail. If only a small percentage of people had them, the market probably could have absorbed the impact with the help of quick-thinking investors. But it *wasn't* a small percentage; by February 2008, 8.8 million Americans had negative equity in their homes.[86] Throughout 2008, prices plummeted amid a flood of short sales and foreclosures. People who could actually afford their payments couldn't refinance because of how far their home values had dropped. Housing prices fell by 30% on average from their mid-2006 peak to mid-2009 (in some areas, 70-80%), and remained at approximately that level for the next four years. Some of the people who actually qualified for their loans, seeing that their homes were valued much lower than what they owed, decided to short sell or request a loan modification with a principal reduction. This created a phenomenon of "strategic defaults," which consisted of people intentionally falling behind on payments in order to force the banks into modifying their loans and reducing the principal balance (after all, if the banks had a choice between reducing the balance and taking the loss vs. foreclosing on the house and trying to sell it at the dismal current market value, they would choose the option that resulted in a smaller loss).

People are quick to blame the "greed" of the mortgage industry, but it's important to understand that not every mortgage lender in business at the time was on board with what they saw happening. The truth is, many of us were far from "predatory." As a lender, I was honest with people. I made sure they understood the pros and cons of these loans. Many times, I tried to talk them out of it — especially people who wanted to get on the dangerous bandwagon of, "Buy a house, refinance to pull out all your equity, buy another house" that was growing in popularity.

You probably saw some version of this phenomenon going on around you: people pulling money out of their house to buy a vacation home or a bunch of toys. Due to the insane availability of credit, people were becoming investors with no knowledge of what they were doing or how to do it properly. In the 2015 film *The Big Short*, there's a scene involving Steve Carrell and a stripper that encapsulates this perfectly. These people were acting like an 18-year-old with his first credit card, and they were borrowing against equity that wasn't going to stay. Who can honestly say they didn't see all of this coming to a disastrous end? But first, there's one more factor we haven't named.

The Federal Reserve. When inflation or other factors bring about an economic downturn, the Federal Reserve may use quantitative easing by printing money, using that money to buy mortgage bonds and selling those bonds on the secondary market all across the globe. During the housing boom, this eased the interest rates and increased access to cash. The supply of cash went up to offset the demand, which kept the interest rates down. The Federal Reserve pumping cash into the economy kept the banks liquid so they wouldn't go into receivership or be seized by the FDIC, but it was artificial inflation of the market — and because trickle-down economics is a very real thing, it influenced a lot more than interest rates. It influenced the stock market; it influenced your 401(k). That's why what happened wasn't just a housing crash in the United States, but a full-blown financial collapse of the global markets.

These are the major factors behind what happened in 2007 and 2008. To explore it further in a more entertaining format, I recommend watching *The Big Short*.

Fortunately, I don't think we'll ever see this happen again in our lifetime. Today, here's what's changed for the better:

- People have to actually qualify for their loans.
- They're no longer using their homes like ATM machines, because they can't. The banks no longer allow homeowners to pull out 100% of their equity.
- Stated income loans are now limited to high credit, self-employed borrowers who have 20 to 30% cash to put down. And even then, they get a higher interest rate

For the foreseeable future, it seems everyone has learned their lesson.

And yes, we got new government regulation to restrict activity. The irony is, it was written by the very people who started this mess in the first place. To stop another housing crisis from occurring, the two members of Congress who wanted affordable housing at all costs wrote the Dodd-Frank Wall Street Reform and Consumer Protection Act of 2010. Unbelievable.

But these changes don't mean we won't have extreme market cycles ever again. If you see those coming on, you need to know how to handle them whether you're an investor or just the owner of your primary residence. What do the market cycles look like? We'll explore them in the next chapter.

CHAPTER 19

Today we're shifting gears. Today...is "greedy bastard" day.
The secret to riches, lab rats, is the same as the secret to comedy: timing.[87]
- A Good Year, 2006

The Real Estate Market Cycle

NOW, IT'S TIME to learn about the real estate market cycle. Understanding it is the key to achieving any degree of success in real estate investing.

Economists say there are four phases to the real estate market cycle: recovery, expansion, hyper supply and recession. That's true, but I want to make it simpler by using terms that new investors are already familiar with. Most people understand the terms "buyer's market" and "seller's market." These are both connected to the law of supply and demand.

- Buyer's market: Supply is high and demand is low, driving prices down.
- Seller's market: Supply is low and demand is high, driving prices up.

If you know these, you're off to a great start. But there are actually two types of buyer's markets *and* two types of seller's markets, totaling four markets in the cycle. There are parallels between these and the market phases economists have identified, but it's important to understand that "cycle" means there's no actual starting point. There is no "first market" or "last market," just a cycle with four markets made up of different conditions.

All four are all influenced by the same factors that naturally occur in any economy: interest rates, the rental market, the stock market, the job market, consumer confidence, national/global events (even local events, which we'll touch on), changes in the law and other external factors. These are things that affect every-body, and yet most people don't recognize them as having an influence over their own economic opportunities.

As a new investor with your eyes wide open, you should start recognizing these influences right away. First, because they play a big role in determining the length of each market in the cycle; second, because your success hinges upon your behavior in each one of these markets. Here's something to memorize:

Good investors make good money in good markets. Great investors make better money in bad markets.

With that, let's identify the four markets, characterize them and discuss how a smart investor behaves during each one.

Buyer's Market 1

Leading into a Buyer's Market 1, you'll notice the following characteristics as you analyze your local market. These are the signs you look for to prepare yourself.

An overabundance of properties. When you see the market flooded with inventory, you are likely in a Buyer's Market 1. Because the markets that preceded it were full of dreamy-eyed homebuyers and excited new investors snatching up properties, builders kept building in order to meet the demand. This has happened in virtually every region of the United States; however, my location (the Inland Empire region of Southern California) earned the dubious honor of being the hardest hit region in the housing crash due to this market characteristic, fueled by the easy availability of credit due to subprime. From 2005 to 2007, demand was high, prices were high, and builders kept building (and building, and building). This behavior created Buyer's Market 1 — and in Buyer's Market 1, you will have no shortage of properties to consider as potential investments.

Historically high foreclosures. Due to the factors that caused the crash, 2008 was the year that more than 3 million foreclosure filings were issued in the United States (one out of every 54 households).[88] As I said, I don't see an event of that magnitude happening again in our lifetime. But foreclosures are a reality of the market cycle, and Buyer's Market 1 is when they are at a peak. That influx of foreclosed properties leads to major opportunities for investors. When you see a price bubble happening, that's the time to start getting prepared for its burst. When the burst happens, you'll want to buy properties that can provide you with cash flow.

Slow or stalled job growth. If people flock to a specific region in search of jobs during a previous market, then job growth will naturally slow down by the time the cycle reaches Buyer's Market 1. It could be because all the jobs have been filled, or it could be because of the loss of a major employer in the area. In 1993, this happened in response to the mass closure of military bases. President Bill Clinton had approved the shutdown of 35 "unneeded military installations" across the country; seven of them were in California, and three of them were in the Inland Empire. In addition to military personnel, these bases employed thousands of defense contractor employees. When they closed, all those residents who had left Los Angeles County to be closer to work and enjoy a lower cost of living in the Inland Empire were forced to sell their homes and move to wherever their next assignment was. Others were simply laid off and left unemployed — and in the neighborhoods where properties were less than 10 years old, people had little to no equity. As a result, we saw short sales, foreclosures and a dramatic price drop in our area. Because the job growth had completely stalled, supply went up and demand went down. This is a practical illustration of how slow job growth creates Buyers Market 1 conditions. For investors, it provides the opportunity to grab up properties at bargain basement prices. After the market collapse, banks were entertaining offers for lower than what was owed — otherwise known as short sales.

So these are the things you'll see happening in a Buyer's Market 1. In this market, here's how should you behave as an investor:

Buy for cash flow, not appreciation.

The fact is, there won't *be* any appreciation in a Buyer's Market 1; remember, there's been a huge price drop. All this means is you can't flip properties. But what you *can* do is buy properties, renovate them and fill them with renters to cover your mortgage payment and generate some cash flow. There's an old adage in real estate investing:

Money is made on the purchase, not on the sale.

What that means is if you were smart enough to find a good deal when you purchased the property, then you set yourself up for success on the purchase; now, when the time comes to sell, you'll make money no matter what. But in a Buyer's Market 1, you're not selling; you're doing a "buy and hold" strategy by renting the property out. So in this case, setting yourself up for success on the purchase means following this advice:

- Don't use every dollar you have to buy the property.
- Research the fair market rent for properties like yours in your area, to make sure that you charge a monthly rent that will cover your mortgage payment, generate cash flow and leave you with a cushion.
- When unexpected expenses happen, use that cushion as your emergency fund.

Any number of unexpected events could happen: Water heaters blow up, air conditioners break, renters lose their jobs. Here's an example using one of my properties, which I rented out for $1,475 per month to a good tenant who worked multiple jobs. When he lost one of those jobs, he fell behind on the rent. After two missed payments, some landlords would move him out right away — but in this case, that would not have been the best option.

The fact was, I didn't want to lose a good tenant. Yes, I lost two months of rent and still had to cover the mortgage. But if I evicted him, I would have to put a lot *more* money into the house to renovate it for the next tenant. It came down to a matter of deciding whether I'd rather lose $3,000 (two months' rent) or $10,000 to $15,000 (renovation costs). See what I mean?

Here was my solution. I told the tenant he could pay back the two months' rent in installments and I lowered his rent to $1,325. Yes, I *lowered his rent*. This was because I was smart enough to put a cushion in between my mortgage payment of $927 and his previous monthly rent of $1,475. Lowering his rent by $150 was not going to hurt my ability to make the mortgage, and it only slightly reduced my cash flow. It protected his ability to make the rent, which kept him in the house. This protected me from having to absorb a vacancy in one of my properties. Later, I added incremental increases to get it back up to the fair market rent.

If I had let him move out, here's what would happen:

- I'd be stuck with a vacancy, which means no cash flow at all for at least a month.
- I'd be saddled with at least $10,000 in renovation costs.
- I'd have to put the property back on the market and find a new tenant.
- It would take much longer to recover the money I had lost.

In these scenarios, I'll find whatever solution is needed in order to preserve good renters, because good renters mean good cash flow. They're what keep you afloat when you have vacancies. You might be able to find a new renter who's willing to pay more, but you don't know what their character is. I knew the renter I already had was someone with good character.

Renters are people, and people have problems. They have their own lives that affect yours. If you have the ability to ease their pain so they'll ease *your* pain, why wouldn't you do it? It may seem like being cutthroat is good business — but in reality, good business requires you to be flexible and being a landlord requires you to acknowledge that nothing is perfect. Here's some of the best advice I can offer new landlords: Drywall, paint and carpet are cheap. Let your renters live their lives. It's your house, but it's their home. If you made money on the purchase, then you already set yourself up for success while you have tenants in the property.

As investors start buying the foreclosed properties in Buyer's Market 1, that creates conditions that lead to the next market in the cycle, Buyer's Market 2.

Buyer's Market 2

In a Buyer's Market 2, you'll notice a gradual shift to the following conditions.

List prices at their lowest levels. After banks foreclose on the properties in Buyer's Market 1 and put them back on the market, this is your last chance to get them at dramatically low prices. Locals have not yet realized the recovery phase is starting; it could take them anywhere from six months to a year to start noticing. But experienced investors smell blood in the water. The more they pounce on the opportunities, the closer we get to Seller's Market 1 — which is when all these opportunities will be gone. You may be a new investor, but you should think like an experienced one and take advantage of this market. It could be years before the cycle is back to a Buyer's Market 2, which means you'll be waiting a long time for opportunities like this to come back.

Rising competition for foreclosures. Because the experienced investors have started to move in, the competition for bank foreclosures is rising in Buyer's Market 2. These investors are not making lowball offers, so you shouldn't either. Good deals will be everywhere, but you should expect to pay full asking price regardless. If you wait too long, you may be purchasing a property from another investor after he's already rehabbed it. This adds value and raises the price, so do your best to enter the competition early.

Rents increasing. I still recommend the "buy and hold" strategy in Buyer's Market 2. As jobs slowly come back to the area, incomes will increase and grown kids will move out of their parents' homes and want homes of their own. This means rents will begin to increase, and that improves your ability to generate good cash flow from renters. You won't be selling until it's a seller's market — and if you made money on the purchase, you may never want to sell.

That's what's happening in a Buyer's Market 2. In this market, here's how should you behave as an investor:

- *Think like an experienced investor.*
- *Buy everything you can that makes sense; get what you can get, while you can get it.*
- *Buy and hold — no flipping.*

Buyer's Market 2 reaches its peak when the area is flooded with investors. As prices plateau, this creates conditions that lead to the next market in the cycle, Seller's Market 1.

Seller's Market 1

As the cycle moves from a buyer's market to a seller's market, there's more homebuilding and rental prices reach their peak; this is what makes Seller's Market 1 the equivalent of the expansion phase in the traditional economic model. Here's what else to expect.

Uneducated investors move in. With all the supply created by the previous markets, uneducated investors start to realize their missed opportunities when prices were at the bottom. However, prices are still low enough to convince these newcomers that the good times are here to stay. So now, they start buying.

Demand reaches its peak. If interest rates are low, then educated investors continue to buy as well. They understand that even if prices have climbed a little, it's still better to buy while interest rates are at 3% rather than 4%. They also know it's better to make profits this way than sticking their money in the bank. If it seems like you're always hearing that interest rates are "historically low," that's because they keep going down! I remember the first time I saw a 30-year fixed interest rate fall to 3.75%. Who would've thought the rates could go even lower? Sure enough, they did. At some point, they'll go back up. While they're this low, that's the time to take advantage. Now that you have both old and new investors flooding the market, demand is at its highest point in the cycle.

Bidding wars erupt. In a Seller's Market 1, properties sell so quickly that you'll often see bidding wars above asking price. If you were to list a house at $450,000 (to give a modern day California example), it would not be uncommon to get offers of $475,000 or $480,000. People are going crazy, because they see how quickly everything is selling. This not only applies to investors, but also to homebuyers intending to occupy the properties they buy.

Prices start rising. This increase in demand makes prices go back up, but it doesn't happen overnight. First, you see the falling prices slowing down. Then, you see them beginning to climb in accordance with the growing demand. They don't hit a peak until the cycle reaches Seller's Market 2.

This is what you can expect to see in a Seller's Market 1. In this market, here's how should you behave as an investor:

- *Buy fewer cash flow properties; look for them in areas where rents are rising.*
- *Be highly selective about "buy and hold" opportunities. Know that by the time you purchase and renovate, there will already be a price jump.*
- *Start flipping. This is the market that's primed for it.*

We haven't talked about flipping much yet. New investors tend to have a wide-eyed view of flipping; they envision making a huge profit by simply buying a property, doing a few renovation tweaks and putting it back on the market. That's not how it works. To understand how it *does* work, you need to understand the anatomy of a property flip. All the costs involved with a flip make up its anatomy. You subtract each cost to calculate your net profit.

Anatomy of a Flip

Potential sale price
Minus the purchase price
Minus the miscellaneous purchase costs
Minus the financing costs
Minus the renovation costs
Minus the miscellaneous selling costs

Minus the sales commissions
Minus the concession/buyer costs
Minus the carrying costs (loan interest from the time you buy until the time you sell)
Equals net profit

That's a lot of costs, right? Now, let's plug in some real numbers. Here's a property that, after renovation, would be listed at $180,000.

Anatomy of a Flip, Real Numbers

$180,000 Potential sale price, then subtract
$110,000 purchase price, then subtract $2,000 miscellaneous purchase costs (title and escrow), then subtract
$5,000 financing costs (points on a hard money loan), then subtract
$25,000 renovation costs, then subtract $2,500 miscellaneous selling costs (seller's title, escrow and transfer tax), then subtract
$10,800 sales commissions (6% of sale price), then subtract
$10,000 concession/buyer costs (including closing costs), then subtract
$7,100 carrying costs (total cost of project at 10% for six months), equals
$7,600 net profit

That's a profit, but it might not be the profit you envisioned before you learned about the anatomy of a property flip.

If You Put Up the Cash Yourself

What if you're now a seasoned investor who no longer needs to borrow with hard money — in other words, you didn't get a loan and you put up all the cash yourself? In that case, you would replace the hard money costs and carrying costs with the amount you pay yourself for the use of your own money (with whatever the going interest rate is on hard money). This is important to do, because while your money is tied up in this project, it's not doing something else. For more on this, I recommend researching Robert Kiyosaki's "Pay Yourself First" rule.[89]

The Role of the Renovation

It's important to recognize the role that proper renovation plays in the success of your flip. Here's one time I learned this the hard way. Partnering with a friend, we purchased a home in a country club neighborhood for $400,000. This was a unique opportunity to buy a tri-level house in an exclusive area. We knew it needed work, and the idea was to turn it around for $650,000 after renovation.

Once we tallied up everything that needed to be done, I started gathering bids from contractors. The best price I was quoted was $140,000. Can you guess the problem? After sinking $140,000 into it and subtracting all the other costs in the anatomy of this flip, there would be no profit left. The only person who would make money on this project would be the contractor.

At that point, the best course of action would be to swallow the pill and move forward with the work. That way, we could at least get our asking price of $650,000 and break even. The bid I got would have made it beautiful: soft close cabinets, quartz counters, tile showers, a new garage to replace the carport. But instead, my partner found a lower bid...that is, he found a lower bid for a lower quality renovation: cheap cabinetry and counters, fiber-glass showers, nothing to replace the old carport outside. In this neighborhood, that wasn't going to fly. Your renovations should always match the quality of the comparable homes in the neigh-borhood — specifically, the homes you're competing with for buyers — and this one didn't.

When we showed the house, the reaction from buyers was pre-dictably lackluster. When they walked around, they expected to see quality that matched the rest of the homes around it — in other words, a comparable product. That's not what they saw.

Did we sell it for $650,000? Of course not.

On the other hand, you can renovate everything perfectly and *still* fall short of your profit goal. This is easy to do if you're coming in as an out-of-area investor, which is one reason why you should start out flipping in a local market you're familiar with. Next, it's also easy to fall short of your profit goal if you get too greedy.

If this next story could happen to me as a seasoned investor, it could certainly happen to you as a new one.

This time, Dawn and I were buying a Palm Springs property — a market neither of us knew much about. We relied on the local agent to tell us what buyers there were looking for. It turned out the answer was white surfaces, large showers and open concepts. So we gave it to them...all of it. We put $50,000 into the work after paying $381,000 for the house. The initial goal was to turn it around for $510,000, based on the value of the house next door with the same floor plan. I thought we could probably sell it faster if we listed it at $499,000. That would still give us a marginal profit. Then, someone we were working with found comparables within a half-mile radius that indicated we could possibly get $549,000. I wasn't sure that was a good idea, and it turned out I was right. For one thing, that half-mile radius bled into other neighborhoods and crossed over a storm drain. We knew even less about those neighborhoods than the one we were buying in.

Because I was in an unfamiliar market, I had to trust someone who *was* familiar with the market. But every time I called the agent, he had some kind of weather-related excuse: "It's summer; no one shops for houses in the summer here. They only do it in winter and spring." But the bottom line was, we were priced too high and he didn't want to admit it.

That house sat on the market for nine months, and in the end it sold for a sad $450,000 — in other words, a massive loss. Here are some lessons that go with this:

- *If your house is priced too high, no one will come see your house. Lower your price.*
- *If your house is priced right, people are coming to see it and you're not getting any offers, there's something wrong with your house. Ask the agent what their buyers thought, or attend the open house yourself and listen to buyers as they walk around.*
- *If your house is priced right and there's nothing wrong with it, people will come see it and someone will write an offer. Congratulations, you've sold your house.*

The Role of the Real Estate Agent

Choosing the agent you'll work with can play a critical role in the success of your flip. If you've already made some agent connections, that's a good place to start — but you shouldn't feel obligated to hire an agent just because you know them, or because you have some mutual friend or acquaintance. That agent who knows your brother-in-law said he'd only charge you a 1% commission, but guess what? Good agents don't work for 1%. When all is said and done, what cost you an extra $2,000 to $5,000 to pay a good agent full commission might get you an extra $15,000 to $20,000 in profits on your flip.

How can you spot a good agent? Look at their reviews online. You want five stars, no exceptions. After all, the success of your flip largely depends on hiring an agent who can help set the right price, advise the right renovations, show the right buyers and help you make a profit.

When you search for agents online, look at how many transactions each one has closed in the last year. A search for agents in any city, anywhere usually gives you dozens of results to go through. The more transactions they've closed in the past 12 months, the better. That shows you their credibility as a real estate professional in the area. Those five star agents with high transactions are the ones you want to call. Whenever I invest in a property in a new city where I don't know any agents, this is how I find one.

In a Seller's Market 1, you'll see investors who flip blindly without taking the anatomy of a flip into account. You'll also see investors who fail to recognize the role their renovation plays in the success of their flip. And, you may see seasoned investors who come from out of town, get greedy and take bad advice. Don't be one of those investors. Be the one who chooses the right renovations, the right advice and the right agent to work with.

How will you know when a Seller's Market 1 comes to an end? You'll notice that things are starting to cool down:

- Although prices remain high, properties are beginning to sit on the market longer.

- Construction continues, but it's getting excessive; new construction sales are slowing.
- Job growth may begin to slow; in the next market, it will become stagnant.

Before Seller's Market 2 takes over, this is the time to sell your properties and count your profits.

Seller's Market 2

Seller's Market 2 is the riskiest part of the cycle because of the following conditions.

Job growth is stagnant. No jobs means low population growth to the area, which is another reason homes aren't selling. Fewer people working in the area means fewer people looking to move into the area. People will move to where the jobs are. As the market continues to cycle, the low demand mentioned above will be met with high supply. Over time, this will eventually lower prices and pave the way for recovery (back to Buyer's Market 1). However, this could be a long way off.

The deals are drying up. The time for snatching up property after property at wholesale prices is over until the next buyer's market. Right now, you're shifting your focus to selling while prices are at a peak.

The buyers are going away. Where did all the buyers go? They disappeared due to lack of affordability. Affordability is a combination of wages going up and prices coming down at the same time. Often, you can find an affordability index that assigns a percentage to the level of affordability in an area. As the affordability index drops in a Seller's Market 2, you have fewer buyers who can perform. That drops the demand for houses, which makes the prices go down.

In California, we saw this happen in 1980, 1989 and 2005. In each of those years, the California Association of Realtors reported the affordability index was at 17%.[90] There has been some indication that when the affordability index is at 17%, that's when the market turns. At that point, investors are supposed to start selling off assets to protect against losses.

Now, you may look at the three years listed above and wonder why there were still buyers in 2005 if there was such poor affordability. The answer is, the subprime environment allowed for it to continue. People couldn't afford the homes they were buying, but they were allowed to simply state their income as high as it needed to be to get into the house they wanted, and a magic wand was waved.

As the market melted down over the years to come, affordability went way up — but by that time, people were 1.) gun shy and 2.) could no longer qualify. As we know now, the market eventually recovered. As an investor, an American and a human being, there's a lesson there:

Don't get too up; don't get too down. When times are tough, things are never as bad as they seem. When times are good, things are never as good as they seem.

You're never going to sell at the exact top or buy at the exact bottom. You try to watch the markets in the cycle and do your best.

Seller's Market 2 is a critical one. How you behave in this market will play a major role in your success as an investor. It's time to lock in gains and protect against losses. You do this by:

- *Selling the rest of your properties (you should have started this in Seller's Market 1).*
- *Moving your money into another market (a city or state you're familiar with).*
- *Or, moving your money into stocks and other investment products.*

Now, here's a caveat: If you still have properties you're renting out for cash flow and things are going smoothly, there's no reason to sell those. You can ride it out and let your renters keep making your mortgage payments for you. You don't need to sell if your properties are cash flowing.

CHAPTER 19

Ways to Lose Money in Real Estate

These are especially important during Seller's Market 2, but they apply in any market of the cycle. For most people who lose money in real estate, they manage to do it one of these three ways.

1. Buying properties that don't cash flow. This can happen by paying too much for a property, or by charging rent too far below market value. It can also happen by being too optimistic on what the market rents are.

2. Refinancing into negative cash flow. If you're holding onto cash flowing properties and starting to see some equity in them, *don't* pull every dollar out of them with cash-out refinances. "Buy a house, pull out all your equity, buy another house" is an unsustainable strategy if you destroy your cash flow by pulling out too much.

3. Selling in a down market. If you make the mistake of refinancing into negative cash flow too many times, then at some point, you'll need to sell — but in a down market, there's a good chance you won't be able to. Unless you have a ton of cash or credit lines as your safety net, you'll be in trouble.

Other Protection Strategies

If you've done your homework before you start investing, you already know Warren Buffet's rules:[91]

- Rule #1: Never lose money.
- Rule #2: Never forget rule #1.

What if you're in a Seller's Market 2, you're losing equity and you didn't sell when you should have? If you followed the adage of making money on the purchase rather than the sale, then you should still have some kind of margin to protect yourself against losses if you have to sell in these conditions — or, as long as your properties cash flow, you can opt to wait it out.

Another way to protect yourself is to incrementally raise the rents on your cash flowing properties. A good rule of thumb is to raise your rents by 3-5% annually. If you're afraid your tenants will vacate in search of a better deal, here's what I've found: Once they start looking around and they see everyone is charging the same rent you are, they aren't going anywhere.

Just knowing the four markets in the real estate cycle isn't enough. You need to learn the characteristics of each one, and be prepared to make your investment behaviors match up to what's happening. If you're determined to make it investing in real estate, this is crucial to your success.

CHAPTER 20

"Fear and panic are two separate emotions.
Fear is healthy; panic is deadly."[92]
- Chasing Mavericks, 2012

AFTER THE MELTDOWN, a lot of full-time investors didn't make it. You might think the opposite would be true — but until it got to the point where banks were taking short sales and the foreclosures went back on the market, investment opportunities had completely dried up.

I was able to stay afloat because of my commercial property and my mortgage business, but that wasn't easy either. Because so many people had screwed up their credit and were upside down on their houses, sales were way down. What helped keep the business going were some of the new refinance products introduced by government-sponsored entities:

- Fannie Mae had the Home Affordable Refinance Program (HARP).
- Freddie Mac had the Freddie Mac Enhanced Relief Refinance® (FMERR).
- For veterans, there was the VA streamline refinance.
- For FHA borrowers, there was the FHA streamline refinance.

Since everybody was underwater, these loans didn't require an appraisal. That's what made them good products. The problem was, not everybody qualified for one of them. If you kept your credit up and made your payments on time, these opportunities were available to you. But as you can imagine, many people *didn't* keep their credit up or make their payments on time. Those things would eliminate them from eligibility. Having an Alt-A loan, subprime loan or even jumbo loan would also prevent eligibility, because those loans are not Fannie, Freddie, FHA or VA. Even those who kept their credit up and still made their payments on time were ineligible, because they were upside down on their house (meaning, their loan amount was higher than the value of the house).

Lessons After the Meltdown

Since the majority of the country was melting down, things were tight in the mortgage business; there weren't many transactions closing. Until the opportunities presented themselves again, I was relying on the cash flow from my commercial building and my other savings to keep from having to adjust my lifestyle. By late 2008, the opportunities started to resurface. You saw all the contributing factors for a Buyer's Market 1 environment: an over-abundance of properties, historically high foreclosures and stalled job growth. With that, I waded back in. My first stop to getting re-engaged was at the Javits Center in New York City, where the The Learning Annex Real Estate and Wealth Expo was being held.

That's where I was exposed to more wealth building ideas from:

- David Lindahl, who created an easy-to-understand model for monitoring the markets.
- Alan Greenspan, former Chairman of the Federal Reserve.
- Tony Robbins, who has a lot more wisdom than people give him credit for.
- And yes, a future President of the United States named Donald Trump.

Since it had only been two years since Alan Greenspan left his position as Fed Chairman, people were interested to hear his thoughts on what we were all now living through. One person asked him what we could do to prevent anyone from committing loan fraud again in the future. In my best recollection of

Greenspan's answer, I recall a takeaway being this idea: Fraud and manipulation are part of our freedoms. In order for us to absolutely guard against the possibility of fraud or the manipulation of rules, we have to be willing to lose freedoms. So as long as we want to be a free country, we have to expect there will be a certain amount of fraud and manipulation going on.

Again, this is my personal recollection of his remarks – and if that was the message, does that mean Alan Greenspan is for fraud and manipulation? Of course not. It means he knows there will always be rule breaking in a free market, but that's the cost of *having* a free market. There's rule breaking in a restricted market, too. Which one would we rather have?

In 2010, Chris Dodd and Barney Frank unveiled their bill designed to overregulate the mortgage industry and gave it a fancy name: The Dodd-Frank Wall Street Reform and Consumer Protection Act. Think about this irony: They passed a law to prevent a future repeat of the very problem *they* had caused. The people who created an environment where fraud and manipulation could thrive were now playing clean-up with legislation that would punish the free market for their misdeeds. It was shameful.

There's Always That One Guy

At any motivational learning event, you're bound to meet someone who lives to attend these conferences but never does anything with what he learns at them. This expo was the first time I met one of those people. Sitting near Dawn and me in one of the workshops was a guy who held a bulky white clipboard on his lap, furiously writing notes on page after page.

We struck up a conversation in between speakers. "I've been to hundreds of these things," he bragged. "I'm learning so much stuff."

"Wow," I said. "So how many properties have you bought?"

"None yet," he said. "But I'm getting ready."

Hmmm.

The next speaker was Tony Robbins, whose remarks should have hit home with this guy. Again, this is personal recollection – but the idea was this: 99% of everybody in this room will do absolutely nothing with what they've learned here this weekend.

It's that kind of wisdom that makes Tony Robbins much more than a motivational speaker.

As I started doing my own investment workshops, I incorporated that wisdom into what I taught people. "Most people do nothing with this," I would say, "because they get overwhelmed." Remember when I made offers on three different properties in one week? Once they were all accepted, I was in a pickle. I was still a new investor who didn't have the experience necessary to anticipate what happened.

Here's the point: If all you can think about is reaching your goal of buying 10, 15 or 20 houses, then you'll get overwhelmed and end up buying nothing. So instead, this is what you should do:

- Focus on buying *one* house.
- Buy it, rehab it, get it refinanced and put a renter in it.
- Take a deep, cleansing breath.
- Collect rent for a month or two.
- Ask yourself what you liked and didn't like about the experience.
- N*ow*, you can start looking to buy the next one.

Do this one property at a time until you reach your goal.

The things I'm teaching in this book are things I learned the hard way – so you don't have to.

The truth is, the properties I bought before the meltdown were ones that a monkey could've picked by throwing darts at a map. That was the market I was in at the time. Once I learned about the four markets in the cycle and the benefits of buying more methodically than I had in the past, I realized:

1. I had made some really good purchases.
2. I had made some purchases I would never do again.

That's when I started staying away from anything that was too big, too small or too far away. Did that limit my options? Not anymore, because the foreclosures were back on the market. There was plenty of inventory, because it was a Buyer's Market 1.

Natural Fear, Healthy Nervousness

The first move I made after the meltdown was on a four bedroom, two bath single story foreclosure. It had a perfect footprint and perfect floorplan that families would love. I drove over to look at it and saw that it was kind of busted up (as opposed to a lot of the area foreclosures that were *very* busted up), so maybe it wasn't worth the full $130,000 they were asking. I called the listing agent and said I would write a cash offer of $120,000.

"Okay," the agent said. "I'll write up the contract while you're driving back to your office. When you get there, you can sign it and send it back to me."

This was 2008; as you know, I had already bought 18 houses, sold 15 and bought a $5 million commercial building by this time. Prior to the crash, I had done pretty well with this real estate investing thing. But there was something about making my first move after the meltdown that had me pretty freaked out.

On my drive back to the office, I started getting the shakes. I was making a leap I hadn't made in a while, and that created a nervous reaction. I asked myself all the questions I should have been asking anyway: *"Is this really the bottom?"... "Did I miss anything?"..."What will it really appraise for after I rehab it?"..."Am I making the right decision?"*

If you aim to be a successful investor, this is going to happen to you. It doesn't have to be your first purchase after a market downturn; it could happen the first time you increase what you put into your existing investments. No matter how seasoned you are, you get nervous every time you decide to make a big move. *Everybody* asks, "Am I making the right decision?" A little natural fear doesn't necessarily mean the answer is no (see the earlier quote from the film *Chasing Mavericks*).

Also, this applies no matter what you invest in. If you're investing in the stock market, and you decide to go from being a conservative investor who puts in a few hundred dollars a month to a speculative investor who puts in a few thousand dollars a month, the nervousness you feel before doing that is healthy. If the investment doesn't interfere with covering your living expenses and you're doing this for the purpose of long-term gains, then questioning yourself doesn't necessarily mean you're on the wrong track. If you made these kinds of moves without thinking it through, then *that* would be a problem.

When it came to this first post-crash opportunity, I realized I wasn't on the wrong track. Once the foreclosures were listed, the market was ready for investors to buy up the properties and usher in the recovery phase. By the time I got back to the office that day, I was feeling good. I signed the contract for my offer, sent it in — and then, I found out the seller didn't accept my offer. Someone had outbid me. The free market takes care of everything.

It Gets Easier

Not getting that house didn't stop me from finding another one. In fact, it actually made it easier for me to plow forward and continue getting back into investing. I found another single story, open floor plan property that was perfect to rent out to a family on a street called Shadybend. I wrote an offer for $117,000 and it was accepted. I rehabbed it, refinanced it, put a renter in it and enjoyed the cash flow until 2021, when it was valued at $460,000. Until then, I rented it out for $1,475 a month and my monthly payment was $927. That gave me monthly cash flow of $548. So was that a good decision? You bet.

One at a time, I bought up more properties like this — properties bought at the bottom of the market that provided both appreciation and cash flow. Here's a look at that post-meltdown part of my portfolio.

Property Address	Year of Purchase	Sale Price	Value Today (2021)
Shadybend	2008	$117,000	$460,000
Mantee	2008	$135,000	$375,000
Foreman	2008	$112,000	$365,000
Tierra Canyon	2009	$108,000	$445,000
Pinzon	2010	$75,000	$465,000

As you can see, these were all bought in a period of two years. I show you that to illustrate that you can buy one property at a time and still grow your portfolio quickly.

That shows the lucrative possibilities after appreciation. Now, what about cash flow? On these same properties, here's the positive cash flow generated after my tenants pay their rent and I pay the mortgage.

Property Address	Tenant's Monthly Rent	My Monthly Mortgage	Positive Cash Flow
Shadybend	$1,475	$927	$548
Mantee	$1,650	$916	$734
Foreman	$1,400	$904	$496
Tierra Canyon	$1,700	$896	$804
Pinzon	$1,650	$1,012	$625

With more than $1.3 million in equity and more than $3,000 in monthly positive cash flow, I'd say those were pretty good decisions. That's how I know that a little nervousness is not necessarily a sign that it's time to hit the brakes. If anything, it means you're on the verge of something big. The key is moving one step at a time; in this case, one property at a time.

The Pinzon House

You may notice that I got the house on Pinzon as a bargain basement steal. That $75,000 price tag is an example of the kinds of deals you can get as an investor if you're willing to take on a little risk.

An agent named Mike told me about a house that had been condemned by the county; they actually had a HAZMAT team come in to remove the drywall that was infested with cats. It was *literally* a cathouse; it was filled with cats (and all the things cats leave behind). It was total squalor, and the neighbors were complaining. Off and on, one of the seller's adult kids would sleep on a cot inside. But since he never paid the property taxes on it, the county had stepped in. "I'm just trying to keep it from going to tax sale," Mike told me. He asked if I wanted to buy it for $75,000.

"Sure," I said without hesitation. "I'll buy it." Yes, I had cash available to me — but even if I didn't, there was always hard money. When you have hard money available, you can make these kinds of decisions on the spot. That's why I'm promoting the idea of using hard money loans for investing. Often, it's the best way to get the properties you want quickly with the strength of a cash buyer.

Mike told me the neighbor said there was no one living in the house at the moment, but I should be able to get inside. So Dawn and I drove over there, walked to the front door and gently pushed on it. The door swung right open — and as it did, a cloud of cat feces aroma whiffed in our faces. Dawn immediately said, "I'll wait in the car." Good decision.

So I went in alone, and Mike was right. There were litter boxes everywhere, and plenty of live cats to go with them. After the HAZMAT team had been in there, they had removed so much contaminated drywall that the cats could now enter the walls and inhabit the ducts. Those felines found every open space in every corner of the house. The concrete under the flooring had to be disinfected, and I learned something from that experience: You can spray paint concrete to seal in the disinfectants and get rid of the smell! Who knew?

I put $71,000 into rehabbing the house, and I'd say it was worth it now that the house is valued at $465,000. I got all that equity *and* $625 a month in positive cash flow because I was willing to take a risk on a property that was a bigger rehab than your average foreclosure home.

That's the story of the Pinzon house.

Moving into Arizona

Dawn and I have always loved Laughlin and Lake Mohave, and eventually there was an opportunity to buy a property there. In 2005, a couple asked me for a loan to save their house in Corona, California from foreclosure. Meanwhile, they still owned a mobile home in Bullhead City, Arizona (see what I mean about the "Buy a house, refinance to pull out all your equity, buy another house" bandwagon? These people were a classic example of that phenomenon leading up to the meltdown).

They needed $25,000 to save their primary residence in Corona, and they had put their house in Bullhead City up for sale. "I'll lend it to you," I said, "but I'll put a lien on the Bullhead City house so that when you sell it, I'll get paid back. You'll be paying me $28,000 in 60 days."

The wife seemed nervous. "What if it doesn't sell in 60 days?"

"Then I'll go 90 days for $30,000," I told her.

"What if it doesn't sell in 90 days?"

"Then you drop the price from $180,000 to $150,000, and I'll buy it from you. The $30,000 you owe me can be my down payment. Then we're even."

I had never even seen the house.

I already knew what the outcome would be. They had a renter in the house, and it's too hard to sell while the renter is still occupying; plus, this renter was trashing the place. So after 90 days with no buyers, they dropped the price to $150,000 and sold me the house. The loan closed in December 2005, sight unseen. Why would I do that? Because the house appraised for more than $150,000. It appraised for $178,000, which gave me a safety net. Six months later, Dawn and I finally went to Bullhead City to see our new investment in person; by that time, the renter had moved out.

None of the keys I was given fit into the lock. But just like I tapped on the door of the Pinzon house to get in, all I had to do was flex in the cheap, single pane window of this house and it slid right open. And in we went.

And, also like the Pinzon house, this house was disgusting on the inside. It turned out that when the renter vacated, he took the furniture that was supposed to be ours in the deal. Once again, it was time to rehab. Whatever we were going to do with this place, it needed to be ready. I hired a local contractor to:

- Install dual pane windows, new cabinets, a Silestone counter and a solid new floor.
- Stucco the outside so it looked like a stick-built house rather than a mobile home (after all, I didn't want my friends to start giving me NASCAR tickets for my birthday).
- Add on a security system, an Alumawood® awning and a fence.

That was a pretty extensive rehab totaling around $70,000. Now, it looked great — so I shouldn't have been surprised by Dawn's idea.

"Let's not rent it," she said. "Let's keep it as a vacation home.

I didn't even know we *wanted* a vacation home in Bullhead City.

But I liked the idea, and I liked it even more the first time we came back to it after a long day out on the lake. That's when I discovered how much nicer it is to have your own little crash pad to come home to, with your fridge full of food and your own clothes in the closet, along with a shower and bed that belong to you (no hotel germs!) after a day of hot sun and Seadoos.

The point is: Once you've become a seasoned investor with lots of properties in your portfolio, there's nothing wrong with deciding to keep one of them. If it's in an area where you'd like a second home, then I highly recommend it once you can afford it.

We enjoyed that house for eight years. In 2013, the neighbor was selling his stick built house for $245,000. I thought I wanted to buy it, until I realized how high it was priced for only being 1,400 square feet; the only advantage was it had an RV garage. Maybe I didn't want another house after all; maybe I just wanted an RV garage. Then, while driving around one day, I discovered a 2,150 square foot house on a 10,000 square foot lot for $225,000...*with* a giant RV garage.

"I already have an offer on it," the agent named Kathy said. "It's a short sale."

I've seen this movie before. "Where I come from, short sales fall out 50% of the time. Can we just look at it?" It never hurts to ask.

She showed it to us the next day, and we wanted it. But there was still that short sale. "How much is the other offer?" I asked Kathy.

"You know I can't tell you that," she said.

"Okay," I said. "As my agent, what do you suggest I write an offer for?"

Kathy wasn't budging. "Why don't I just keep your card," she said calmly, "and I'll call you when the bank comes back on this one." She knew the short sale could fall through, but her fiduciary responsibility required her to let it happen on its own.

Six weeks later, I got a call from Kathy. "Ed," she said, "the bank came back on it. They want $230,000 and my other buyer's offer was $200,000. He wants 72 hours to think about it. In 72 hours, we'll lose the deal. The bank says take it or leave it. Do *you* have to think about it?"

"Well, maybe," I told her. "Will it appraise?"

"Yes."

"Then I'll take it." That was the extent of me "thinking about it."

We put the other house up for sale; we had bought it for $150,000, put $100,000 into it and sold it for $140,000. Yes, we took a loss. Here's why: The house we were buying was built with a $550,000 construction loan from the original owner. I was getting it for $230,000. A small loss on the first house was no big deal, because of what we were gaining.

Here's the lesson: *The moment the first house became a vacation home, it became a different kind of property.*

When you're looking for an investment property, it's all about the rate of return. But as soon as Dawn decided it should be our vacation home, it was no longer about trying to make a profit from it. We were buying a house to live in. If you're a man, then your only concern when you're buying a house to live in is what makes your wife happy. If you're a woman, then good news: You're in full control.

Some investments aren't just about profit.

CHAPTER 21

I'M TELLING MOST of these stories in chronological order, but I'm going to backtrack for this one. Like I said, I started buying properties around Mammoth in 1996 and launched my long-term plan with local properties in 2003. But there was a chapter in between those two, and it taught me some valuable lessons about real estate investing.

Four-Way Flipping Venture

It started in 1998, when I recruited a fellow arm wrestling competitor named Felix who was interested in getting involved with "any of the fantastic opportunities that are real estate" (as I say on my weekly radio show).

Since he was new to the industry, Felix wasn't exactly sure what part of real estate he wanted to work in — but since my business is mortgage, the only position I could offer him was loan officer. After about a year of commuting from Orange County to Riverside County to learn from me, Felix decided all the minutiae involved with qualifying people for home loans (helping them clean up their credit, showing them how to file their taxes, etc.) wasn't for him. In fact, he didn't want to be on the mortgage side of the business at all. He decided he'd rather be a real estate agent, handling sales contracts and showing properties to buyers.

That's not what I do, but I still thought I might be able to help him. At that time, we were doing tons of business with people who were buying properties and flipping them (this was 1999. Remember when everyone you knew thought they could flip houses?). Jim, Dan and I decided it was time for us to get in on this movement; after all, I had great credit, Jim had great credit and Dan had great credit and were involved in the real estate business. What none of us had, however, was time to go out and find properties to flip because we all had to mind our full-time businesses. That's where Felix came in.

Since he was no longer going to be employed as one of my loan officers and he had just earned his real estate broker's license, Felix needed a real estate job — so, why not hire him to find us properties, coordinate the rehab work and facilitate the sales transactions? The three of us would put up the money, we'd split the profits four ways since Felix was doing the legwork, and we'd deduct Felix's sales commission out of his cut. He was on board and we got going.

At the time, there was no shortage of inventory. In 1999 and 2000, there were tons of HUD repos, VA repos, Fannie Mae repos, Freddie Mac repos...you name it. Plus, we were still coming off the aftermath of the military base closures. It was a classic Buyer's Market 2.

As we got started, it looked like Felix was doing great. He'd give us full analytic presentations for each property, including what needed to be done in terms of renovations (and when it came to the HUD repos, some of them needed full gut rehabs). When each transaction was complete, we'd tally up what we paid for the property, what it cost to rehab and what we made off the sale, including the commission Felix was paid. From there, we'd calculate what the four-way split would be. Since Felix got his commission upfront, we would deduct that from his split. It worked out great for a while. But eventually, the law of cause and effect set in.

Because he was making money based on the rest of us buying the properties, Felix's priorities shifted. Remember, he was supposed to be finding the properties, buying them, coordinating the rehabs and making sure they got sold. That was a lot of work, which is why we made him a full partner.

The problem was, Felix began prioritizing the "find and buy" part of his job over the "rehab and sell" part. Once he realized that he made more money on the commission than the profit split, he was only focused on finding more and more properties to buy (with our money). That put the rest of us partners in a bad position. The less Felix sold, the more mortgages we had to pay until he started selling again.

Plus, he wasn't following my rule of only buying three bedroom, two bath homes (but to be fair, I actually hadn't figured out that rule myself yet. I was still okay with houses with fewer than three bedrooms or fewer than two baths at this point). Because of this, there were times we didn't make as much profit and Felix would be in the hole. Then, he'd end up owing us money.

One of the transactions that spelled out "the beginning of the end" for this venture was on a rural area manufactured home Felix had found. He thought it was a good investment because the title said it was a four bedroom, two bath with a second story (what manufactured home buyer wouldn't be excited about having two stories?). But what nobody knew — including us, until after we'd already bought it — was that the owners had disconnected the second half of the home before they foreclosed (why? Who knows). Felix, for some reason, couldn't tell by looking at the property that this had happened. It was boarded up, which made it too dark to see everything — but Felix was who we trusted to find the properties, so we didn't question him when he said this was a four bedroom, two bath, two story manufactured home.

After we bought it, took the title and started the rehab, we discovered that not only was the second story gone — but also, losing the second story meant this house was actually a two bedroom, one bath. All I could think was, *I know it was dark...but how did Felix get confused about this? How do you stop counting at one bathroom?* We fixed it up as best we could, but we ended up losing a big chunk of cash in the process. Because we bought a product that was different than what we thought we had, our numbers were all skewed. And that was because the one guy who was supposed to be putting his eyes on the property was more concerned with making sure the money came in on his end, because that was his only source of income. When you work for someone else, you can't do that. You have to "make sure you're making sure," because that's what you're getting paid for.

At this point, most of the cash we were making on the properties we sold was going into making the payments on the properties we were carrying. Since Felix still wasn't selling, we would typically carry anywhere from 10 to 20 properties at a time. This headache went on for over a year before we stopped buying, and about two years until the last of all our inventory was sold.

Wrong Strategy, No Profits, Big Lessons

Over the course of two years, we bought 48 properties. When we finally liquidated, each partner's share was about $150,000. That alone isn't much for four dozen properties. Divide that by 48 properties and you have about $3,125 per house. But by the time we paid the taxes on the profits, the amount of cash pocketed was insignificant. It ended up being inconsequential in any of our lives — except for Felix's life, since he made commissions the entire time.

I learned three lessons from this experience:

1. *You can't do things on a grand scale unless you're prepared to turn your units faster.* Being prepared means having a clear strategy. "Buy, buy, buy" is not a great strategy.

2. *Don't get in over your head.* It didn't make sense to have 20 houses when our rehab crew could only complete the work on two houses a month. Having too many properties sitting meant having too many mortgages to pay.

3. *You need someone with skin in the game managing the project.* This is the most important lesson, because the first two mistakes could be avoided if we just had this one figured out.

If any of us with more skin in the game had set aside time to manage the venture, then "buy, buy, buy" would not have been the strategy. But I can't put *all* the blame on Felix, because he was the new guy. The rest of us were supposed to be his mentors. We never stepped in to get him to change course.

What the Strategy Should Have Been

At the end of 2003, when I was introduced to *Rich Dad's Prophecy* and learned the strategy that led to owning seven houses in the first year, I had an epiphany about that previous venture: *What if we had just put renters in them?* After all, most of them were ideal rental homes. I realized that if we had done the same strategy I was now doing by renting out the houses after rehab, things could have been very different. Instead of making an insignificant amount of money, we would've had consistent positive cash flow amounting to about $1.5 million per person.

Here's how that would have worked:

- Let's say we bought a property with a $100,000 loan at a 7% interest rate (the going rate at the time). This would give us a mortgage payment of about $800 including taxes and insurance.
- Renting it out for $1,200 a month with an $800 a month mortgage would have given us $400 a month positive cash flow per property.
- Multiplying that by 48 properties would give us $19,200 a month.
- Divide that by the four partners, and each of us would have had $4,800 a month in positive cash flow. That would have amounted to $230,400 in positive cash flow per person over four years.
- Then, if we had held the properties for four years until 2004 (prices had doubled by then, and we were still not at the top of the market), we could have sold them and profited an additional $6 million.

But this didn't happen, because we couldn't see past the end of our noses. We didn't take a long-term approach based on the market cycle.

When I tell that story in workshops, people gasp when they hear me say we left $6 million on the table. I tell them, "Don't feel bad; each person's cut would've only been $1.5 million." Still, a million and a half dollars is a million and a half dollars.

It's like the story of the old bull and the young bull sitting up on the hill together.

- The young bull says: "Look at all those cows in the field. Let's run down there and have our way with one of them."
- The old bull says: "No, let's *walk* down there. Then we can have our way with *all* of them."

In other words, let's not try to have all the profit now. Let's pace ourselves, so we can have *more* profit.

When I did the calculations that led to the $6 million figure, it was in 2004 when I was trying to figure out how we could buy that apartment building. If we had held them until the top of the market in 2006 when values jumped another 30%, we'd have *more* than $6 million and easily could have bought the apartment complex. We just didn't have the foresight.

Flipping and Short-Term Greed

If you're not careful, then flipping and short-term greed can go hand-in-hand. If we're being honest, a *lot* of people were short-sighted during the flipper craze. It just made a bigger impact on us because we were trying to bite off so much more than we could chew. We thought all we had to do was keep our credit clean and send Felix out to do the legwork. What we *should* have done was set up an LLC, collect the rents and make the payments, pressing on until we would sell at the top of the market. We were short-term greedy. We should have been long-term greedy.

If you're a new investor full of adrenaline and thinking of flipping properties, here's what my experience should teach you.

- Don't ask yourself: "How many properties can I buy?"
- Instead, ask yourself: "How many properties can I carry at one time?"

Remember, you still have to pay the mortgages while you're waiting for the rehabs to be complete. If you're making payments on more houses than you can rehab at one time, you're defeating the purpose and doing it wrong.

Every company only stocks inventory based on how much the inventory sells, because 1) they only have so much warehouse space, and 2) carrying products for too long will drag down the bottom line. A good retailer understands he can only sell x number of units per day, and he doesn't stock more than he can sell. Don't stock more inventory (properties) than you can keep in your proverbial warehouse. It will kill your profits as an investor.

CHAPTER 22

*"You can't never let anything happen to him.
Then nothing would ever happen to him."*[94]
- Finding Nemo, 2003

WHEN THE KIDS were growing up, Dawn had a sign on the wall that said, "Kids: Tired of having to obey rules and being harassed by your parents? Act now! Move out, get a job and pay your own bills while you still know everything!" Of course, my kids aren't the only ones who thought they knew everything. Your kids did too (or they will, if you haven't had them yet) — and when you and I were growing up, we thought we knew everything too. When I look back on those days of working in restaurants and going to high school, I remember how smart I believed I was. But it's only after we get older that we get wiser.

Eventually, things become crystal clear — and it's a shame that you can't have that kind of clarity while you're young, energetic and still have a body that can climb mountains or jump out of airplanes. But apparently, that's the way God wanted it. I think it's so we wouldn't question his plans.

Where Wisdom Comes From

When William was my partner, we balanced each other out; he had put off having a family until he was older, so he had some business vision I didn't have. Meanwhile, I had my family young; that meant I had some life wisdom *he* didn't have.

My human resources director would sometimes tell me, "William can't figure out why employees don't react to him the way they do to you." To understand the cause of that, I reverse engineered what she was saying:

- Employees reacted to me differently than they did to William.
- That's because I interacted with employees differently than William did.
- I interacted with them differently because I saw things differently.
- I saw things differently because I had more life wisdom.
- I had more life wisdom because I had raised kids to adulthood.

When the partnership with William ended, I was 55 and he was 59. My youngest kid was 30; his oldest kid was 12. There's wisdom that comes from raising your kids to adulthood.

But when I say "raising them to adulthood," I don't just mean raising them to age 18. I mean raising them to be successful adults with careers, their own homes, and bills that they pay themselves. But wait a minute: When you're a young adult, doesn't the process of learning to do those things *yourself* give you wisdom? It does, but that's not always enough.

The fact is, you learn more about a subject by teaching it to other people. You can learn how to do something, and you can even get good at doing it. But that's just knowledge. Wisdom comes when you're in the process of teaching it to others. That's when everything crystallizes.

Like a lot of you, I took algebra in 8th grade, geometry in 9th grade, trigonometry in 10th grade and pre-calculus in 11th grade — and like a lot of you, I wondered: "When am I ever going to use this in real life?" It wasn't until pre-calculus that I finally understood the practicality of algebra. By then, I was helping other students. And that's how I came to understand it all more fully.

Historical Applications

For most kids, the "how does this affect my real life" question is usually associated with learning math. But if you're like me, you may have asked yourself the same question when you learned history and social studies: "Why do I need to know what the Pilgrims went through? Why do I need to know about the first Thanksgiving?" Later, I realized it was because the Pilgrims' first economic system at Plymouth (as well as the settlers' first economic system at Jamestown) — collective ownership of farmland, also known as a communal "sharing economy" — was the first experiment in socialism. And it was a failed experiment, because it led to widespread famine. At some point, they saw that everyone was starving to death and realized, "This isn't working."

From that experience, they determined that a better system would be each family owning their own parcel of land. This parcel goes to the Monroes, this one goes to the Andersons, this one goes to the Jeffersons. Now, everybody is expected to work on their own land and grow their own stuff. And everyone was successful, because they all realized this: "If I don't produce, then I don't eat." They figured out that each farmer had his own crop or livestock he was good at producing. As they watched each other work, they realized:

- This guy is great at growing corn, but he doesn't have any potatoes.
- This other guy is great at growing potatoes, but he doesn't have any meat.
- That guy is a great hunter, but he doesn't grow any crops.

They realized that they could each produce their own harvest and barter with each other. Now, *everyone* had corn, potatoes and meat. It was the beginning of free market capitalism. Unfortunately, we don't learn the story of the Pilgrims that way in school — and even if we do, we probably don't fully understand it at that point. We're still growing kids with forming brains, sponging off our parents.

But once we're grown up, working on our own "land" and participating in the free market, we can understand what all that history really meant. Our kids still learn the story in school — but just like us, they aren't being taught the lesson. That's why so many of them think socialism is a great idea: free healthcare, free college, free food programs. If they were taught the lesson, they would be able to learn from the mistakes of the past. You don't have to *only* learn from the people you encounter in your life. Learning from the mistakes of history can be just as valuable.

When Kids are Lied To

This is why I believe politicians who say things like, "Trickle-down economics has been tried and failed" are lying (Hillary Clinton, Barack Obama, Joe Biden and Bernie Sanders all come to mind). They know it's succeeded, because they've seen what happens in economies that don't use it. They just don't want to disappoint the younger Americans who will only vote for them if "free stuff" is promised. It's actually evil, because it's lying to kids for your own gain.

If it's true that supply-side economics (the technical term for "trickle down") has truly failed, then we wouldn't still have it as our primary economic proposition today...but we do. It's still the foundation of our economy *because* it works. And the politicians who say it doesn't work are lying for their own gain.

The simplest way to explain it is this: Companies create jobs. They hire people who *need* jobs. Now, those people are employees. When the company's profits are rising, they trickle down to the employees in the form of increased wages or expanded hiring.

The only time this system fails is when the government fails to create an environment for companies to prosper.

If someone is lying about this, they're doing it to manipulate our kids. And that's evil.

God's System for Hindsight

We all know the expression, "Hindsight is 20/20." This means it's easy to see how things worked after you've already done them.

After you've tried something, it's easy to look back and say: "Hey, based on the results, maybe that wasn't a great plan" (or, "Hey, based on the results that was a pretty good idea").

God set up this system that allows you to have kids when you're young, dumb and don't know anything about how to do it right. It's a system where it naturally happens, either on purpose or by accident, with no license or training required. Now, here you are. You try to do the best you can, but you know you're making mistakes (even if you don't necessarily know what those mistakes are).

But when your kids grow up and have their own kids, you can see *exactly* what mistakes they're making. Now that we're done raising kids and our son has his own, we can see what we think he's doing right and wrong. But they're not our kids; they're his.

Plus, I don't have the energy to keep up with them. "Grandpa, come play with me upstairs. Where's Grandma? She's downstairs? Okay, let's go get her. Now let's go back upstairs." Up, down, start, stop...they have so much energy, and you don't anymore. When you raise your kids, you have energy but no wisdom. When you have grandkids, you have wisdom but no energy. It's ironic, but it's God's way.

Wisdom vs. Knowledge

Knowledge is something you can acquire at any time of life, but the act of raising kids to adulthood produces wisdom. You definitely acquire knowledge as you're growing up, and you think that knowledge will transfer while you're raising your kids. Then, you find out that your kids have to learn their *own* lessons.

When we learned lessons growing up, it wasn't because we just arrived at a bunch of conclusions. It was because we made our own mistakes. Likewise, your kids have to make *their* own mistakes or the things you teach them won't be internalized. Looking back on the challenges that taught me lessons (divorce, failed businesses, sleeping in my car, you name it), I would never want my kids to go through those things. But as I told them, God won't give you the desires of your heart without you paying the price first. *Everyone* has to pay their price; your price will be different than mine. Along the way to gaining wisdom, wealth and happiness, you'll pay *your* price. When you have challenges, it's not necessarily about who you are or where you live or what your skin color is. It's about that challenge being part of *your* price for success and happiness.

When my kids were born, I was 23 and 24. I didn't know squat. I gained knowledge as they grew, but I didn't consider myself wise until they were out of the house, in their careers, with their own lives. Your knowledge only becomes wisdom once you've practiced it, seen the results and made the necessary adjustments.

When Dawn and I were first together, my kids were two and three years old. I was recently divorced from their birth mother and doing it on my own. As Dawn and I developed our relationship and we both knew it was about to become forever, she said, "I'd love to raise those kids with you." That was good, because her wisdom was much more developed than mine! She had already raised a daughter to age 14 (who tragically died from cancer), and a son who was now a teenager as well. As a single dad of two toddlers, I needed her experience — whether I knew it or not. God made our paths cross because we needed each other.

Up to that point, I was just focused on keeping food in their bellies. I hadn't learned that was just the beginning — that they also needed guidance and unconditional love, and that they needed a parent rather than a friend. Dawn taught me that our only job is to create responsible adults and good humans. She helped me remember that they're only going to be kids for a short time, but they're going to be adults for the rest of their lives.

She also helped me realize when I made mistakes. One of the biggest mistakes we make as parents is rushing to judgement to protect our kids. Once, my daughter was carrying her clarinet at school and a kid kicked it out of her hands and broke it. My knee jerk reaction was, "Someone's got to pay for this," which means I went directly to his parents. I said, "This is the story, this is what it cost, and your kid is going to pay it." The parents agreed, and the kid reimbursed us out of his piggy bank with a big bag of change.

Unfortunately, the story didn't end there; down the road, I found out my daughter may have provoked him. But I didn't even think about holding her responsible for her clarinet breaking. I jumped straight to holding the other kid responsible. That's when Dawn reminded me this: Teaching that kid a lesson was not my job. Teaching *my* kid a lesson was my job.

Now that my son is a dad, he and his wife deal with the normal challenges that come with having two sets of grandparents, each with their own opinions about how kids should be raised. If you have a spouse and kids, then you know there's conflict when your parents and your spouse's parents are constantly imposing their own differing opinions on you, informed by their own backgrounds and cultures.

When it comes to this, here's what I told my son: "You can listen to your mom and me, or not. We don't matter here. You can listen to your wife's parents, or not. They don't matter here either. Your priority is not to keep any of us happy. We can all take care of ourselves. The only one in this equation who can't take care of themselves is your daughter."

Once he had his own kids, his right to be selfish ended. Too many parents don't realize that, and that's why so many young adults today are selfish. Because their selfish parents raised selfish kids.

Fortunately, I was able to rescue my kids before it happened to them (or maybe Dawn rescued all three of us). In the early days, I shared custody with their birth mother. I arrived to pick them up one day and found nothing but an empty bottle of wine, an empty carton of milk and a bottle of mustard in the refrigerator. I told her, "Instead of paying child support, I'm going to buy you groceries."

"You can't do that," she said.

"Yes I can," I said. "It's not called 'you support.' It's called child support."

Of course, the courts wouldn't allow that. So instead, I fought repeatedly for sole custody and eventually won. My kids never went without food from that point on.

Shielding Kids from Stress and Instability

In the subprime mortgage years, I did my best to reason with people about what they were trying to get themselves into. When they asked about every trick in the book to manipulate their stated incomes, I explained what would happen if they went down that path. Once, a client attempting to buy a $600,000 house; he said he wanted to put it in his wife's name. His plan was to keep the house they were living in (which was in his name) and buy this next house in her name. I told him to look at the numbers. "I can get you the house," I said, "but I have to state your wife's income at $13,000 a month. How much do you guys *really* make? Because you have to *really* make the payments."

He said she made $45,000 and he made $55,000.

"So you're telling me you make $100,000 a year," I said. "That's $8,300 a month. You take home 70% of that, which is $5,833 a month. Your house payment is going to be $4,200 and you still have another mortgage. Do you have any car payments?"

"Yes, two."

"Do you carry any balances on your credit cards?"

"Yes."

"Do you have kids?"

"Yes."

"Do they like to eat?"

He seemed surprised. After all, this was a time in history when everyone else was handing out home loans like candy. "Um...yeah."

"Okay," I said. "Then listen to me. I see this as a foreclosure waiting to happen. And in my years of experience, along with a foreclosure comes a divorce. You get into a nice, big house and everything's happy and wonderful. But in a few months or a few years, when you're tired and stressed over living to make your house payment, you have no breathing room in your budget to take your wife out to dinner or replace the balding tires on your car — *and* you're behind on all your bills — that's what's going to happen.

It becomes stress in the marriage...and the next thing you know, it becomes a divorce."

That's just one example. In those days, I found myself leveling with people like this pretty often.

Remember what I explained about my own dad? He was an accountant who never became a CPA, which he blamed on us kids for being born. He'd take the money he got from buying someone else's business and use it to furnish his office instead of paying bills. Melvin never worked very hard, refused to take responsibility for anything, and rarely finished anything he started. As a result, there was an endless supply of stress and instability in our home.

Once, my parents bought a big, brand new Westinghouse refrigerator. It was a big deal to replace our old, slowly dying fridge with this beautiful new model, and all of us were excited. What we didn't know was that my dad didn't make the payments on it, which of course means it was soon repossessed. It's a scary thing for a bunch of kids to see someone come in and take the refrigerator out of your house. And we saw it all. Other times, we saw the repo men come to take our cars away. I was determined to never let my kids see those things. Even as a single dad with financial challenges, my kids would have stability.

Once, I was late on the electric bill and knew we were on the verge of shutoff. My intention was to go to the electric company and pay with a check (that I knew would bounce) to keep the lights on for the next few days until I got paid. Then, I'd rush the cash over there as soon as my commission came in. I thought I could time it perfectly for the day the check came back from the bank. Unfortunately, I got busy on that day and forgot to take the check over. So when the kids and I pulled up to a house with no lights on, I had to improvise.

"Oh man," I said. "The lights must be broken. We'll light candles tonight and get them fixed tomorrow." This isn't lying to kids; this is doing what it takes to protect them from stress and instability. Today, they say they remember the "broken lights" — but they don't mind, because I kept them from being scared when it happened. I borrowed some cash from someone to pay the bill, the lights came back on, and it never happened again.

The difference between this and what I grew up with was that my dad let these incidents happen over and over again, and nobody tried to insulate us from the instability. I call it "not letting them see me eat a peanut butter sandwich," which is what my mom did when there was no food in the house. She'd feed the rest of us a hot hamburger meat casserole while she ate a peanut butter sandwich (she'd always say, "A house without peanut butter isn't a home," which means that as long as you have a jar of it in the house, you'll always have something to eat). Today, I appreciate her sacrifice. But back then, I felt a lot less secure seeing her eat that sandwich, because I knew it meant things weren't stable. And I was determined to shield my kids from instability.

I also wanted to protect them from what happens when parents are so financially strained that they can't function properly. My dad was short-tempered by nature — but any time his failures caught up to him, he became completely unhinged. I remember walking out of my bedroom once to see my dad choking my mom with the dog leash, and later realizing that it probably wasn't the first time. I remember when the ambulance came to pick up my brother after my dad used an eight-inch carving knife to stab him within a half-inch of his lung, and everybody lied about how my brother had "accidentally backed into the knife" to keep my dad from going to jail. What was the reason he stabbed his own son? Scott had probably committed some minor teenage infraction, like leaving out some tools or letting his car drip some oil in the driveway. *Instability.*

My dad always had a knack for distorting the truth. When clients would call and he'd say, "Tell them I'm not here," I never understood why he didn't want to talk to them. Then he'd call them back and say, "I'm in Phoenix." He was in our house in Lakewood, California; I didn't even know where Phoenix was yet. *Instability.*

Obviously, my dad had more going on inside than financial stress. But it's undeniable that the stress of not pulling your weight creates an unstable family. This became obvious to me growing up as I watched all his failed attempts at businesses, all the unfinished projects. It became even *more* obvious when, as an adult son who had just finished paying him back for a loan (out of his inheritance; he still didn't have any money of his own), he pulled a gun on me while insisting it wasn't paid off. Every month when I sent him a check, I calculated the balance in the memo to prevent an argument with him. I didn't know I needed to prevent him from shooting me, too. This happened to be the first time I took Dawn to meet my parents. What a way to make a great impression on your future daughter-in-law. Dawn informed me she was never going back. My sister tried to explain it away, the way we'd always been taught to: "This isn't unusual for him. It's no biggie." She didn't understand when Dawn said, "No. This is not normal for *any* family." My dad never stopped creating instability.

After a lifetime of living with the instability, my brother Scott killed himself. It was three weeks before his 36th birthday.

All those years, my mom would say, "I'm staying with him for the kids" — and we'd all think, "Mom, we'd be happier if he wasn't here." The men on her side of the family would say, "Sharlene, leave him...we'll help you support you."

"But I love him!" she'd say.

That black eye really shows how much he loves you, I'd think. *Instability.*

Protect your kids from it.

When Kids Become Teenagers

We all know kids think they're smarter than their parents, and we all know it isn't true. But some parents are truly naive to what their kids are doing. My parents sure were.

When I started coming home drunk at 15, they didn't seem to notice. When my friends and I split whatever malt liquor the store owner sold us or a bottle of Bacardi 151 that we snuck into the football game, my parents seemed totally unconscious of it. When I came home drunk, parked at the curb and fell asleep in the front seat, I'd spring up when my mom came outside and tapped on the window. "Just listening to the radio," I'd say, and she apparently believed me. How do I know? Because when it came to the kids, my mom was the type who dealt with something if she suspected it. And my parents weren't permissive when it came to drinking. My dad would buy a six pack, and one year later there would still be two cans in the fridge. He had a lot of issues, but alcohol wasn't one of them.

As my kids became teenagers, I decided that my parents' naivety wasn't the best approach — but at the same time, I knew that kids are going to find a way to do the things that kids do. The things I know now were things I suspected when they were happening, but you have to hope that you've instilled enough values in them so that they don't do anything truly stupid.

When they turned 17, we gave them each a four-banger car for their driving lessons. When they turned 19, both kids got hand-me-down cars, each one worth about $10,000. We said, "These are the last cars you're getting from us. You're on your own from here." They still lived under our roof, but the rules now included:

- If you aren't going to school, you have to work.
- You don't have a curfew anymore, but you need to let us know where you are.
- You're not allowed to come home drunk or messed up.
- You can't have sex in this house unless you're married. So that excludes everyone but Mom and Dad.

If they didn't like those rules, they had to move out. So at 19, they both did. At that point, I told them, "If you can afford an apartment, you can afford college. If you *can't* afford college, you can get student loans. If you graduate, I'll pay them off."

Eventually, both of them decided to go on other paths without finishing college *and* paid off their own student loans for the time they spent there. They learned their own lessons by making their own mistakes, which was hard to watch without intervening too much...but it was necessary. It doesn't mean we let them lose their homes or have their utilities shut off. It means we let them struggle and exhaust all other options before they asked us for money. It shouldn't be *you* asking *them* if they need money; you want to show them that your expectations are high, which means you know they can figure it out on their own. And then — if they truly *can't* figure it out on their own — they can ask you. But because you made it hard for them to ask, they'd rather not do it again. When they learn the lesson that Mom and Dad aren't going to save them every time, they learn to take charge of their own lives.

Hiring Your Kids to Work for You

Over the years, employees have asked me if I would hire their kids. As long as we needed the extra help, I would say yes. We'd hire an employee's daughter or son to be a receptionist, then train them to be a loan opener or processor. Over time, their responsibilities would increase to the point that these kids (young adults) would become valuable employees.

It would work out well for a while, until (for whatever reason), the parent would leave the company. Once the parent left, the child would leave too. This started to get me thinking about hiring my own kids. If I was going to invest in *someone's* kid, I'd rather it was my own so that their loyalty is to me and my company (as opposed to another person's kid, who is only loyal to their *own* parent, who will eventually leave.) There's nothing wrong with that when you're a business owner. At some point, if my kids leave my employment for the betterment of their lives, that's what I want anyway.

At the 2016 Republican National Convention, Donald Trump Jr. said something that got me thinking about the value of having your kids watch you work. He explained, "We didn't learn from MBAs. We learned from people who had doctorates in common sense."

Then, he described how his dad turned him and his siblings over to the superintendents on the job sites — the guys who worked their way up through the ranks to become Donald Trump's most trusted advisors in real estate development. These people taught the Trump kids the value of hard work and how things get done from 1,000 feet above the ground (as opposed to where their dad was, 10,000 feet above the ground). They taught them how small tasks completed by many people come together to complete larger tasks, and eventually the larger task completes an entire project. They involved them in work on the job sites: how to drive heavy equipment, operate tractors and use chainsaws. "It's why we're the only children of billionaires as comfortable in a D10 Caterpillar as we are in our own cars," Trump Jr. said. "My father knew that those were the guys and gals that would teach us the dignity of hard work from a very young age. He knows that at that heart of the American dream is the idea that whoever we are, wherever we're from, we can get ahead, where everyone can prosper together."

Although I wasn't overseeing construction sites, I would use my knowledge of how things worked to teach my kids practical lessons they needed. Instead of letting them rely on a mechanic to diagnose every noise a car might make, I made sure they knew what a clicking noise meant vs. what a stalling noise meant. I made sure they knew how to change their own tires.

While thinking about this, I asked my kids to remind me of some valuable lessons I passed on. My comments are in parenthesis.

- *You taught us that even if you can afford to pay someone to do something for you, you should still seek to have an understanding of how things get done so that you can have respect for the people doing it and understand why you're paying them what you're paying them* (and to help you understand when they're just trying to get their hands in your pockets).

- *You taught us that we should not be so self-absorbed to think there is anything that others do that does not impact us. This gave us respect for others and for their skills and training, and it gave us respect for our differences* (from politicians, to contractors, to restaurant workers, to police officers).

- *You taught us that we should strive for luxury, but that we should not step on the heads of others who helped us get there.* (Striving for luxury and expecting it are not always the same thing. You can't expect to drive a luxury car if you've only paid the price to drive an economy car. Like the assistant coach tells the football team in *Remember the Titans*: "Champions pay the price").

- *You taught us to respect how hard things are to do and learn, and that made us respect others for the things they can do that we cannot.*

- *You taught us that we all have something we can do that others do not, and it is our job to share those blessings with the world, just as we need mechanics to fix our cars and plumbers to fix our pipes.*

This reminds me of a story. Dawn and I lived in some interesting situations in the early days, including one in which we had bought a house, but needed to move in with our sellers for a couple of months while they waited on the house they were buying in Oregon. We had bought it on contract from them, because I had crappy credit at the time (this is why I can relate to many of my clients today).

It was almost time for the house to be ours, and that meant it was time for all the fun stuff, like buying furniture for that living/dining area of the house no one ever uses. But in order for that furniture to look its best, the room needed a new coat of paint; Dawn wanted it bright white. I said "no problem" and went straight to Home Depot, because I thought it would be a great idea to do this project myself.

This would save money, right? Right. And it looked great, right? Wrong.

It *looked* like I did it myself, and that's not a compliment. By the time the weekend was over, the carpet was covered in dried paint specks and it was evident there were entire sections of wall I had missed (how'd that happen? Who knows). The bottom line is this: *I can paint something, but I'm not a painter.*

Before I could go on to the next room, I was given a life raft by a client named Mark. Mark was $4,000 short to close escrow on his loan. Mark was also a painter. Suddenly, a lightbulb went on.

"I'll tell you what, Mark," I said to him. "If you can come up with $2,000, I'll pay you another $2,000 to paint my house."

Mark was excited and relieved. He came over that weekend and painted the entire house in two and a half days. Watching how smooth and easy it was for him, I saw that some people are just painters. I could do his loan with my eyes closed and my hands tied behind my back, because loans are what I do. He could paint my house just as easily, because painting is what he did.

The point is, you should understand how to do something so you can appreciate why you're paying someone else to do it. If you've ever tried to do it yourself, then you know how hard it is. That was a lesson I learned myself, and I passed it onto my kids.

Here are some more of my kids' recollections of lessons I taught them:

- *Nobody should write a book before they're 40* (good thing I passed that milestone a while ago).

- *Learn how to do things the hard way, but pay someone else to do it anyway so you can spend time making more money* (what do you know...both of them remember that!).

- *Everyone has a price to pay to live the life they want to live. Your price will be different than my price, but you'll pay it* (didn't I say that earlier? See, I'm consistent).

- *Greed is good, but be long-term greedy and do good by your clients. Short-term greedy is bad* (sound familiar?).

- And, most important: *If momma ain't happy, no one is happy. Happy wife, happy life.*

Eventually, both of my kids came on board at my business. But it wasn't immediately, and it was never something that was promised to them growing up.

My son had tried culinary school, restaurant management and other ventures — some successful, some not, but he always learned his own lessons. After a few years of this, he had a new family to support and decided it was time to explore other options.

Since he knew from listening to me that the richest people in the world made their money in real estate, he had given that some thought. "Dad, I could be in the real estate business if *you* weren't in the real estate business," he said. "But I don't want to ride on your coat tails. I want to blaze my own trail."

"You don't have to ride on my coat tails," I said. "I know you have the street smarts to succeed at whatever you want. But I'm teaching a lot of other people's kids how to make money in this business, so I'd like to show my *own* kid how to do it. Then, you can decide if it's for you. You don't have to get any more guidance than I would give anybody else."

He said yes to giving it a try, and it worked out. Now, he's a high six figure earner and has no problem supporting his family. But he had to learn his own lessons first.

My daughter was blessed with natural intelligence; when she was young, she could read a book like *War and Peace* in a weekend. But she had the same struggles a lot of young women do in terms of relationships and careers, which meant she was still finding her way throughout her 20s. Still, I knew she had the determination to conquer just about any challenge — so when the timing was right, I suggested she come work for us too. It won't be forever, because eventually I'll retire. But now, she's gained skills she could use at just about any job (or any business venture she might want to start herself).

Here's my caveat, though: You should never hire your kids when they're in trouble. At one point, I almost did this. But if I had, she never would have learned how to get herself *out* of trouble. It was Dawn who reminded me of this. As I contemplated which position I could offer our daughter at the company in order to get her out of her pickle, Dawn gave me this valuable piece of wisdom: "Ed, be a parent first and a corporate president second." She was right. If my daughter came to work for me only to get herself out of trouble, then she'd never learn how to get herself out of trouble any other way. I've never stopped learning how to be a parent from my wife.

Eventually, our daughter did come to work for me — but it was later on, once she had found her footing and was ready. This part is important if you're a business owner, so pay attention: *There has been no nepotism or special treatment.* In fact, because she used her married name and we never made an "announcement" about hiring her, a lot of employees didn't even know she was my daughter (for a while). As a leader, you can bring your grown kids into your organization while still promoting a fair environment for your employees.

Dawn's son, who completed a degree and found professional success in his father's company, hasn't yet accepted my offer to come on board. But in the meantime, I'm grateful for the relationship we have as buds. And if he ever decides the time is right, the opportunity is still there.

I didn't rescue my kids; I provided opportunities to help them succeed. Ultimately, we want them to have productive lives once we're no longer on this planet. When they're young, you should let them struggle and find their own solutions so that they learn how to make this happen. But if you have the ability to give your kids certain opportunities where you know they can be successful, why wouldn't you do it? The most important thing is that you don't shield them from having to pay the price.

The journey of raising your kids will be the greatest source of wisdom in your lifetime. It's important to recognize that journey so you can retain the wisdom it provides throughout your life. The truth is, you'll never stop learning; when you think you know everything, you probably don't — especially if your kids aren't yet grown. As you help them become responsible, successful adults, you'll continue to learn as long as you're willing to.

If you think "I'm there," you probably aren't. There's always something to learn.

My parents, Sharlene and Melvin
Hoffman, early 1990s.

With my siblings in 1968, clockwise
from top: Scott, Rene, Lori and me.

Tying the knot with Dawn,
New Year's Eve 1996.

Dawn with Ryan and Kacie, 1989. I'll
never forget her saying, "I'd love to
raise those kids with you."

Meeting Rocky in Philadelphia!
A dream come true.

Dawn and our daughter Kacie on
Lake Mohave.

Boys night out with our sons Ryan and
Brett, Los Angeles Forum.

Recording my weekly radio show,
The Main Event,
from the KTIE studio.

Arm wrestling with grandson Nolan, 2017.
Our grandkids are our pride and joy.

With granddaughter Rowan,
growing so fast. Our grandkids
are our pride and joy.

Dawn and me. One of my
all-time favorite photos.

Hoffman Family Christmas 2014,
including my best buddy Tank (RIP).

With both grandkids out on
Lake Mohave.

CHAPTER 23

"Geez, that information might have been more useful to me yesterday."[95]
- The Wedding Singer, 1998

WHEN JIM AND I started Wholesale Capital Corporation, we worked out of a 2,700 square foot suite. Within a few years, we were in need of another 800 square feet to accommodate our growing staff. Now, we were at 3,500 square feet and it wasn't long before we needed to double that. Since the offices next to us weren't available, the only way to get 7,000 square feet of office space was to move some of our staff into a building 20 yards away in the same plaza, which had been recently vacated by an escrow company. Now, we had the space we needed. It seemed like this would be a building we could stay in long-term as the company continued to grow.

However, it wasn't long before some new issues surfaced. These are things you'll inevitably end up dealing with if you ever lease office space or a storefront.

First, there was a change in building ownership. This can be a good thing or a bad thing, and in our case it was the latter. We had a triple net lease that included our rent, utilities, property taxes and prorated share of the common areas. For the first eight years, the settlement bill we received from the owners was usually in the neighborhood of a couple thousand dollars — never very significant. But when the new owners came in, they failed to bill us for those things for the first two years. Then sometime in the beginning of 2001, they sent us a bill for $35,000 that was due in 30 days. They claimed it was for what we owed them back in 1999.

Well, that was unexpected. It hurt, but we paid it. Then 60 days later, another bill came for the very same amount: $35,000. Supposedly, this was for what we owed them in 2000. What we were accustomed to with the previous owners was a bill at the end of the year that was due in 90 days. That's how reasonable building owners operate.

I called the new owners up. "I can't do this," I said. "I don't budget this way."

Now, why did our annual bill for upkeeping the building go from roughly $2,000 to $35,000? It was because these owners had made what they believed were "improvements." I consider improvements to be resurfacing the parking lot, repairing the roof or upgrading the lighting. But to these owners, improvements meant tearing down buildings to make it look less crowded in the plaza. Then, they painted everything to look "visually pleasant" (but I wasn't impressed). And then, they handed all the tenants the bill.

Next, there was an issue with parking. When a physical therapy practice moved in across the plaza, we discovered that their patients preferred our parking lot to theirs. Their parking area was on the side of their building, but their front door was straight across from our front door. Before long, all their patients were parking in front of our building because it was a shorter walk. This meant our mortgage company parking lot was filled with people on crutches and walkers, which they would frequently bang into our cars (and our clients' cars) on the way in. Not a good look. Plus, a bunch of us had all just purchased our first luxury sports cars. That made every ding a huge aggravation.

I asked the owners if it would be possible to install a sign that designated our parking area as "Parking for Wholesale Capital Corporation Only." They said no. After that, it seemed like there was only one logical solution: *Why don't we just buy a building?*

There's nothing wrong with leasing office space — but when you own the building, there's a lot more you can control. I give these examples to help you think about the kinds of challenges you might encounter as you grow your own business.

Decisions, Decisions

Finding a building to buy might seem like an easy endeavor as long as you have the money to do it. But believe me, there are plenty of decisions to be made that have nothing to do with the money. First, I found an 11,000 square foot building for $795,000. It had no parking issues and was located right next to an El Pollo Loco, which happens to be where my lunch comes from three to four times a week (priorities!).

However, the property wasn't in the greatest neighborhood. Also, I discovered that a real estate agency we did a fair amount of business with was occupying a portion of it. I didn't want to displace them, as this would almost certainly mean losing their business. Plus, there was one decision that was at least *partially* about money: The building would need a facelift on the outside and a reconfiguration on the interior, which would easily cost another $500,000. I wasn't sure I should spend that kind of money to reconfigure a building that wasn't in the neighborhood I wanted to be in (whether it was adjacent to El Pollo Loco or not).

At that point, someone asked, "Why don't we build our own?" I couldn't think of any good reason why we shouldn't. So we got started.

Planning a Project

I knew nothing about constructing a building, but I knew a contractor would. Of course, the contractor informed us that we should be speaking to an architect first; he couldn't build something until an architect designed it.

The architect, Ray, wanted to understand our business in order to design the right building for us. He asked questions about our workflow: what documents go to which departments, and in what order. He asked about our current square footage; by that time, we had determined 7,000 still wasn't enough. Having already looked at the 11,000 square foot building earlier, I knew that was our minimum target. We agreed with the architect that a range of 12,000 to 14,000 square feet was what we actually needed.

Now, it was time to start looking for dirt. The first lot we found was off the freeway, visible from the main boulevard and a full acre. But unfortunately, it was on the curve of a cul-de-sac. That wouldn't work unless we got the rectangular lot next to it, which was owned by the seller's ex-wife. He wanted $300,000 for his lot, which was just a smidge over one acre. She wanted $300,000 for hers, which was only ⅝ of an acre (but she knew that we wouldn't buy his lot without hers; therefore, she could charge the same price. Smart lady). In total, it was 1.7 acres.

But $600,000 just for the dirt? That seemed like a lot.

Then, there was a third option. There were two adjoined half acre lots, located about a block up the street. Ray didn't think it would be large enough for our needs unless we constructed a two-story. But the land was only $400,000. I trusted Ray on the two-story proposition and was happy to save $200,000 on the dirt.

So Ray went to work on designing plans, creating flow charts, making elevation drawings...all the things architects do. There were no construction costs attached to any of it; that's because he was an architect, not a contractor. There's a lesson here, so hang onto that piece of information.

With my background, I knew you could build a house at $50 to $75 per square foot at that time. Knowing that, it seemed logical that you could construct a commercial building at $100 per square foot. For a 12,000 square foot building, that would be $1.2 million. Add in the $400,000 for the dirt and another $400,000 for incidentals, and that brought us to $2 million.

I could live with that.

But at this point, Ray still hadn't asked us what style we wanted. When he asked me to show him styles that appealed to me, I thought of the new buildings going up in the North Village area of Mammoth. "Oh, that's Craftsman," he said. Great! Show me a Craftsman. And he did, along with two others. Ray drew up the design in these options:

- Craftsman style, which I was most interested in.
- Spanish style, which is the same building with a stucco exterior instead of planks or wood siding.
- Modern, concrete tilt-up style with mirror glass windows.

For whatever reason, Ray was adamant that a concrete tilt-up wasn't a great deal unless you're constructing a much larger building. "That's only worth it if your building is at least 25,000 square feet," he said. I'm not sure how he arrived at that conclusion, because what he *didn't* tell me was that the concrete actually cost less than the Craftsman — about $1 million less, to be exact. The Craftsman would be $2.5 million to construct, and the concrete tilt-up would only be $1.5 million. Had I known each of these styles came with different costs and the difference was $1 million, I would have chosen the less expensive one.

In my mind, this building was going to cost the same no matter how we dressed it up...and no one told me anything different. But remember, we were still just talking to the architect. Only the contractor could tell us how much each of these would cost to actually *build*. No one was telling me each of these three options had different costs — and as the customer in this scenario, I wasn't asking yet.

The lesson: *Assume nothing.*

Why did Ray say the concrete tilt-up wasn't a good option? Probably because he wanted a cool Craftsman design to put in his portfolio and figured we could afford it. But whatever his intentions were, I should have gone in with my eyes open.

That's the overarching lesson for this entire chapter: *Always go in with your eyes open.*

But I didn't. I gave Ray the greenlight on the Craftsman, paid him his $50,000 fee and started signing everything he put in front of me regarding the plans and permits. Everything from the foundation, to the frame, to the finish on the composite siding had to be approved by the city. Meanwhile, I was proudly telling everyone in town about our new building.

I trusted our accountant, Kathy, to keep me updated on the costs. But things were moving so quickly, we still didn't have a contractor estimate and we hadn't yet applied for the construction loan. Once we were planned, permitted and ready to break ground, Kathy came into my office. "You know how much you have into that piece of dirt across the street?"

"No," I said. "How much?"

"$1.1 million."

"$1.1 million?! Where did I get *that*?" I genuinely didn't know.

"All the profit the company's making right now...plus, you and Jim aren't taking any bonuses."

She was right; we had done well that year, and Jim and I had passed on bonuses in order to fund this project. But I had no idea we were anywhere near $1 million in this project before we'd even stuck the first shovel in the dirt.

Too Late to Turn Back

Obviously, we were way overbudget. But at that point, I was too emotionally connected to the project to turn back.

Why didn't I just ask the contractor for a construction estimate while Ray was still working? For one thing, the first contractor we met with wasn't the one who ended up doing the work — and I didn't have a choice in the matter. When the bank made our massive construction loan, they dictated which contractor they were "most comfortable with." At *that* point, we got an estimate.

That's when I learned even more about building things, like the fact that contractors bid your job to try to *get* the job. Along the way, as you see your vision materialize, they're banking on you getting more ideas: what's too big, what's not big enough, where there needs to be another door or extra square footage (in our case, we ended up with 14,000 square feet). Based on your ideas, the contractor makes "change orders." And this is where all their profit is. It's like going to the movies; your $10 ticket seems like a lot, but where the theater makes their *real* money is on your popcorn and soda. You didn't know you wanted popcorn and soda at first, until you walked in and saw the brightly lit concession stand. That's a change order. With a building, most of your expenses are in the final phases and finish work: cabinets, counters, fixtures... that's where the lion's share of your cost is. Now, we were over budget by more than double. Our $2 million project was now a $4.5 million one. Jim and I had stopped taking bonuses near the beginning — but eventually, we stopped taking paychecks too. By the time the project was finished, neither of us had taken a paycheck for almost three years.

And every time we saw that what was designed was different from what we were actually building, the contractor and the architect pointed fingers at each other. Nobody wanted to take responsibility, and I just had to keep writing checks.

But the project was done. Now, it was time to maximize every inch of space with office equipment. Were we going to move our old furniture into our new building? Even if we did, we'd be 7,000 square feet short. A few trips to some furniture manufacturers and $350,000 later, we had furnished the whole building. Then, we needed a sign; after all, we were right off the freeway. When I was asked, "What kind do you want?" the only logical answer was, "I guess an electronic one." How else would it get anyone's attention from the freeway? I wanted a high quality sign, and the first bid was $110,000. That was for average quality. A high quality one turned out to be $181,000.

Then, we realized that you can't run a 14,000 square foot office on a phone system maxed out for 7,000 square feet. So we needed a new phone system, and that was $161,000.

And obviously, you have to secure your brand new building. For security equipment and services, which included alarms, cameras, access control and the monitoring service, it was $55,000.

These were all the little things I hadn't thought about. I was just trying to build a building.

When I talk to a new client about their home loan, I use a spreadsheet that outlines *all* their costs (I call it an LEF sheet, which means "lender estimate of fees"). Many mortgage lenders don't do this, which is why people come to me upset that they're seeing figures the "last company" didn't tell them. "They only told you *their* fees," I explain. "These are *other* fees, but they're still fees you will have to pay." I make those fees clear to home loan borrowers upfront, because I'd rather do that, than have them pissed off when they get to the closing table. And that's what I hoped my vendors would do with me. But they didn't.

Hindsight is 20/20

Stepping out of the circle and looking back on this with the perspective of 15 years, I'm not sure I would have built the building at all. We were mortgaged to the hilt, didn't take a paycheck for three years, and accumulated a heap of debt. We designed it for what we were using it for at the time, but we didn't anticipate the ways technology and progress would eventually change our processes. By 2019, we had merged with another company and offloaded 70% of our staff. You never know what the future will bring. That's why it's important to make big decisions carefully and conservatively.

So what would I have done if I didn't build the iconic Craftsman I ended up with? There are a few different options, and all of them sound like better ideas than what I chose to do.

Option #1—Still build the building, but hire a design/build firm for the project. This is a company that has both the architect and the builder under one roof, working together. It would have kept everyone on the same page and could have easily saved me $1 million on construction alone. Plus, it would have also saved money for the long-term. Had I known what it would cost to keep lights and air conditioning running full-time in a two-story building, I would have gone with the slightly more expensive 1.7 acre plot, built a one-story building and saved a lot of money.

Option #2—Still build the building, but ignore Ray's advice about concrete tilt-ups and tell him that's exactly what I wanted — one that's a two-story cube with an elevator in the middle. That would mean that when we later downsized, the unused offices could be easily converted into suites to rent out.

Option #3—Continue looking for an existing building to buy, like a one-story that was already designed for renting out sections to other tenants (this is how my commercial investment property is, but I didn't own it at the time we were building). Like the previous option, this would also allow me to adjust according to our size at different times. You can always take an existing building and make it what you need.

I believe this same thing with residential properties. I've talked a bunch of people out of building a house. It's the same concept: Rather than building from the ground up, you can always buy an existing house and remodel it to be what you want. It already has the hardscape, landscape and other things that are easy to customize to your needs. It's a lot less costly than putting them in yourself.

It's easy to see your mistakes after you've made them. Hopefully, the lessons I learned the hard way can help you make decisions with clearer vision than I had.

CHAPTER 24

"Having dreams is what makes life tolerable."[96]
- Rudy, 1993

AS WE GROW up, most of us are put into a sport at some point. This is good for kids, both boys and girls, because it's through sports that they learn about healthy competition. My parents never put me in the programs that cost money, like Little League or Pop Warner football. I always played park leagues, because that's what the kids who didn't have money got to do.

Every summer was park league baseball; every fall was park league flag football; every winter was park league basketball. This started at eight years old, and you could stay in those leagues until age 15. By that time, you could try out for your high school's team if you want to continue playing.

I tried doing that by going out for the baseball team in 9th grade (which was technically still junior high, since that's how the schools were structured back then). I was a good player (but not *that* good), and I still hadn't experienced my final growth spurt. Plus, park league kids were rarely as good as Little League kids because Little League was a much better program. I was the last guy that made the team and spent the season on the bench (with the exception of one game). And if a kid was never called up to play in 9th grade, there's no way the coach of the Lakewood High School CIF champions would have him on the team the next year. So that was the end of my baseball prospects.

I wasn't devastated, since I wasn't one of those kids that was in love with baseball. What I *was*, though, was a kid who wanted a letterman's jacket. Back then, everyone knew you couldn't get girls to go out with you if you didn't have a letterman's jacket. But I couldn't get one from baseball, so what was next?

Football was the same drill; if you didn't have the experience, you weren't going to make the team. And I was too short for basketball. So where did that leave me?

I realized there might be some promise in the swim team. I wasn't sure what it entailed, but I knew that I liked to swim. What I *didn't* know was that swim team kids didn't just join the swim team in January; they also played water polo in the off season. It was the only way to stay conditioned throughout the year. "If you don't play water polo, you won't be anywhere close to where you need to be at the start of the swim season," the swim coach told me. "All the swimmers play water polo from summer through December."

I wasn't excited about it — I couldn't tread water with no hands, and it seemed like that might be a requirement — but it didn't matter in the grand scheme of things. My goal was to make a team, play a sport, get a letterman's jacket and go on dates. That was all that really mattered to me at that time. Then, I found out that if you tried out for water polo, and them beating the shit out of you didn't get you to quit, you were on the team. So that's how it worked out for me in 10th grade. I made it through the tryouts unscathed. Now I was officially a water polo player.

Soon, I saw my body trimming down, my baby fat coming off, and muscles showing up that I didn't recognize. It wasn't long before I learned how to tread water with no hands. By the end of the season, I was a starting player. By Christmas break, water polo season was over and I had my letterman's jacket. Mission accomplished!

So did I continue playing? I did not. It wasn't because I was short-sighted; it was because now, I had to do *more* work to maintain my goal. It turned out there was more to getting girls than just wearing a letterman's jacket. Obviously, you needed a driver's license. I got one...and then I found out about paying for my own car and insurance. So I got my work permit and that first job at Seafood Broiler, and now there was no extra time for sports. Between school and work, I could keep my grades up and have money for fun on the weekends. I could have fun whether I was out on dates, or out with my friends looking for girls who would actually go out with me.

Of course, in order to get dates you *also* needed to stay in shape. Lucky for me, kids who dropped out of sports were put into zero period P.E. class, where you'd get ripped running obstacle courses and lifting weights with the head football coach as your trainer. From then on, I got just enough dates to keep myself in the game, made just enough money to keep gas in my car and had just enough muscles to keep myself from getting picked on. I never played on another high school team again, but I still competed in high school...in a very unconventional way. Let me explain.

Arm Wrestling for an A

What I'm about to describe is something you would never see in a high school classroom today. Today, you'd have parents filing frivolous lawsuits. It was June 1978, the last day of 11th grade, pre-calculus class. The teacher, Mr. Minor, was telling us our final grades, and I was on that fine line between an A and a B (probably 89.75% or something like that). Remember, I was the math whiz in my family. I wasn't about to let my mom see me bring home a B in my best subject. Being the ballsy kid I was, I asked Mr. Minor if he wanted to arm wrestle me for it. If I won, he'd give me the A. If he won, I'd get the B.

Mr. Minor was the kind of teacher who wouldn't say no if we started arm wrestling in class during some downtime. So this wasn't totally out of the blue, but I don't think he believed for one minute that he would lose to me. He was also one of those teachers who made sure kids knew how much he worked out (which may seem a little creepy today). He probably had just as much cockiness in him as I did. But my will to win (and to not have to deal with my mom's disapproval) was stronger — so to the delight of my cheering Lakewood High School classmates that day (including a bunch of seniors and football players), I beat Mr. Minor at arm wrestling that day. He gave me the A.

That's when I realized this lesson: *Winning isn't just about being the biggest or the best. It's also about heart.*

My heart was in this, because I wanted that A. And I got it.

A New Opportunity

One year later, I was a high school graduate who was missing the physicality and competitive atmosphere of high school. What do most kids do in that position? They join a gym. It was there, at Holiday Health Spa in Downey, that I found my next opportunity to compete. On the locker room wall, I saw a poster for the American Cup, a triple event of arm wrestling, powerlifting and bodybuilding. But I didn't just see a poster; I saw an opportunity.

I called the number on the poster to find out how this all worked. How did I sign up...how much did I have to pay...where did I have to be, on what day and at what time? I got the information, and for the next few months, I started doing whatever seemed like it would help me prepare: pumping weights, doing curls, whatever seemed logical.

The day of the event, I arrived at the Shrine Auditorium in Los Angeles with my mixtape of songs from the *Rocky* soundtracks blasting in my ears. I was pumped. The arena was set up into three sections for each event. I'm looking around at the other guys in the arm wrestling section, feeling intimidated. One of them was Terry Busk, who would later become a world champion, and this guy was ripped. No way was he in my weight class, right? Wrong. He most certainly was. Terry was huge on top, but he had pigeon legs. Meanwhile, I had dinosaur legs, with an upper body not half as big as his. So I guess we balanced each other out, but he terrified me nonetheless. And guess who my first match was against?

Terry had what I later learned were called "table manners": all the etiquette that arm wrestlers are expected to uphold in terms of grip, leaning, pulling...there are standards for all of it. Table manners also entails all the tricks you're supposed to know, and

I knew none of them. All I knew is what I had done in Mr. Minor's classroom.

You guessed it; I lost my first match, and I lost it fast. Maybe this wasn't going to be my thing after all. My second match wasn't against Terry, but I lost it too.

Only one thing saved me from throwing away the whole idea of competitive arm wrestling: the admiration of a female. Like most guys, I remained motivated by girls even after high school. And it just so happened that I had brought one with me to the event that day. "You can do this," she said. "I know you can figure this out. Just keep trying."

So I did.

I entered five more tournaments, getting a little better each time but still losing. I'd start off strong, and each time I'd get so close to bringing the other guy down to the pad. Why couldn't I just finish him? It was a mental thing. Here's how I overcame it.

Pretty soon, my buddies and I started turning my new hobby into a hustle. Still underage, we needed to find a way to score drinks — so we'd go to one of those bars where there was a video game table, places with names like The Rusty Nail or The Starting Gate. The hustle involved putting on an impromptu match at the Pac-Man table and getting the attention of some other group of guys. They'd see Steve, Jimmy, Adam or Dave going against me and get interested in playing too.

What they didn't know is that we had the whole thing planned out, and that I was losing on purpose to hook them. When we saw them watching us, we'd ask if they wanted in. "Let's play for a pitcher of beer," we'd say, and they'd always bite. They had no idea my friends and I had rigged the game they'd just watched, so these guys would be full of confidence. And of course, I beat them every time. We scored a lot of beer that way.

It was just kids' stuff, but focusing on that hustle is how I eventually overcame the mental block that kept me from winning tournaments. When I was in a real match and it got to the point where I almost had my opponent on the pad, I would close my eyes. I'd say to myself, "Just think of the Pac-Man table." And it worked. I started slamming guys down, winning matches regularly. Now, I really was a competitive arm wrestler. It wasn't long before I started moving up the ranks, going from middleweight to light heavyweight.

Breaking Bones

There was a tournament at the National Orange Show Fairgrounds in San Bernardino. It was my first time in the new weight bracket, and I had just learned a new technique: Instead of loading back, you were supposed to push down and sweep into your opponent. I was going against this guy Randy Yamel, and he would be my first guinea pig for the new move.

Focusing on what I had just learned, I swept into him as planned — and as I did, Randy bent my forearm back. What happened next is something I can only describe as a "wham, wham, wham" motion onto my arm...and then, he took a half-second stop. I thought he was taking it to rest, which is when, adrenaline and heart pumping, I turned my face away from my arm and wound up in preparation to take him down. Randy was *not* resting, though. As I turned away, he went in hard in the opposite direction. I found my body going to the left and my forearm going to the right. The humerus bone that runs from the shoulder to the elbow will only twist so far before it snaps, and I heard the sound as he snapped it. I saw a flash of light, realized what was happening and grabbed onto my hand to stabilize it while we waited for the medics to come get me.

My sister Lori had been at the tournament with me; she drove me to Loma Linda University Medical Center, where the orthopedic doctor set it in a giant hunk of plaster held by a sling until I could get a regular cast. "Look how swollen his arm is," the doctor said to her. My sister wasn't impressed. "His arms are always that big," she said. I rolled my eyes.

Luckily, my Sears job provided decent medical coverage. I just hadn't realized it yet. I had a card in my wallet that said "employee health insurance" — but being 22, this was the first time I had used it. My doctor moved the arm into a fiberglass brace, and I spent the next couple of months sleeping on the sofa; I was supposed to sleep sitting up, so that gravity would pull the bone back into a straight position. But because of the way the arm hung while I was sleeping, it healed in an angled position instead (which the doctor called "an acceptable angulation"). My bicep had shrunk down to nothing, but my forearm was huge. I looked like Popeye. Eventually, I started working out to get things back to normal. But I still thought my arm wrestling career was over.

Then, I had an idea. I had started driving again, learning to push in the clutch and reach over with my left hand to switch gears. So why not start entering tournaments again, but this time as a left-hander? Not all events had a left-hand division, but enough of them did for me to get started. So that's what I did.

And that worked out for a while. I did pretty well as a left-hander, and in fact found some internet evidence of my wins while researching for this book (how about that?). But then came the big announcement about an event I *needed* to be at...and there was no place for left-handers there.

Over the Top

Over the Top is a 1987 movie in which Sylvester Stallone plays a trucker who yanks his snooty son out of military school and goes to Las Vegas to compete in arm wrestling. It was a big deal to everyone in the sport at the time, and Stallone was my hero. The promoter, Marvin Cohen, spent 18 months putting on tournaments all over the world to get extras for the film, starting in 1985. You had to qualify at one of these tournaments to go to Vegas and be in the movie, and none of these tournaments had a left-handed division. "Work on your right hand," Marvin told me. "The last tournament's in the L.A. area." When the day came, I went to whatever hotel in whatever peripheral city off the 210 freeway was hosting the tournament (Arcadia? Monrovia? Who knows). I was still gun shy — but if I broke my arm again, at least I gave it my all. I wanted a shot at *Over the Top*.

I won my first few matches that day, but those weren't the ones that qualified you for the movie. The final match of the day is what would send me there...and as I approached the table, I couldn't believe who was across from me. It was Randy Yamel, the opponent who snapped my arm. After all these months of rehabilitation, I couldn't believe he was the only thing that stood between me and the opportunity to be in a movie with Sylvester Stallone.

Randy knew I was the guy whose arm he had broken, and he wasn't careful the second time around either. But as I found myself unable to get past his shoulder while we struggled, I devised a quick strategy: *Just push into him until he fouls out.* It worked, and I won second place (or maybe it was first place). I don't really remember, because all that mattered is I qualified to go to *Over the Top* in Las Vegas that summer.

What Happens in Vegas

Rocky IV was still a new release. Stallone was the hottest thing in movies at the time, and *Over the Top* was capitalizing on that. It has been called "the biggest event in arm wrestling history."[97]

Everybody who was anybody in the sport was there in the basement of the Las Vegas Hilton on July 26, 1986. I remember hearing there were 700 competitors from 25 different countries, both amateurs and pros. They had a trucker's division, and the winner would get the actual rig from the movie. I was still in the light heavyweight division.

The tournament started at noon on Saturday and ended at 5:30 AM on Sunday. It was the most disorganized thing I'd ever been part of; one stage had eight arm wrestling tables. As a scorekeeper, I had been responsible for two tables in the past; that alone was difficult. Eight was pandemonium. Still, it was a blast, and they were filming everything.

I won three matches and lost two that weekend. My objective was to act professional and try not to look like a groupie. Maybe that was the wrong strategy, because it was the groupies who ended up with actual roles in the movie. One of them was my friend Clarence Edwards, who showed up in blue tights with white tassels on the side, his Afro picked high off his head with a sequined red, white and blue headband around it. I had seen him dressed in a suit and tie for his job at United Grocers, but now he looked like Black Captain America.

"Hey Clarence," I said. "I guess you're trying to get into the movie?"

"Absolutely," he said.

Now *that* was the right strategy.

For the first match, Clarence was on the table right next to me. His opponent had curly red hair, freckles and glasses; he stood out too, but only because he was going against Clarence. Clarence, trying to look like a wildman, pulled out every trick in the book to get noticed during the match. He yelled. He grunted. He ripped off his shirt (he must have rigged it with Velcro. Nice touch!). He had thought of everything. Guess which one of us got actual screen time in the film? Not me.

When I watch *Over the Top* now, I know exactly where I was standing. I'm behind some guys, I'm next to some guys...I'm everywhere except in front of the camera. But I didn't make a spectacle out of myself. So the lesson is: *If you want to be noticed, you have to make a spectacle.*

I was trying to be professional. That worked great for arm wrestling, but it didn't work great for movies. But it did mean I won three of my first four matches. And Clarence went to all that effort to be a showman, but he actually lost against the red-haired guy. So maybe there's a lesson there, too.

At some point between winning my matches and 5:30 A.M., I got to meet Stallone and shake his hand — and that was the *real* point of making it to the event. In real life, he probably couldn't have beat me at arm wrestling. But would I have *let* him beat me, just to be in the movie with him? You bet I would.

Becoming a Promoter

It was at *Over the Top* that I met Rick Zumwalt, who played the character Bull Hurley in the movie. At that time, there were two major organizations I competed in: the National Arm Wrestling

Association and the Southern California Arm Wrestling Association. One of them was run by a guy who competed in the tournaments he put on, which left the rest of us wondering whether he was manipulating the brackets so he would only go against people he knew he could beat. That was hardly fair.

I saw an opportunity there. What if I could put one of these things on myself? If it worked out, I'd do more of them. I knew we wouldn't get as big as the other organizations; I just wanted to create something where all the competitors would feel appreciated.

So that's how I started Pacific Coast Arm Wrestling. We did tournaments in illustrious venues like Round Table Pizza in Chino, but it was fun and I made a little money. My friend Randy (remember him?) had come to a few of them and was impressed. He knew Rick Zumwalt a lot better than I did, and Rick was now pretty famous thanks to the movie. Rick had his own organization, All American National Arm Wrestling (rumored to be named so that the initials would be a tribute to Alcoholics Anonymous and Narcotics Anonymous). Randy thought I should merge my organization with Rick's.

"You know how to put on a good tournament," Randy said. "I can help you, and Rick can bring the celebrity factor." I was intrigued, and to my surprise Rick was interested. We joined together and started putting on tournaments in open air markets and big saloons.

The division of labor was as follows: Randy and I planned the events, booked the venues, bought the trophies, created the marketing materials, bundled the flyers and printed the t-shirts. The day of the event, Randy would run the referees and I would run the brackets. Rick would show up to sign autographs, act like an asshole and leave. For this, we gave him one-third of the profits.

So as you can imagine, it didn't take long before we decided it wasn't working out with Rick. Luckily, it was easy to break the news to him; he was more interested in pursuing an acting career than anything else.

Next, Randy and I changed the name of our organization to United States Arm Wrestling (mostly so Rick wouldn't think he was entitled to more money, but by putting "United States" in there, we were strategically making ourselves sound bigger than we were). The strategy paid off, because pretty soon, we were doing tournaments at actual event venues all over Southern California. People looked forward to our annual Father's Day tournament and we were making a name for ourselves. It was hard work. Sometimes I even slept in my car at the venues (this is while working at A.L. Williams, before I saw very much success). I was never homeless for very long, but I was doing a lot of couch surfing with friends.

One of those times, I had the kids with me for the weekend. I told them we were camping at Calico Ghost Town where the event was, and lucky for me, they didn't question why we were doing it without a tent. I parked in the campground area around the tents and RVs, and the kids slept in the hatchback of the car. To them, it was fun (remember how I handled the electricity going out?). This was all just part of the adventure.

Overall, Randy and I enjoyed what we were doing — but there were exceptions, and those exceptions are what eventually convinced us it was time to move on. A lot of the guys who were doing these tournaments were new to the sport; some of them would sign up for the first time at the event. We would use our big P.A. system to lure them in, appealing to their wives or girlfriends ("Don't you want your man to show everyone how strong he is," stuff like that). These were guys who were first timers; they hadn't learned anything about "table manners" or the rules of arm wrestling, and a lot of them acted like it. A few of them broke their arms, and that's when I started refereeing the matches myself. Because of my experience, I knew how to coach people away from what came to be known as "broken arm position." I didn't want to see another guy turn white and get carted away in the ambulance, knowing how hard it would be for him to live with one working arm for the foreseeable future. Plus, we didn't want to get slapped with a lawsuit; although we had everyone sign a waiver before competing, we knew it probably wouldn't hold up in court if someone was really motivated to sue us.

After five or six years, I hit a breaking point. We were doing one of our annual tournaments for Huck Finn Days in Mojave Narrows Regional Park. This was a huge event that drew big crowds. The second place winner thought we had made a bad call; in his mind, he was first place. When we awarded him the second place trophy at the end of the day, he took it from us and smashed it right there on the stage in front of hundreds of spectators. So much for having competitors who appreciated our efforts.

At that moment, I decided this thing was way more work than it was worth. We certainly weren't getting rich off this, because the entry fees for an amateur tournament were only $25 and most of what we brought in went into marketing. For most events, we worked 50+ hours to net about $300. I told Randy he could continue on if he wanted, but I was out.

Being Busy vs. Being Productive

Once I had won the Amateur World Championship and became "the one to watch" (at least in California), I became choosier about which events I participated in. I only entered tournaments when it was convenient; if it wasn't convenient, I didn't go. One that I decided was convenient enough was at a bar up in the High Desert.

A guy named Tom, who lived in Victorville and whose last name sounded like a body part (I won't say what it was, but just know that I called him "Tom Rectum from Sphincterville"), was my opponent for one of the matches. Tom was one of those guys who got extremely intense about competing. For this match against me, he warmed up by breathing heavy and loud, his face reddening as he got himself more and more psyched. I had seen him get like that before — but this time, I decided to use it to my advantage.

"Tom," I said. "Take it easy, man. It's only arm wrestling."

He didn't respond; if anything, he got *more* intense. His eyes were huge and bulging, his face was beet red and his breath now sounded like hyperventilation. Tom thought this was the approach he needed to win, and maybe you think the same thing. But it's not true.

As we got into our grip, I warned him one more time.

"Tom...chill out, buddy. It's only a trophy. You're gonna give yourself a heart attack."

I knew he had no intention of chilling out, but I figured I could use that to my advantage by trying to throw him off his game.

The referee got our arms straight and the match began. What I did next is the reason I won.

First, I let Tom think he had the advantage. He squeezed my hand and held it for about one second. I'm not sure why he thought that would win the match for him, because he didn't move my arm anywhere; he just held it.

Then, I delivered the psych-out he didn't see coming.

I looked right at him, making my eyes the same size as his to mirror his intensity. I sucked in a huge, loud breath, just like he was doing...and "whoosh," my arm pushed down on his, right onto the pad. The whole match was less than one minute.

The referee didn't waste any time saying, "Ed Hoffman wins!"

I went back to my table with Dawn to enjoy our appetizers. Tom walked over.

"Good match, Ed. What did I do wrong?"

Here's what I told him. "Tom, you didn't do anything *wrong*; you just didn't do *anything*. All you did was squeeze my hand." (Okay, I may have imitated his breath too). "You forgot that the object of the game was to move my hand down to the pad."

The lesson is this: *Don't get so focused on being busy (or "so intense about being intense") that you forget what the object of your game is.*

In sales, some guys will get so into the busy-ness of their business. I hear it all the time:

"I have to organize my emails."

"I have to put meetings on my calendar."

"I have to make sure my business cards are perfect."

And of course, they obsess over finding the perfect digital marketing strategy.

What they don't realize is that being busy is not the same as being productive. What they really need to do is get out there and meet people who need what they have.

Tom didn't do anything wrong. He just didn't do *anything*. It's the same thing for a sales guy who's focused on busywork.

The major takeaway here is: *Focus on what you're trying to do*. If you're trying to build a real estate empire, the first thing you have to do is buy a house. Don't figure out how to buy 10 houses; focus on buying one. We've already touched on this, but it's important enough to repeat: Do everything one step at a time, but always keep the end goal in mind. In the next chapter, I explain how my first experiences with charity work taught me this lesson too.

When people say, "You don't understand what I go through," they're usually wrong. I understand what it's like to figure out how to survive. It's humiliating, depressing and defeating. But the only way to turn it around is *to turn it around*.

Lessons from Our Hobbies

Arm wrestling was a chapter in life that brought me a lot of fulfillment. It fulfilled my innate desire to compete (I believe all people have this desire), it taught me some great life lessons, and it gave me the title of Amateur World Champion six times. When I was young, it got me free beer. A few years later, it helped me meet Sylvester Stallone. It even gave my kids some cool memories, since I continued doing it until 2002. I just discovered an old LA Times story that mentioned my daughter doing her homework while I competed at an event. She was 10 years old then; she's 35 now. That's pretty cool! But as life goes on, supporting your kids becomes more important than whatever your hobby is: being on the softball team, racing motocross, playing chess or arm wrestling. When I had arthroscopic surgery on my shoulder, the doctor suggested I stop arm wrestling. He made a point of saying it in front of my wife, and that effectively sealed the deal.

That doesn't mean you have to regret the years you spent on your hobbies. Our hobbies can teach us a lot. Once I became a promoter and saw everything that goes into putting on an event, I learned not to be critical of things that other people work hard on. Life isn't perfect for anyone; we need to go easy on people.

Also, competing in arm wrestling set the stage for becoming competitive in my career. It taught me what it felt like to win and made me want to help others learn the thrill of winning, too.

This is why my management style is to challenge people to be all they can be. Some people have told me, "I just don't respond to that kind of pressure." My response is to tell them to go work somewhere else. If you aren't competing in your career, how can you ever win at it?

Why is it that so many people who claim they aren't competitive enjoy watching *other* people compete? So many people spend their lives watching other people make money playing baseball, football or basketball that they forget to make money for themselves. I've seen people actually who *lose their houses* while never missing a Dodgers or Lakers game. I enjoy going to a game as much as the next guy, but I'll never understand why someone else's success would matter so much to you. It's just not worth it. If you enjoy watching them and caring about their success, then you obviously have the urge to compete within you. Pay attention to that. It's trying to tell you something about your own will to win.

CHAPTER 25

"The most important thing a man can take into battle is a reason why."[98]
- 12 Strong, 2018

WHEN YOU'VE STARTED to reach your goals and see some success, it's time to start thinking about how you'll give back. On my way up, I looked forward to the day that I'd be able to give back to the community and causes that meant something to me. For some people, it takes time to figure out how you want to engage when you start being charitable. For me, figuring out what I *didn't* want to do came first.

My company used to get approached to participate in a charity golf tournament put on by some local Realtors. We'd be asked to sponsor a hole, which we would. We'd be asked to buy some foursomes, which we would (they would use "you can network with the agents" as an incentive, but usually that just meant you could network with whatever agents were in the foursome right behind you or in front of you). We'd be asked to donate a raffle gift, which we would (and everyone expects an expensive one). When all was said and done, our total amount spent was somewhere around $2,000 — and, all our employees had spent an entire day tied up at the golf course.

The first time we did this, I was shocked to find out at the end of the day that the entire event raised $2,000 total for the local food bank — the same amount we had spent just to be there. I would have rather written a check to the food bank for that amount and kept my employees working. Instead, I paid $2,000 for everyone to get drunk and play golf all day. I'm not saying a day on the golf course isn't fun sometimes, but I could have taken a day to golf with one or two employees rather than shut the whole company down for a so-called "networking" event. The people putting on this event were making the same mistake Tom did back in that arm wrestling match: Forgetting what the objective was.

Once again, I saw an opportunity. *I could put one of these things on myself.* I'd do a better job, raise more money, decide where that money goes and keep my employees productive. In order to do it well, we'd need to add a philanthropic arm to the company. We decided to call it WCC Charities.

For our first event, I decided to do what the local Realtors couldn't: put on a golf tournament that actually made a difference. Here's what I tell people: If you're going to do something for charity, then *do something for charity.* If you just want to put on a social function, have one — but don't try to pretend it's a charitable fundraiser. I wanted an event that would focus on what we were actually trying to do, and do it as efficiently as possible.

Most of the people who entered the Realtors' tournament showed up to play golf, eat their dinner and leave. They paid $300 for a foursome that actually cost $200, which means they only raised $100 for charity. They didn't stay for the raffle, if they entered the raffle at all. No wonder the whole event only made $2,000. I was determined to do it better.

Bigger and Better

For our first event, we booked the local 27-hole SCPGA course and got enough sponsors to cover the cost. We charged more for the foursomes (but of course, we had to pay for them upfront). We made the clubhouse party something people would actually want to stay for, and I got Outback Steakhouse to cater the lunch for free. We gave away shoebags and other cool swag, a lot of it donated. I got Colleen Williams (from our local NBC news affiliate) to be our emcee.

Both were big hits with the participants. The first year, we netted $43,500 in funds raised, which we split between the

Ronald McDonald House in Loma Linda and Moreno Valley Community Hospital.

If you're going to raise money for charity, then raise money for charity.

Still, I was disappointed by how much we had to spend to raise that much. We probably raised $80,000 that day, but it cost $35,000 to pay for the 144 golfers, dinner, marketing materials, conditional use insurance and incidentals. When we netted that $43,500, I was actually a little discouraged.

Dee, the liaison for Ronald McDonald House, told me something that opened my eyes. "Ed, don't feel bad," she said. "You did great. Most people have to write a check to break even for their first event."

The second year, I tried to see if I could do it more efficiently. Colleen Williams came back, and I also asked the most famous client I had: Tony Burton, who played Duke Evers in the Rocky films. Tony did a great motivational talk and everyone had a great time. That year, the whole event raised $125,000 but we only netted $75,000. I had done what I set out to do — raise more money and put on a better event — but it still seemed like a lot of work and upfront cost.

I started to wonder why golf tournaments are such popular charity fundraisers. When it costs so much and takes so long to raise any money, how much good are you actually doing? After two years of putting on that massive event, I decided to look for a better, more efficient way to give to charity. After all, it's hard to feel good about what you're doing when you get in over your head.

When I worked at Sears, they used to tell us that they operated on a loss all year until Christmas. That meant they made all their profit for the entire year in the month of December.

I would imagine that's how a lot of retailers operate, and I'm not sure any non-retail businesses could do that. My point is: When you're raising money for charity, you don't want to put on something that takes all year to pay for.

Choose a cause that matters to you and fundraisers that are doable for you and your organization. You'll feel a lot better about what you're doing.

Choosing Your Causes

There's no shortage of charities out there willing to accept your money, but you want to choose a cause that really matters to you. A lot of people go straight to cancer charities. I got skeptical about cancer a long time ago, but not because I don't want to help people who have it (after all, the Ronald McDonald House helps families affected by cancer and of course the hospital does as well). But at some point, I decided that organizations like the American Cancer Society aren't necessarily interested in curing cancer. That's because cancer is a big business. So are a lot of diseases. Jerry Lewis did an annual telethon for muscular dystrophy for 44 years...how are we doing on that disease? Is it cured yet?

I decided to start raising money in places where I could see the results. This was during a time when we were sending thousands of young people off to war for this country, and they were coming home missing entire parts of their bodies. I wanted to help them and say thank you.

Locally, we had an explosion of kids entering the foster system. Unless the community stepped up, many of them wouldn't have a Christmas at no fault of their own (it was the fault of their shitty parents). By giving those kids Christmas presents, I could see where our donations were going.

We keep the whole experience very simple. Employees and friends who want to participate are given a wish list for a specific foster child or children, depending on how many kids they want to sponsor (the foster agency provides this). They bring the gifts in to work on the collection day, and we deliver them to the agency on the day of the Christmas party they put on for the foster families. It costs us nothing as an organization, and people can decide how many kids they want to buy for. Dawn and I always buy for a minimum of 20 kids, but most employees choose one or two. People are doing good from their hearts on an individual level. The best part is attending the Christmas party event where the kids receive the gifts. Some of them have just separated from their biological families and are hurting. They don't know who bought them the gifts, but the looks on their faces when they open them up are incredible. In that moment, they aren't hurting anymore.

What Giving is About

It's amazing how your giving can inspire others to give too. After seeing the good we were doing with WCC Charities, my employees decided to choose an organization to support based on my interests and surprise me with the donation. They chose The Independence Fund, a nonprofit that helps catastrophi-cally wounded veterans and their families. Pooling their money together, my employees raised $28,250 for the Independence Fund to purchase a track chair for a paraplegic vet and send care-giver spouses on a retreat. They made the presentation, giant check and all, at the company banquet in 2016. I was blown away by the surprise, but more blown away that I had inspired them to do this.

After that, I was able to make a connection with actor Gary Sinise, who runs his own organization for wounded veterans. That expe-rience opened my eyes to even more of the deep needs our sol-diers have when they come home. Just like in business, every door you open will lead to another when you get involved in a cause you care about. Here's how I got involved with the Gary Sinise Foundation; maybe it will inspire you to think about what organizations you'd like to support.

Not long after our donation was made to the Independence Fund, I got a call from Silver Star and Purple Heart recipient Army Sgt. Tommy Reiman; he extended an invitation to Gary's annual Lieutenant Dan Weekend event the following September. All I knew was that the event would be in South Carolina, and that it was a time for vets and supporters to interact and enjoy music from Gary's Lt. Dan Band.

I thought that Dawn and I would just be going to party, meet a great actor and hopefully shake the hand of the veteran who would receive our track chair. But it was so much more than that. First, I'll say this: Anyone who's ever been in the top three on American Idol doesn't hold a candle to the singers and musicians in the Lt. Dan Band (named after Gary's iconic character from *Forrest Gump*). Not only are they incredibly talented, but they also put on the most patriotic 90-minute set of cover songs you'll ever see.

More importantly, I was able to meet many brave heroes who have sacrificed life and limb for our freedom. In our conversations, I discovered that many of them share connections with each other. In some ways, the wounded American veteran community is like one big family. That's pretty inspiring.

When I told them where we were from in California, some of them started naming their brothers who were being helped by the foundation in our local area. One of them was USMC Cpl Juan Dominguez, who lost both legs and his right arm in Afghanistan. The Gary Sinise Foundation and the Tunnel to Towers Foundation had worked together to build a retrofitted smart home for Juan and his family. A home like this is designed to make everything from showering to cooking to housework easier for the disabled vet who lives there. I had heard of Juan before; I had watched local news coverage of his family receiving their house, and I had attempted to contact the foundation to see how I could get involved with the next one. Since I never heard back, I figured this was my chance to cut out the middleman and go straight to the top. I asked Tommy if Dawn and I could meet Gary Sinise. "Sure," he said, and he led us backstage.

Gary couldn't have been nicer, but he almost seemed surprised that I came to him asking how I could help. For many of these organizations, they have full-time teams dedicated to finding new donors because there just aren't enough people stepping up unsolicited. So when someone volunteers to get involved without being chased down, that's a big deal . "I want to build a house like that," I told Gary. "Well, I don't want to *build* a house; I'd like to raise the *money* to build a house."

Gary's response was this: *"Really?"*

Like I said, he was surprised.

He called over his development director Brenda, and she told us they were doing one other house in California that year. It was located in San Diego, and they had already bought it for $600,000; now, they had to pay to get the retrofit done. Even after Home Depot donated the flooring, a second company donated the windows and a third company donated the roofing, it would still cost another $100,000 to complete.

Being the efficiency-minded giver I am, I asked Brenda, "Couldn't you have done it in a more cost-effective place than San Diego?"

Her response taught me something new. "Here's what happens when you take wounded veterans out of their environment and away from their support system," she said. "They might get a free house, but they also get depressed. And that's not what they need." That opened my eyes.

Then, she explained that because they need to have their prosthetics adjusted so often, it's best if wounded veterans can live near a high quality military hospital. There are only a few of them in the country, and one of them is the Naval Medical Center in San Diego. That helped me see why it was important to sit back and let the foundation do what they do; they have the knowledge to make these things happen the right way. The recipient of the house, US Navy EOD1 Andrew Bottrell, was already living in the San Diego area — and because we weren't going to pluck him out of that comfort zone, he would be gifted a house that truly met his needs.

At some point, clients started finding out what we were doing and told me about another important organization. This one had its own model for an easy fundraiser with low overhead. It's The Boot Campaign, a veterans' support organization that has an annual campaign called Pushups for Charity. People ask others to sponsor them for a specific dollar amount to match the number of pushups they can do in 90 seconds, kind of like a walk-a-thon. It's an opportunity to experience (even if it's only for a minute and a half) the intense physical regimens that a member of the military goes through.

We had some overhead, of course — we brought in an outdoor stage, paid for a hot dog vendor and had some banners made — but compared to booking a PGA golf course, this was a piece of cake. Employees and community members came on a hot Saturday afternoon, brought their friends and did pushups while we blasted music and had our own people emcee. It was an electric, patriotic atmosphere and we netted $70,452 for deserving veterans and their families (overhead was $5,000, so that came out of the $75,452 raised). Nobody got drunk, nobody missed work, we didn't have to spend twice as much as our targeted goal and we met the objective.

That was rewarding enough. But I didn't count on getting a great friend in the process, too.

Sergeant Johnny "Joey" Jones, an amazing advocate for veterans, was working with the Boot Campaign at the time. Joey is a double amputee who sustained injuries in Afghanistan; you may recognize him from his appearances on Fox News. His story is so inspirational that I brought him in one day to speak to my employees, and they loved him too. In 2016, we gifted him a customized motorcycle so he could continue riding as a double amputee.

Around that same time, some of my neighbors asked if we would get involved with helping our local VFW post. It was poorly run and badly in need of rescue. With broken air conditioning, it was so hot inside that no one wanted to go there anymore. I sent my HVAC guy over, and he said the wiring was so old that there was no way he could install new air conditioning technology without rewiring first. So I sent over my electrician, and now I had two professionals working on quotes. Putting them together, it amounted to $13,000 and change.

I've found that one of the best resources to fill a charitable need can be your employees. They care about the community too; they just may not have the same financial resources as you. But when I told them I would put in the first $3,000 myself, it only took 24 hours to get enough commitments for the entire $13,000. I called the professionals and told them to do the job. Just like that.

Once it was done, we stopped by to say hi and check things out. Now, the air conditioning worked great — but I was seeing all kinds of other issues, too. The flooring was in disrepair, the parking lot was a mess and there was a dangerous lack of fencing, which meant homeless people were trying to camp out. Once again, I put out the call and my employees stepped up, along with other friends in the community. It's amazing how much you can accomplish when you make an effort to inspire people, and put your money where your mouth is. Sometimes, participating in charity gives you opportunities to see and do some pretty cool stuff – like when we got to play with the simulators for the Reaper and Predator drones used by our military in Afghanistan, or watching Juan Dominguez play drums like a rock star with one arm.

Supporting so many different causes was the point of establishing our own charity — so in 2017, we held an event that would support all of the funds we were now donating to. We had dinner, dueling piano entertainment and a silent auction that raised $100,000 for the Gary Sinise Foundation. We called the event a R.E.D. Tie Gala; R.E.D. stands for "remembering everyone deployed."

Dawn and I have donated a lot of our own money to help these causes, too — but it's amazing how, when you're passionate about helping a cause, you can get other people inspired. If you can show someone why a cause is worthy of their support, you can get them to feel good about opening up their wallets. You can get them to see that giving isn't just about making a donation; it's about making a difference.

Golf tournaments and galas are popular, but they aren't the only ways to raise money. Another event that's pretty popular is a Mash Bash, where everyone dresses like they're from the TV show M*A*S*H for a big dinner and auction. The one Dawn and I participate in is at March Air Field Museum to raise money for local hospitals. One year, I got a call from a guy named Rich, who was with the sponsoring organization. Rich said they wanted to make me Citizen of the Year. I attempted to joke with him by saying, "I guess this is what happens if you open your wallet for a certain number of years in a row."

Rich said something that surprised me. "Ed, this is not about what you did. This is about who you are." That blew me away, but he kept going. "You're generous with your blessings and you inspire other people to be generous too. That's who you are, and that's who they want to be like. They see something they admire and need."

I was a little embarrassed, but very flattered. I accepted the award at the Mash Bash with local officials and Congresswoman Mary Bono in attendance, and it felt great. But what felt even better was what Rich had said: *My generosity had inspired others to be generous.*

When you feel inspired to start giving, don't keep it to yourself. Share it with others and inspire them too.

Street view of the Craftsman
style corporate building.

Dawn and me at the MASH
Bash, where I was awarded
Citizen of the Year.

The digital sign to attract
new clients from the freeway
(and it works!).

Interior lobby of the building.
Paintings by Gregory Adamson,
who also illustrated this book cover.

With Brett and his bride Nicole on their wedding day.

Back in the competitive days. Universal Studios, 1990.

Christmas shopping for our local foster kids. Always the highlight of our year!

Father-son competition at Push-Ups for Charity, 2015. We raised over $75,000 for deserving vets.

With two of my favorite vets,
Andrew Bottrell and Joey Jones at
Pushups for Charity 2016.

With Lieutenant Dan himself, Gary
Sinise. Proud to have supported GSF.

With Dawn, Ryan and Kacie at our
WCC R.E.D. Tie Charity Gala, 2017.

With Pastor Matt Brown of Sandals
Church, a great spiritual mentor
and friend.

With the 43rd President of the
United States. "We miss you,"
I told him.

CHAPTER 26

I DON'T KNOW EXACTLY when I got so passionate about politics in this country. I suspect it was the same for me as it is for others: a process that began in my younger years and developed over time as my eyes were opened to what was going on around us.

Growing up, my Jewish, Democrat dad was always talking about "Tricky Dicky" Nixon. And, growing up, we were always hearing about the war in Vietnam. Anyone who grew up in the 60s will tell you: From kindergarten through sixth grade, our elementary years were dominated by the news about Vietnam. But in sixth grade, something happened that inspired me to form my own opinion about Richard Nixon based on how he handled the war.

It happened at Camp Hi-Hill, which I didn't remember the location of until checking it out while writing this. Apparently, it's on 13 acres of government-leased land in the Angeles National Forest and every student in Long Beach Unified School District has the opportunity to go there at some point. So that's why I was there, and that's where I formed my first independent political thought.

We were all eating dinner in the big cafeteria hall. I remember one of the counselors coming in and saying something like this: "Those of you with brothers in Vietnam...they just ended the war and your brothers will be coming home!" And a bunch of kids started cheering. Maybe some of them had brothers over there; others, like me, probably didn't. But they were excited the war was ending, and so was I. That's an awesome memory I'll never forget. If I didn't know anything else about Richard Nixon, I knew he ended the war in Vietnam.

But then, life went on and you kept being a kid. I recall starting to pay more attention as a teenager. At the time, I knew two things about Jimmy Carter:

1. I didn't like waiting in gas lines.
2. I didn't like hearing the president talk about how we might have to replace our cars with bicycles.

Even as a kid, no part of that seemed American to me. And it still doesn't.

I was 15 when Carter got elected, got my driver's license on my 16th birthday and bought my first car just before I turned 17. At that age, there's something about having poor parents that turns you into a Republican really fast (even if you don't realize that's what's happening). Here's how it works:

- Your mom and dad can't afford to pay for your gasoline and fun.
- You have to work to pay for your *own* gas and your *own* fun.
- You see how different your life is from your friends whose parents have money; they get to go to school, come home and watch TV. Any money they get from parents is a handout, and you can tell they feel entitled to it.
- You accept that you do not have access to these handouts. But as it makes you more mature and responsible, you see your entitled friends not keeping up. And you know it's because of the handouts.

That's more or less why I became a Republican and cast my first vote, in my first presidential election, for Ronald Reagan in 1980. Maybe that's not how people get converted to conservatism when they're older — but when it happens at a young age, sometimes it can be that simple. Remember, I had lied about my age to start working before I turned 16, because I had to. I understood that:

- No work equaled no money.
- No money equaled no car.
- No car equaled no girls.
- No girls equaled no fun.

Conclusion: If I wanted to have fun, I'd have to be a Republican.

I won't pretend like I understood the value of Reagan as a leader back then. I *was* still a regular teenager. But just like I had done with Carter, I was paying just enough attention to form an opinion about this new candidate who had already accomplished a lot in his life, from being a successful actor to the governor of California.

I recognized the difference between the positive, uplifting message of Reagan ("It's morning again in America") and the sad sack message of Carter ("Woe is me, we might have to walk or take the bus").

I also paid enough attention to see Carter's failure with the Iran hostage crisis. It bewildered me that some other podunk country in another part of the world was holding Americans hostage, and Jimmy Carter couldn't do anything about it for 444 days. That didn't seem very presidential.

Reagan also had the kind of short, memorable diplomacy taglines that everyone can remember, including young people. They were simple but significant:

- "Peace through strength."
- "Trust but verify."
- "Tear down this wall."

The one that gets quoted the most is one that Reagan doesn't even get credit for. Most people think it was said for the first time in 2016: "Let's make America great again."[100]

Reagan said it first, and most people don't realize it. That's part of his greatness.

Plus, Reagan had no problem joking about his age. Democrats made a big deal about it back then, when he was 73 and running as the incumbent against Walter Mondale. They did it again with other candidates; remember what a big deal it was that John McCain was 71 in 2008? But today, the guy who's in office was inaugurated at 78 — and Democrats don't give a crap, because they just wanted to get rid of a disruptor who was bucking their old establishment rules (we'll get to him later).

Reagan's Real Legacy

One of my most poignant memories during the Reagan years is the Space Shuttle Challenger disaster: January 28, 1986. As Americans, we were all excited to watch the Challenger as it blasted into space — until it broke apart 73 seconds into its flight, killing all seven crew members on board. I remember being at work as it played on the TV, and watching the faces of Christa McAuliffe's parents; their expressions made it clear it wasn't registering with them just yet. It was like their faces were silently saying, "What happened?" along with the rest of us as we watched this rocket ship disappear into a cloud of smoke. Their daughter was supposed to be the first teacher to go to space. Now, she was gone in an instant. Having a one-year-old child at the time, I could only imagine what it was like to go from being so proud to so horrified in a matter of seconds.

The president was supposed to give the State of the Union Address that night. Instead, he postponed it to give an Oval Office address on the tragedy. It's still documented as one of the most significant speeches of the 20th century, and no one can take that away from him. Reagan assured the nation:

"We'll continue our quest in space. There will be more shuttle flights and more shuttle crews and, yes, more volunteers, more civilians, more teachers in space. Nothing ends here; our hopes and our journeys continue."

The most memorable part is the conclusion, which includes lines from the poem "High Flight" by John Gillespie Magee. It goes like this:

292

"We will never forget them, nor the last time we saw them, this morning, as they prepared for their journey and waved goodbye and slipped the surly bonds of Earth to touch the face of God."[101]

Now that's a president with dignity. He continued displaying it during the memorial for the crew members at the Johnson Space Center. I remember wondering how he could meet with all those families without bursting into tears. It was the saddest thing I'd ever seen, but also the most inspirational. The most memorable part of that address was:

"Sometimes, when we reach for the stars, we fall short. But we must pick ourselves up again and press on despite the pain."[102]

Talk about inspiring. *That's* what made Ronald Reagan a great president.

But as he neared the end of his second term, I noticed the mainstream media and entertainment industry portraying him as a senile old warmonger. In his song "The End of The Innocence," Don Henley (someone I'm otherwise a fan of) referred to the president as "this tired old man that we elected king."[103] In their video for the song "Land of Confusion," the band Genesis made him look like a dementia-induced bonehead (and they aren't even American!). It was disgusting, even *if* he did have early onset signs of Alzheimer's disease (and I don't think he did yet; remember, it was not announced that he had the disease until 1994). The truth was, Reagan was the wisest guy out there. Not a "wise guy," but *the guy with the most wisdom*. He saw things for what they were. He had a crystal clear vision of where we were, where we had been and what we needed to do to keep going to where we wanted to be. That's the real legacy of Ronald Reagan.

The First George Bush

Reagan's vice president, on the other hand, was not quite as inspiring. When George H.W. Bush ran against Michael Dukakis in 1988, the only thing anyone remembers is, "Read my lips; no new taxes."[104] And it wasn't even a promise he could keep.

When we led the war known as Desert Storm, I remember hearing this was to protect Kuwait from Iraq. At 28 years old, I had never even *heard* of Kuwait — but neither had a lot of Americans. Most of us didn't even know the difference between Iraq and Iran yet. One of the guys at my A.L. Williams office was in the military and stationed in the UAE. I asked, "What's the UAE?" I didn't know whether the United Arab Emirates was a country or some other kind of territory (if you're old enough to remember life before 9/11, then you remember that a lot of us back then were clueless about the Middle East).

Since I was selling mutual funds at the time, I saw how the uncertainty of what was about to happen made the stock market take a dump. People who were buying mutual funds started calling us to find out what was going on. I didn't know what to tell them; this was my first time seeing up close how the market was affected by world events.

Then, things took a turn for the better. Once the news broke that we were dropping laser-guided smart bombs down smokestacks with no American casualties, the stock market rallied. That's how I came to a better understanding of how the government's every move can affect the private market. When we go to war, everyone's worried and the market goes down. When we're victorious at that war, it starts to go the other direction as soon as the reports come back. That's a perfect illustration of why paying attention to the news is important for anyone in business.

Bush was enjoying high approvals for a while, but that was short-lived. Things changed after we liberated Kuwait and the president stopped short of ordering our military to take down Saddam Hussein. As *Time* magazine would later note:

"It's a sad story of false hopes and serious miscalculations. After the U.S. evicted Iraqi forces from Kuwait, George Herbert Walker Bush had no intention of marching the U.S. Army to Baghdad to topple Saddam. He had promised the Arabs in the war coalition that he would push Saddam's army back into Iraq. That's all."[105]

Bush was fine with the Pentagon preparing to finish Hussein off with an Air Force bombing or special-ops commandos, if they could find him. But Bush also made it clear that if the Pentagon *couldn't* find him, he would be happy to let someone else take over. That came as a shock to Americans who had come to believe we were going to finish the job by taking out Saddam Hussein... including me. Many of us were disappointed in him.

Bush announced the end of the war in a speech on February 15, 1991, at the plant in Massachusetts that manufactured the same laser-guided missiles used to eject Saddam's forces from Kuwait. "There's another way for the bloodshed to stop," Bush said. "And this is for the Iraqi military and the Iraqi people to take matters into their own hands and force Saddam Hussein, the dictator, to step aside."[106]

Wait a minute...I thought you said that was going to be *our* job?

The war ended 100 hours after the ground campaign started. Bush declared a ceasefire on February 28. He also declared that Kuwait had been liberated. That was true, but the "Iraqi people" Bush referenced in his speech (the Shi'ites and Kurds) had taken his words to heart. They revolted against Saddam Hussein themselves, starting the very next day on March 1. But they were no match for Saddam's Republican Guard, which quickly attacked the Shi'ites in southern Iraq; meanwhile, the Kurds In northern Iraq didn't stand a chance against the rest of Saddam's forces. So now, America had inadvertently helped Saddam Hussein annihilate somewhere between 30,000 to 60,000 Shi'ites and 20,000 Kurds. They begged us to stay, but Colin Powell said no; he didn't want us mired in their civil war any longer. Eventually, Bush sent troops and relief supplies to protect the thousands of fleeing Kurds who were in danger of freezing or starving to death. The war had started out nobly and successfully — but by the time it was over, the result of Bush's misstep was not a good look for America.

So when it was time to campaign for 1992, it was too late for George H.W. Bush. He just looked tired. I think he ran for president out of obligation. I also think the outcome of the election had *less* to do with the coolness of Clinton and *more* to do with Bush feeling defeated.

Slick Willie vs. Ross the Boss

That doesn't mean Bill Clinton wasn't a force to be reckoned with. In comes this governor no one outside of Arkansas has ever heard of, and he's got all kinds of scandals going on (sexual and otherwise). Plenty of people loved it (about 45 million, on election day) — but the more I heard about all the slimy things "Slick Willie" was involved in, the more I gravitated toward a guy named Ross Perot.

Ross Perot was a billionaire who would go on TV as often as possible to explain why we needed to turn our country around. Perot would talk about how much debt we'd accumulated by Reagan and Bush building up our "war machine" and working to break up the Soviet Union with economic weapons rather than tanks and bombs (and that was when we were only $4 trillion in debt; at the end of 2020, it was near $28 trillion).

- He also told us Americans would soon hear the "giant sucking sound" of manufacturers leaving the U.S. for Mexico because of the North American Free Trade Agreement (NAFTA).[107]
- He spelled all of it out with pictures, graphs and common sense.
- He was skinny and goofy-looking, with a Texas drawl and a military haircut.

I was sold.

A lot of smart people support third party candidates, especially if the candidate is the only one running who truly understands money. I knew we needed to keep the country healthy financially, because I was a 31-year-old who was finally starting to understand what financial health looked like in my own life. Perot said that in order to diagnose all our economic problems, he'd have to "get under the hood and tinker with the engine" of America.[108] And I thought we should let him. (Dana Carvey's *Saturday Night Live* impression parodied this as, "feel it, touch it, smell it, eat it, and pass it through my lower intestine").[109] Either way, Ross Perot made all the sense in the world to me.

When he bankrolled his own half hour primetime TV special, Perot said he wouldn't take any money for the job of president *and* only serve one term. I cheered him on the whole way. I even sent the kids to school with "Ross the Boss" t-shirts.

I looked at the three candidates this way:

1. George Bush: Did some great things, but too tired to continue.
2. Bill Clinton: Smooth talker, good looking guy, slimy as hell.
3. Ross Perot: *This* was the guy.

But then, the establishment tried to attack him (he first claimed it was a "mafia-like" pro-NAFTA group, and later said he believed it was someone from the Bush campaign). There were also threats to disrupt his daughter's wedding. So in July, Perot dropped out — only to re-enter the campaign 11 weeks later in October, one month before election day. He said it was because the threats to his daughter had passed.

But by that time, Perot's most influential supporters had moved on. I wondered: If this was the smartest guy for the job before, why isn't he the smartest guy *now*? I knew he shouldn't have dropped out, but I was trying to think with some humanity.

In November 1992, I cast my vote for Perot despite his long odds and the dufus he had picked as a running mate, Admiral James Stockdale. That guy probably didn't help the campaign either, because his opening line at the vice presidential debate ("Who am I?" Why am I here?")[110] gave off the impression that maybe Perot wasn't so serious about being president after all (if Perot only planned to serve one term, was this *really* the guy he felt good about handing things off to?). I thought he should have chosen Jack Kemp, who had already been a congressman, a cabinet member and a presidential candidate himself. But I guess Perot didn't think to call up his 31-year-old supporter in California to ask for my opinion. By staying in, Ross Perot took enough votes away from Bush to hand Bill Clinton the presidency.

Pros and Cons of the Clinton Presidency

So now, we had a president who was *still* slick and slimy, but also smart enough to reach across the aisle. Clinton never refused to work with the Republican-led House when Gingrich became Speaker in 1995. From that, we got welfare reform and some other good economic progress. We also got the Contract with America.

Unfortunately, he was not a good guy. He was a sex addict, but it was more than that; he couldn't stay focused. When our military had its first opportunity to kill Osama Bin Laden in 1998, what was Bill Clinton caught up in? You already know the answer. But the fact is, there were *nine separate times* that we could have captured or killed Bin Laden before he masterminded the largest attack in history to occur on American soil. From the Washington Post Fact Checker:

Philip D. Zelikow, the executive director of the 9/11 report, actually identifies nine key moments in Clinton's presidency when a different decision might have led to Bin Laden's death. "On every one of these nine choices there are people who believe the president could have made a different choice," Zelikow said.[111]

One missed opportunity from March 1999 was described in the 9/11 Commission Report:

According to CIA and Defense officials, policymakers were concerned about the danger that a strike would kill an Emirati prince or other senior officials who might be with Bin Laden or close by... The lead CIA official in the field, Gary Schroen, felt that the intelligence reporting in this case was very reliable; the Bin Laden unit chief, "Mike," agreed. Schroen believes today that this was a lost opportunity to kill Bin Laden before 9/11.[112]

Who knows if Clinton would have made the call if he hadn't been so wrapped up in defending (and denying) his actions with a young female intern. It may not have seemed like that big of a deal at the time when we were all listening to the juicy details on cable news every night, but it sure turned out to be a big deal on September 11, 2001.

Although he was charged with two articles of impeachment (perjury and obstruction of justice), Clinton was acquitted because the necessary two-thirds majority vote in the Senate wasn't met to convict or remove him from office.

Then-Congressman James Rogan (now a California Superior Court Judge) was chosen to be one of the 13 impeachment managers. He took thorough notes during Clinton's impeachment trial, resulting in the book *Catching Our Flag: Behind the Scenes of a Presidential Impeachment*. Rogan's book explains that the Senate knew removing Clinton from office would give Vice President Al Gore the power of an incumbent in the 2000 election — and this would almost certainly result in him winning. So Clinton finished his second term, and Al Gore still ran in 2000. But he wasn't an incumbent, so he lacked the tremendous advantage an incumbent would have in those days.

As an aside, James Rogan represented California's 28th District. This seat is the one now occupied by Representative Adam Schiff (I have lots of great nicknames for him). Schiff is currently best known as the member of Congress who spent about five minutes working on behalf of his district from 2016 to 2020, because he preferred to devote the majority of his time and efforts to impeaching Donald Trump. I'm getting ahead of myself again, but the point is this: James Rogan was defeated by a relatively unknown state senator named Adam Schiff in 2000 because Democrats made unseating Rogan a mission in their congressional race targets. One report said Rogan was "targeted for political extinction by the Democratic Party for his aggressive and compromising role as a House manager in the impeachment of President Clinton."[113]

Boy, are Democrats vindictive.

During his campaign, Schiff made frequent references to Rogan being absent from his district. At the time, the Los Angeles Times reported:

Schiff said Rogan's pursuit of impeachment blinded him to the needs of constituents. "The record shows that persistent local needs have never held much interest for our local congressman," Schiff said. "They've never been able to compete with the lure of being seen with [former Speaker of the House] Newt Gingrich and Henry Hyde," the chief House manager.[114]

Fast forward 20 years, when Schiff proceeded to do the exact same thing. His constituents could never compete with the allure of being seen with Nancy Pelosi or sparring with Devin Nunes.

Vindictive *and* hypocritical.

The 2000 Presidential Election

I remember being in Reno for an arm wrestling tournament in early 2000, where some guy at the casino was droning on and on to me about John McCain: "He's the man, he's such a great person," that kind of thing. I wasn't that in tune with it and I don't even remember who I voted for in the primary (sure, I was 38 by that time, but none of these guys were Ross Perot). Plus, I knew California didn't have much of a stake in the primaries because most candidates drop out before we vote in June. When I started paying attention in the general election, the first thing I noticed was how Al Gore would always say, "Bill Clinton and I"...as if they were one and the same person (maybe you noticed the 2020 Democratic candidate doing the same thing).

This was also around the same time I became aware of Al Gore's obsession with the environment. On my drive to work in the mornings, Rush Limbaugh would talk about Gore's fixation on banning aerosol spray cans. "Algore," as Rush called him, wanted us all to switch to puff spray products for our hair care and such. I thought, *this* is what the Democratic nominee for president cares about most?

Gore made sure he got some left-leaning scientists on the task of debunking Limbaugh's claim that volcanic ash could repair holes in the ozone layer (even though a Harvard study has since proven it to be true).[115] The more the climate change doctrine was shoved in our faces by Al Gore and the people he helped get rich, the more I came to understand that God created the earth to be a living thing — and we can't screw it up no matter how hard we try. He made it to be a place for us to live. It's designed for us; we're not designed for it. I wasn't buying what Al Gore said then, and we shouldn't buy it now from the environmental prophets of doom.

I realize I haven't said a word about George W. Bush yet. At first, the only thing that stood out to me was this: Bush seemed like a good man and Gore seemed like a pompous asshole. The end.

Saturday Night Live did a great job parodying those debates, making fun of Gore's Social Security "lockbox" just as much as Bush's pronunciation of the word "nuclear." They even captured what had now become my favorite Gore-ism: "Bill Clinton and I..."

It was amazing how Gore tried to take credit for everything Bill Clinton did right, and nothing that he did wrong. He was right there with Bill for welfare reform, but nowhere to be found when Bill was locked in the Oval Office bathroom with an intern.

I was excited for Bush's victory in 2000 — even though, for the next two months, all we saw on TV was people talking about hanging, dimpled and pregnant chads. What was the difference? You had reporters demonstrating it with their fingers. It all seemed so stupid. I just was ready for a straight up guy to be our president.

But like a lot of Americans, I wasn't *that* worried yet about the future of the country. And then, eight months after Bush's inauguration, came the morning of September 11.

There's no way the government didn't know that Osama Bin Laden was on his way to becoming the most dangerous man in the world. He began forming Al Qaeda in 1988 and made no secret of his enthusiasm for the World Trade Center bombing in 1993 (fun fact: It's been documented that Bin Laden may have paid one of the World Trade Center bombers, Ramzi Ahmed Yousef, to assassinate Clinton on a trip to the Philippines in 1994.[116] But as the story goes, the plan ended up being thwarted when Yousef determined it was a "logistical nightmare"). As we already know, Clinton didn't make the call to rid the world of Bin Laden in 1999 because he was too busy dealing with an impeachment. And two years later, the Twin Towers fell. Our Pentagon was attacked. A third plane crashed in a field in Pennsylvania before it could hit its target; there is evidence that the target was either the U.S. Capitol Building or the White House.[117]

The Day the World Changed

Everyone remembers what they were doing that morning. I was at the gym, glancing at some of the wall-mounted TVs as I walked around (as one does at the gym). On every single TV was a live news broadcast of New York City. The World Trade Center had a giant hole in its north tower, and black smoke was billowing out of the hole. Everyone was asking each other about it. The consensus among us strangers at the gym was that this was an accident; it had to be that a small private plane malfunctioned and just happened to career into one of the tallest, most high-profile buildings in the world. But as it turned out, it was actually a Boeing 767 that had been hijacked by jihadis affiliated with Al Qaeda, Osama Bin Laden's organization of Islamic extremist militants.

The north tower crash happened at 8:46 AM Eastern Standard Time (in California, it was 5:46 AM). I knew what happened wasn't good and that there had to be some casualties, but it still didn't register as alarming — until 17 minutes later, when the same thing happened to the south tower. By that time, I was probably doing wrist curls on a bench or something. What I remember is someone who had been watching the TV with me walked over and said something about "planes."

"What are you talking about?" I said. "There's only one plane."

"No," he said. "A second plane hit."

"Really?" I was probably thinking the same thing every other American adult watching this was thinking. "I gotta go."

I got in my truck, where my cell phone was still sitting (those of us who had them in 2001 weren't keeping them on our bodies at all times just yet). Dawn had been calling for the last hour. The kids would be getting up soon for school. What do you tell them? This was the question every American parent was asking that morning. My kids were 16 and 15, which meant they were old enough that I had to tell them *something*.

Kids are so interesting. As we drove to school, none of us said very much as we listened to the radio reports — but as he got out of the car, my son (who was two months away from turning

17) asked a question that showed me he definitely understood what was happening.

"Dad," he said. "Does this mean they're going to start the draft?"

"Don't worry about it," I said. "Just go to school."

I wasn't intentionally trying to get out of a teachable moment with my son. I truly believed that kids shouldn't have to worry about that yet — not to mention the fact that most of us adults weren't sure what was happening yet either. We knew it was terrorism, most likely committed by some organization from the Middle East. What else did we know? The FBI announced the names of the 19 hijackers on September 14, and the rest of the facts were reported in pieces over the next several months.

While we were on that drive to school, American Airlines Flight 77 hit the Pentagon. I didn't know it at the time, but my high school buddy Chris Newton was on that plane.

Like everyone, I watched the day's events unfold on TV. I recalled that the last time everyone in the country was glued to their TVs in unison for a history-altering event was the Challenger explosion. When that happened, no one knew they were about to see a tragedy happen right in front of them. This time, no one was watching until it *was* a tragedy. People can say this happened "on Bush's watch," but he had been president all of eight months. The truth is, the groundwork of plotting 9/11 happened on the watch of the president before him. But that president had other things on his mind.

When Bush gave an Oval Office address to the nation that night, that's when he "became" president in the eyes of most Americans — including many who didn't even vote for him. Seeing and hearing our relatively new president say this was comforting:

Today our fellow citizens, our way of life, our very freedom came under attack in a series of deliberate and deadly terrorist acts. The victims were in airplanes or in their offices: secretaries, business men and women, military and federal workers, moms and dads, friends and neighbors. Thousands of lives were suddenly ended by evil, despicable acts of terror.

The pictures of airplanes flying into buildings, fires burning, huge structures collapsing, have filled us with disbelief, terrible sadness, and a quiet, unyielding anger. These acts of mass murder were intended to frighten our nation into chaos and retreat, but they have failed. Our country is strong.

A great people has been moved to defend a great nation. Terrorist attacks can shake the foundations of our biggest buildings, but they cannot touch the foundation of America. These acts shattered steel, but they cannot dent the steel of American resolve. America was targeted for attack because we're the brightest beacon for freedom and opportunity in the world. And no one will keep that light from shining.[118]

It was obvious that he was holding back righteous anger and profound sadness, choking up and holding back tears in order to present himself as professional and presidential. This was George W. Bush at his best: serious, strong, emotional. It was when people loved him the most, because deep down that's what we all want in a president.

Later, we saw that morning's footage of him in that Florida classroom where he was whispered to by his Chief of Staff. Apparently, he had already been informed of an aircraft hitting the north tower; however, he was briefed that it was probably just a small propeller plane (the same thing my fellow gym goers and I were thinking). But a short time later, as he read a story called *The Pet Goat* to that room of first graders, Andrew Card interrupted the president to whisper in his ear: "A second plane hit the second tower. America is under attack."[119]

Bush was later criticized (by propaganda filmmaker Michael Moore, and then by his 2004 opponent John Kerry) for continuing to read to the kids and deflecting a reporter's question about the attack in the classroom. But unlike the president that came after him (we'll get to him later), Bush didn't give knee jerk reactions to the press's questions until he had all the facts. He also wanted to keep everyone calm. This wasn't a room of government officials; it was a room of everyday American teachers, parents and kids. And George W. Bush knew how to read a room.

That's what people want from our leaders in times of crisis. He continued to show strength and help unify America over the next year. He did it while standing on top of the rubble at Ground Zero with that bullhorn: "I can hear you! The rest of the world hears you. And the people who knocked these buildings down will hear all of us soon."[120] He did it by throwing out the first pitch of the season at Yankee Stadium. How important was that for America to see? It was symbolic, but sometimes symbolism is everything. These were rally calls for America to come together.

On the night of September 11, even Congress was able to unify for a moment of silence on the Capitol steps, and it turned into a spontaneous performance of "God Bless America."[121] That was unity we haven't seen since and may never see again. I certainly don't expect to see it in my lifetime.

Speaking of my lifetime, I wasn't sure what to expect in the world of finance. No one was. The New York Stock Exchange stayed closed until Monday, September 17. This was the single longest closure since 1933.[122] At the end of the day, it was declared the single worst day in the Dow's history in terms of points lost (684), and it was the 14th worst day in terms of the percentage drop.[123] But the market quickly bounced back. By December 11 — exactly three months after the attack — the S&P 500 was trading 3.8% higher than it was prior to September 11.[124] The stock market rallied and the bond market was stable. It showed America's confidence in the country and in the president.

At the end of his presidency, all we heard about were Bush's "historically low" approval ratings. But in the weeks after 9/11, they were historically high — up to 90%, according to CNN and Gallup polls.[125]

Unexplored Territory

Over the next few years, those approval ratings would change as we lost thousands of troops in war and the president would start delivering bad news with a smile on his face (this always bothered me). I know he was doing the best he could with an impossible situation, but I think people saw it as a projection of weakness.

Still, this president was dealing with totally unexplored territory. Where's the rulebook for this?

My stepson, Brett, was 27 and wanted to enlist. This scared his mother, of course. I told her maybe this wasn't a bad thing, and that, "If I was young enough, I'd go too." And that's how lots of people felt in those days; you heard them talking about it everywhere you went. After all, watching these kids be willing to go fight an enemy they knew so little about was inspiring. They knew the enemy was evil. They knew enough.

By 2004, the Bush administration was being hit with criticism about these same kids "torturing" the people who did this to us — people who couldn't care less about rules of engagement or the Geneva Convention. The soldiers at Abu Ghraib are now labeled war criminals for the rest of their lives for something they did in their early 20s (only one was in his 30s). All they knew is they were being sent to this part of the world to make those people pay. They were punished severely for it, but so was the president's administration.

Visiting Ground Zero

In October 2002, there was an arm wrestling tournament in New York City. Just like *Over the Top* back in the 80s, this was one you had to qualify for by placing first or second in a regional event. I had never been to New York yet, so I set my sights on winning in San Diego and took second place. Good enough! The event was October 10; Dawn and I got there two days early so we could see up close what the whole world was watching from afar.

We checked into the Holiday Inn on Wall Street and went straight to Ground Zero. This was just after the first anniversary of the attack; although the hole in the ground had been cleaned out, you could still smell the stench of death, asbestos and rubble. I had no idea that old, collapsed buildings would smell so...weird. In addition to that, the Financial District of Lower Manhattan is essentially dead on the weekends; at night, the businesses close

and the people disappear. All of this made for an eerie atmosphere. It was an interesting way to visit New York City for the
first time.

Surrounded by a big iron fence across the street is St. Paul's
Chapel, the oldest continuous use building in New York City. It
was built in 1766, and they say George Washington worshipped
there on his inauguration day in 1789. Around the fence were all
the signs and posters for the missing, most of them homemade
by their loved ones, that are in the September 11 Memorial &
Museum today — only today, the museum has redacted many
of the personal details that were on them originally. They would
say where the person worked and when they were last seen; of
course, most of them were last seen on September 11, 2001.
There were letters to heroic parents from their heartbroken kids.
There were fire department t-shirts from every place you could
imagine, from Hemet, California to Tokyo, Japan. They were put
there by emergency workers who came from all over the world to
help. There were vendors selling artifacts from the attack, which
was odd. When it got dark, they turned on lights and people
roamed around all night. It was hard to leave. Somewhere, there
must have been a sound system set up; it was playing the R.E.M.
song "Everybody Hurts." It was sad as shit. I don't know any other
way to describe it.

The arm wrestling tournament was at the South Street Seaport,
which is walking distance from the World Trade Center. We took
advantage of the proximity to return again twice (with a visit
to Friendly Gourmet Pizza in between, which I highly recommend). Time to read more signs, more letters and more tributes
around St. Paul's; once you started, you couldn't stop. I remember
thinking, "I'm glad no one here knows me," because I was crying
like a baby behind my sunglasses.

Then out of nowhere, this guy comes zipping out of the subway
terminal on his skateboard. "Hey, Mr. Hoffman! How are you?" I
was quickly snapped out of my teary-eyed trance. Was this the
biggest coincidence of my life: running into someone I knew from
home on the streets of Manhattan at the worst possible time?

It wasn't. It was just the kid who had checked us in at the hotel.

"Hey!" I said, tears dripping down my face as he zipped past. "How are you...good to see ya...just checking things out...see ya later!"

It was a moment of comic relief in an otherwise somber weekend.

We headed to the tournament, where I got one of the bigger ass-kickings of my arm wrestling career. It was hard to focus on competing after seeing all that. But I got on TV, because Fox Sports was carrying it. And after my defeat, where do you think we went again? We had to. This was the most important place in the world at the moment.

It wasn't a one-stop experience; you could walk around and see something new every time.

Maybe this is symbolic, maybe it isn't...but at one point, when we got lost walking around some desolate part of Lower Manhattan late at night, the lights of Ground Zero helped us find our way back. That was pretty meaningful.

Going to the site while it was still Ground Zero made me appreciate being American, the freedoms that we have and the vulnerability we could find ourselves in anytime we took down our guard. Now, we were fighting the people who caused this on the other side of the world — and like a lot of Americans at the time, I wasn't even sure why they hated us. As we found out more and more about the Religion of Peace (cough cough) and what the goals of those hijackers were, we found out that these people worshipped death the way we worship life.

Kids today (who were either too young to remember or born after 2001) aren't paying attention to these differences. I didn't either, when I was a kid — or even as an adult, for that matter. From September 11, many of us got a really clear picture of how the world is. It was a time to decide what your values were. But we shouldn't have to wait for an event like that to decide; we can decide *now* what really matters to us, and pass it onto our kids with the hope that they'll never have to live through anything like that again.

Decision Time

As we amassed more casualties in Afghanistan, failed to find weapons of mass destruction in Iraq and started a second war in that country based on intelligence that may or may not have been reliable, Bush's approval ratings fluctuated. But here's what he always stood fast on: You're either for us or against us. If you're harboring terrorists, we're coming for you. As he said on September 21, 2001: "Every nation, in every region, now has a decision to make. Either you are with us, or you are with the terrorists."[126]

Contrary to what some Democrats wanted America to believe, Bush didn't authorize our military to invade Iraq "because Saddam tried to kill his dad." He did it because there was intelligence that Saddam may have sponsored training for at least one of the 9/11 hijackers, in addition to harboring the mastermind behind the first World Trade Center attack.

Let's look at a present-day application of this: No one ever saw George Soros break into the Capitol Building on January 6, 2021 or show up on the streets of Portland in the summer of 2020. But if he was paying people to create chaos around the time of these events, then he's the problem that should be dealt with first. And that's where Bush was at in 2003. He believed that whether you *are* the terrorist or you're supporting the terrorists, you're the problem.

Here's where I believe his dad *did* factor in: Bush 41 failed to finish a job and left the Kurds to starve. Bush 43 didn't want to repeat that kind of consequential mistake. So he hunted down Saddam Hussein (*and* his sons with their strangely rhyming names) and finished the job. It was a decision he stood by.

As for the extent of the war, that was complicated too. Bush got a lot of flack for standing in front of a "Mission Accomplished" banner on the USS Abraham Lincoln in 2003. The idea was to announce the end of major combat operations in Iraq, and he never *said* the words "mission accomplished" in the speech. But he has since admitted the banner was a misstep. "To some, it said, well, 'Bush thinks the war in Iraq is over,' when I didn't think that," he told CNN in 2008. "It conveyed the wrong message."[127]

He didn't think the war was over. But there's no question Bush was presented with a challenge unlike any president before him. September 11 was the deadliest day in U.S. history. Bush saw that the enemy we faced didn't wear a uniform, and that was what made it even harder to fight. His administration understood we were in an ideological war above all else.

In his memoir *Decision Points*, he wrote: *There are things we got wrong in Iraq, but the cause is eternally right.*[128]

George W. Bush is a good man; as a president, he made decisions based on what he thought was best for the country.

Case in point, another incident he was slammed over: Hurricane Katrina. When Air Force One flew over New Orleans and a photo was released of the president surveying the damage, the spin from the left was that "George W. Bush didn't care." Never mind that landing the plane and putting the president smack in the middle of the devastation would result in a media spectacle, which the left would then spin as a photo opp gone wrong (he was damned either way). But guess how many times he visited New Orleans after that day? A total of 13 times. Also in *Decision Points*, Bush wrote:

In my 13 visits to New Orleans after the storm, I conveyed my sincere sympathy for the suffering, and my determination to help residents rebuild. Yet many of our citizens, particularly in the African American community, came away convinced their president didn't care about them. Just as Katrina was more than a hurricane, its impact was more than physical destruction. It eroded citizens' trust in their government. It exacerbated divisions in our society and politics. And it cast a cloud over my second term.[129]

Bush is a good man, and he was a good president. He didn't make decisions based on what seemed popular; he made them based on what he thought was best for the country.

Another way he demonstrated his good character was with his presidential vacation decisions. Bush typically vacationed at his personal home in Crawford, Texas, or the official presidential retreat, Camp David (the White House calls it "the president's country residence").[130] He did that because he's a considerate person. Unlike the First Family who moved in after him, Bush understood our tax dollars weren't his to spend however he wanted.

What do I mean by that?

Judicial Watch filed a Freedom of Information Act (FOIA) lawsuit to obtain Secret Service records from Barack Obama's presidency. Those records report that the total spent on the Obama family's travel was $105,662,975.27.[131]

You're reading that right. It was "one hundred and five million, six hundred and sixty-two thousand, nine hundred seventy five dollars and twenty seven cents" of taxpayer money the Obamas spent on their travel. But I'm getting ahead of myself. The point is, George W. Bush didn't spend our money so he could recreate all over the world, requiring a massive Secret Service fleet to accompany him. As much as possible, he wanted the agents to go be with their families on holidays. Because, like I said: He's a considerate person.

When I met George W. Bush at a conference in 2017, I told him, "We miss you, Mr. President."

"Aw," he replied in the classic Bush drawl. "You're just being nice."

"No," I said. "I'm serious. We miss you."[132]

And I meant it.

Enter The Anointed One

In July 2004, the star of the Democratic National Convention was a young, fresh-faced state senator from Illinois. No one had ever heard of him, but for some reason he was chosen to deliver the keynote address — not just of the night, but *of the entire event*.

Why? What did the Democratic party have planned? Well, now we know that this was the beginning of their plan to make this unknown newcomer the The First Black President.

It didn't matter whether he had experience (he didn't). It didn't matter whether he had a track record in business (he didn't...in fact, he never had a real job to begin with. What's a community organizer? That sounds like a job that's pretty much a continuation of college). He becomes a state senator and makes one really good speech on a national stage. Less than one year later, he's elected to the U.S. Senate (probably because people knew him from that speech). And three years after that, he's already qualified to be President of the United States. Because why? Because as Joe Biden said, he was "bright, clean and articulate"[133] (and how is *that* not racist)?

Day after day for eight years, Democrats and their media allies smugly claimed that the *real* racists had to be the Republican voters who didn't like The First Black President's policies...or wondered about his true faith...or took issue with the fact that he flew around the world on apology tours to bow to other leaders and trash America. If you dared to question the presidential actions of The Anointed One, you were a very bad American. If you didn't like being lectured to by The First Black President, you were even worse.

We found out through these lectures that Barack Obama liked to invent his own slogans. I'm not even talking about the campaign slogan, "Yes we can," or memorable lines in speeches he only said once or twice. These were things he said so frequently while wagging his finger at the rest of us that they sounded like things he wanted us to memorize. Things like:

- "Let me be clear."[134]
- "It's the right thing to do."[135]
- "That's not who we are."[136]

How do *you* know who we are? Not only have you never had a real job, but you don't think we should get any of the credit for our own success. Remember this? "If you've got a business, you didn't build that. Somebody else made that happen."[137]

Excuse me???

Obama also had a habit of chiming in about things prematurely. If he was asked about something, he had to answer in that moment, whether or not he had any of the actual details. He also loved to make a personal connection between himself and the victims of various local incidents throughout the country. He'd say things like:

- "Not having been there and not seeing all the facts...I think it's fair to say...that the Cambridge police acted stupidly."[138] *(He should have stopped after the first part.)*
- "If I had a son, he'd look like Trayvon."[139] *(How could he even know that?)*
- "If I had a son, I'd have to think long and hard before I let him play football."[140] *(How many hypothetical sons does this guy have?)*

These kinds of comments were made over and over by Barack Obama. I'm not coming from a place that's racist; I'm just making observations about the agenda of a president. I understand African-Americans wanted a president who represented them — and if you want to comment after the facts come out about a case, then fine. But how about representing *all* Americans, period? That includes Americans overseas who were getting their heads chopped off by ISIS, some of them on video that their families had to see. Some of those videos ended up on YouTube. As I write this, one outgoing president was just banned from YouTube because he supposedly "incites violence." There was *actual* violence — bloody, gory, disgusting violence against Americans — during Obama's administration that YouTube allowed to remain on their platform.

Those Americans include journalist Daniel Pearl, radio tower repairman Nicholas Berg and journalist James Foley. How about coming off the golf course long enough to make a speech about *their* innocence, like he did for Trayvon Martin?

Obama declared he was "heartbroken" after hanging up the phone with James Foley's distraught parents, who had just been told about their son's beheading in Syria at the hands of ISIS. But that's not the end of the story. Even the New York Times was bothered enough by what Obama did next to report on it: *"But as soon as the cameras went off, Mr. Obama headed to his favorite golf course on Martha's Vineyard, where he is on vacation, seemingly able to put the savagery out of his mind. He spent the rest of the afternoon on the links even as a firestorm of criticism erupted over what many saw as a callous indifference to the slaughter he had just condemned."*[141]

As I write this on Inauguration Day 2021, I still can't believe there are Americans who claim to "miss" Barack Obama enough that they would vote in his vice president (who, by his own admission, told Obama to "wait" on killing Osama Bin Laden in 2011).

And when 14 people were shot dead in San Bernardino, California — not far from where I live and work — by a local couple who were eagerly radicalized in the wife's home country of Pakistan (she was able to come into our country because of Obama's chain migration policies like the so-called "fiancé visa"), here's what Obama said.

"We cannot turn against one another by letting this fight be defined as a war between America and Islam. That does not mean denying the fact that an extremist ideology has spread within some Muslim communities. This is a real problem that Muslims must confront, without excuse."[142]

That's the best this guy can do???

On the other hand, Obama had a *lot* to say when a killing had nothing to do with Islamic extremism and the victims were African-Americans involved in some kind of police altercation.

When people talk about the Ferguson Effect, we have Obama to thank for that. When Officer Darren Wilson was acquitted for the killing of Michael Brown in 2014, Obama told Americans who were "deeply disappointed, even angry" with the grand jury's verdict that their emotions were "understandable."[143] Well, they *would* be understandable if the evidence didn't point squarely to Wilson's innocence — but it did. Here's what the grand jury was working with:

- The testimony of six black observers at the scene, all of whom struck down the early reports that Wilson attacked Brown "in cold blood" and shot Brown in the back when his hands were up (these early, untrue reports are what started the first wave of the Ferguson riots in August, which lasted for 16 straight days. Obama's comments after the grand jury verdict in November kicked off the second wave of riots, which lasted for eight days).

- Physical evidence that showed Brown had attacked Wilson first. When Wilson approached Brown regarding the liquor store robbery he had just committed, the evidence showed that Brown tried to grab the police officer's gun. The Department of Justice (DOJ) report on the investigation states: "As detailed throughout this report, several witnesses stated that Brown appeared to pose a physical threat to Wilson as he moved toward Wilson."
- Autopsy evidence that disproved the prosecution. The DOJ report further states: "Wilson did not shoot Brown in the back as he was running away because there were no entrance wounds in his back."[144]

The public reaction to the incident was notorious; most notably, there were two riots in Ferguson, Missouri that year. The second wave erupted in protests in 130 cities across the U.S. in St. Louis, Philadelphia, Seattle, Albuquerque, New York City, Cleveland, Los Angeles, Oakland, Minneapolis, Atlanta, Chicago, Boston and many more. And no, they were not all peaceful. They may not have even been "mostly peaceful" (something we heard a lot six years later in 2020, after George Floyd was killed in Minneapolis). There were blocked roads and highways, officers were accosted, and protestors chanting the catchy anti-cop slogan, "Pigs in a blanket, fry 'em like bacon" was now an expected part of these demonstrations.[145] The Black Lives Matter and ANTIFA-led riots that dominated the entire summer of 2020 might not have happened if the violent, racially charged climate Obama permitted in the summer of 2014 didn't happen first.

After those reflections, this 2016 Rasmussen poll should come as no surprise to anyone. It found 60% of Americans felt "race relations have gotten worse since Obama's election."[146] Weren't we told the exact opposite effect would come from electing him? But what else did we expect from the man who sat in the church of Reverend Jeremiah Wright, the pastor whose church (by his own admission) was founded on extreme black liberation theology? This is a preacher who is best known for making the following statements:

- "God damn America for treating our citizens as less than human. God damn America for as long as she acts like she is God and she is supreme."[147]
- "We are indignant because the stuff we have done overseas is now brought right back into our own front yards. America's chickens are coming home to roost." (He was talking about September 11. Talk about shameful. And if you listen to him say it, his dramatic cadence and pauses make it even more upsetting.)[148]
- "So many folks are hating on Barack Obama. He doesn't fit the model. He ain't white, he ain't rich, and he ain't privileged."[149]

Well, that's debatable.

- First, he is half-white; that's just a fact.
- Second, he was raised by rich white grandparents in Hawaii — and he's *incredibly* rich now that he's an ex-president (as all politicians are the moment they leave office).
- And Barack Obama is the poster boy for privilege, because he was elected to the highest office in the land with zero experience, the backing of every billionaire in Hollywood and dozens of nonprofits that were created for the sole purpose of funding his campaign.

I would say he's a secret Muslim born in Kenya, but I don't even have to. I think I've just made the case against him quite nicely without it.

Remember Bush's simple, low-cost retreats to Camp David that saved taxpayers money and didn't disrupt anyone? Yeah, Obama didn't like those. He preferred to rack up the highest travel bill in presidential history. Let's revisit that Judicial Watch lawsuit and the FOIA release of Obama's travel expenses. Here's some of what it documented:

- Michelle Obama's trip to Morocco cost $128,108.47 in hotels; $88,725.60 in car rentals; $1,476.07 in gas/oil and $972.22 in cell phone charges for a total of $244,218.01.
- Michelle Obama's trip to Liberia cost $55,220 in hotels; $44,000 in car rentals; $2,500 in gas/oil and $1,000 in cell phone charges for a total of $107,890.
- Michelle Obama's trip to Spain cost $79,764.49 in hotels; $81,750.99 in car rentals and $4,547 in staff overtime pay for a total of $166,062.48.[150]

None of that was for the president. That was *only* for his wife.

As a family, the Obamas trotted around to the most luxurious vacation spots in the country: Hawaii, Palm Springs, Martha's Vineyard. Every time they descended on these destinations, there were reports of the streets being clogged by Secret Service fleets and the White House Press Corps (the reporters got to go on vacation, too; although their employers paid for the trips, they were actually reimbursing the White House travel office.[151] That happens no matter who the president is, but Bush's Crawford vacations cost a lot less upfront than Obama's trips to Hawaii).

Judicial Watch found that:

- Secret Service expenses for the Obama family vacation to Honolulu in Christmas 2013 cost taxpayers at least $316,698.03. The total cost of the entire trip was $8,098,060.33.
- Obama's June 2015 golf outing to Palm Springs at the private course of Oracle magnate Larry Ellison required 10.6 hours of flying time at $206,337 per hour, costing taxpayers $2,187,172.20.
- The Obama daughters' July 2015 trip to New York City with their president father required 1.5 hours of flying time at $206,337 per hour, costing taxpayers $309,505.50.

- • The Obama family's August 2015 trip to Martha's Vineyard required 3 hours of flying time at $206,337 per hour, costing taxpayers $619,011.[152]

Remember: The total taxpayer bill for all Obama family travel over eight years was $105,662,975.27.

And they say the President of the United States only makes $400,000 a year.

Elections have consequences. And electing Obama twice is what paved the way for a president who made no secret about his agenda, had his own money for his own travel, and showed *all* Americans he cared about them. You know who I'm talking about.

CHAPTER 27

"You don't want the truth because deep down in places you don't talk about at parties, you want me on that wall. You need me on that wall."[153]
- A Few Good Men, 1993

IN 2008, NOBODY really knew who Barack Obama was. But we should have, because he told us himself. He never tried to hide it. From his own mouth, we knew he was bent on "fundamentally transforming" America. He said it October 30, 2008 — just one week before election day, at a campaign event in Missouri. Why didn't America listen then?

Here's the lesson: *When people tell you who they are, believe them.*

But by the time his first term was up, no one had any excuse. There was no reason to re-elect the president who:

- Made it pretty clear his favorite activity was apologizing for America.
- Did nothing to recover the economy after the subprime mortgage crisis his own party had created.
- Didn't care about helping Americans keep their jobs, unless they were "green jobs."
- Appointed more "czars" to head up various government offices than any president in history (including, of course, a "Green Jobs Czar").

Again, this was the president who said, "You didn't build that" to Americans who owned their own businesses. Barack Obama actually said that while running for a second term. This not only showed his incredible lack of respect for average American entrepreneurs; it also showed his convoluted ideas about where jobs actually come from. Obama truly believed that it was the role of *government* to create jobs, rather than to create an environment where the *private sector* can create jobs. This had to mean one of two things:

1. He was too ignorant to understand he had taken away the incentive for Americans to grow and expand their businesses, or;
2. He completely understood he had taken away the incentive for Americans to grow and expand their businesses

Which one is worse?

Then, in comes Mitt Romney. He was the former governor of Massachusetts and a venture capitalist. He clearly knew how the economy worked — and from a moral standpoint, he was basically a 60-year-old Boy Scout.

The 2012 election was not Mitt Romney's first rodeo; he had run in the Republican primary four years earlier. In fact, Romney's first run for president lasted for exactly one year, from February 2007 to February 2008. He had polled first among Republican voters multiple times, but came in second in the Iowa caucuses (because those people were bent on former Arkansas governor Mike Huckabee). He lost the New Hampshire Primary to John McCain (this was as much a surprise to John McCain as it was to everybody else), but finished fourth in South Carolina and Florida. McCain ended up with the most delegates and was the front-runner as Super Tuesday got closer, which is why Romney then ended his first presidential campaign.

The point is, America had plenty of exposure to Mitt Romney prior to 2012. We knew he was rich enough to run the economy, experienced enough to run the executive branch and moral enough to preserve the dignity of the presidency. When it came to that last one, the Democrats were grasping at straws. The only dirt they could come up with in his entire life history was one relatively mean prep school prank (kids being mean in school? Hard to believe that happens). The bottom line was that it was 50 years prior. If you're in your 60s, do you still do things you did 50 years ago? If you're younger than 60, do you expect you'll still be doing things you did 50 years before when you get older? That's doubtful. It was a pathetic attempt.

Democrats also made an attempt to portray Romney as sexist (let's be honest, though... they do this to every Republican candidate). In the second debate on October 16, Romney told a story that illustrated his support for men and women earning equal pay for equal work. In that story, one phrase was plucked out and twisted into some kind of odd, almost perverse context. That phrase: "binders full of women."

So, here's the actual context in which it was said. It started with Obama talking about what he believed he had done on pay equity issues in the workplace (of course, Obama believed he had done a lot just by signing one executive action back in 2008). Now, it was Romney's turn. Moderator Candy Crowley asked him to talk about his history with the same issue. Here's word-for-word what Romney said:

"Thank you. And – an important topic and one which I learned a great deal about, particularly as I was serving as governor of my state, because I had the – the chance to pull together a cabinet and all the applicants seemed to be men. And I – and I went to my staff, and I said, how come all the people for these jobs are – are all men?

They said, 'well, these are the people that have the qualifications.' And I said, 'well, gosh, can't we – can't we find some – some women that are also qualified?

*And – and so we – we took a concerted effort to go out and find women who had backgrounds that could be qualified to become members of our cabinet. I went to a number of women's groups and said, can you help us find folks? **And I brought us whole binders full of – of women.** I was proud of the fact that after I staffed my cabinet and my senior staff that the University of New York in Albany did a survey of all 50 states and concluded that mine had more women in senior leadership positions than any other state in America."*[154]

"Binders full of women" got a bad rap on Twitter as being some kind of sexist trope, as if Romney was talking about hiring women to work while they were zip tied to their beds. And the Obama campaign ran with it.

"We don't have to collect a bunch of binders to find qualified, talented, driven young women ready to learn and teach in these fields right now," Obama told supporters in Mount Vernon, Iowa.[155]

Then-Vice President Joe Biden said, "What I can't understand is how he has gotten in this sort of 1950s time warp in terms of women."[156] Really? If you know anything about Joe Biden's history with women, you already know how laughable this is.

As you can see, what Romney actually said was completely inoffensive. But Democrats play dirty tricks to make Americans question what they're hearing with their own ears. They do everything they can to keep people from thinking for themselves. They know they can get away with it because most of America doesn't pay attention. This means they can take small phrases and twist the context into whatever they want it to mean, because too many Americans don't know any better.

Three weeks before that, Romney had taken another hit; when it came to getting Obama re-elected, Democrats weren't waiting until October for their October surprise. On September 17, a video was released from a private fundraiser in the home of a major Romney donor in Florida. The event, which had happened months before on May 17, had a bartender. And that bartender had secretly recorded Romney with his phone. Romney later said his remarks were an answer to a question from someone in attendance. The question was, "Do you believe in a government-centered society that provides more and more benefits? Or do you believe instead in a free enterprise society where people are able to pursue their dreams?"

Here is, word-for-word, Romney's response.

"There are 47% of the people who will vote for the president no matter what. Alright, there are 47% who are with him, who are dependent upon government, who believe that they are victims, who believe the government has a responsibility to care for

them, who believe that they are entitled to health care, to food, to housing, to you-name-it. That's an entitlement. (They think) the government should give it to them. And they will vote for this president no matter what. And I mean the president starts off with 48, 49...he starts off with a huge number. These are people who pay no income tax. 47% of Americans pay no income tax. So our message of low taxes doesn't connect. So he'll be out there talking about tax cuts for the rich...My job is not to worry about those people. I'll never convince them they should take personal responsibility and care for their lives. What I have to do is convince the 5 -10% in the center that are independents, that are thoughtful, that look at voting one way or the other depending upon, in some cases, emotion, whether they like the guy or not."[157]

Romney's remarks were called everything from a "slur"[158] and a "dagger," to "elitist" and "kibble for the political news media."[159]

The Obama campaign pounced immediately with this response: "It's shocking that a candidate for President of the United States would go behind closed doors and declare to a group of wealthy donors that half the American people view themselves as 'victims,' entitled to handouts, and are unwilling to take 'personal responsibility' for their lives. It's hard to serve as president for all Americans when you've disdainfully written off half the nation."

What do Republicans do when they get blowback like this? Too many of them put their tails between their legs, and Mitt Romney was no exception. Two weeks later on October 5, Romney walked back the entire remark with this:

"Well, clearly in a campaign, with hundreds if not thousands of speeches and question-and-answer sessions, now and then you're going to say something that doesn't come out right. In this case, I said something that's just completely wrong. And I absolutely believe, however, that my life has shown that I care about 100% and that's been demonstrated throughout my life. And this whole campaign is about the 100%."[160]

He should not have apologized. He should have stood by his words like a man — a man who wanted to be president.

Sometimes, things that fictitious presidents say in the movies would make great statements from *actual* presidents or presidential candidates. I wonder, if Romney had stood by his remarks and explained them like the president in the movie *Dave*, whether it would have worked out for him. The line is:

"If you've ever seen the look on somebody's face the day they finally get a job...they look like they could fly. And it's not about the paycheck; it's about respect, it's about looking in the mirror and knowing that you've done something valuable with your day. And if one person could start to feel this way, and then another person, and then another person, soon all these other problems may not seem so impossible. You don't really know how much you can do, until you stand up and decide to really try."[161]

Mitt Romney clearly doesn't watch enough movies.

Like all high earners, Romney understood that the government taxes the crap out of the rich (and that whether lower earners like it or not, that's just a fact). He didn't have to say it in an angry tone; that wouldn't have earned him their vote. But he could have used it as an opportunity to say the truth about taxes: If everybody paid a little, nobody would have to pay a lot. And if high earners are paying lower taxes, they can hire more employees or give raises to the employees they already have. It would have been another great opportunity to explain the benefits of trickle-down economics.

Maybe Romney didn't talk about taxes in a way most Americans could relate to. There was another candidate before the primary who did: the late Herman Cain. Cain's "999" plan – 9% income tax, 9% sales tax and 9% corporate tax – was both sensible and easy to understand. Most people didn't take it seriously, but I did. They thought he was just being entertaining; I understood how it worked.

I knew that if I had to pay 9% sales tax on everything I bought and my income tax rate was 9%, I would probably be in a slightly worse spot in terms of the taxes I paid at the time — and yet, it would be a lot more fair than the current taxation rate. No one would have to pay a lot, but everyone would have to pay something.

Herman Cain was smart, personable and lively. But Republican voters decided to go with Mr. White Wonder Bread from Massachusetts (or is it Utah? I'm not even sure anymore), and we ended up losing.

Before the 47% remark, the election was Romney's for the taking. He almost had it in the bag. Personally, I was devastated and I know a lot of others who were too. We had a great candidate and we lost. But did we channel our anger into concocting a hoax involving the Russian government? No, because that's not how Republicans think. What's funny is that we probably could have, because Barack Obama himself mocked Romney's concerns about Russia on the debate stage: "The 1980s called; they're now asking to get their foreign policy back..."[162] (that's not so funny anymore, is it?). The truth is, Mitt Romney was right all along when he said Russia was America's biggest geopolitical foe. Well, maybe he was half-right; there is one other country that proved they wanted that title for themselves, and that would be China. The person who saw it from the beginning is the president who came after Obama. He's the one who was later blamed for everything both Russia and China did. Who are we kidding...he was blamed for everything, period.

The 2016 Election

When campaigning for the primary kicked off in 2015, Republicans started with an insanely large field of 17 candidates:

1. Texas Senator Ted Cruz
2. Florida Senator Marco Rubio
3. Businessman Donald Trump
4. Ohio Governor John Kasich
5. Dr. Ben Carson
6. Former New York Governor George Pataki
7. Former Florida Governor Jeb Bush
8. Kentucky Senator Rand Paul
9. Former Arkansas Governor Mike Huckabee

10. Businesswoman Carly Fiorina
11. New Jersey Governor Chris Christie
12. Former Virginia Governor Jim Gilmore
13. Former Pennsylvania Senator Rick Santorum
14. South Carolina Senator Lindsey Graham
15. Former Louisiana Governor Bobby Jindhal
16. Wisconsin Governor Scott Walker
17. Former Texas Governor Rick Perry

Like most conservatives, I was only impressed by a handful of them. In chronological order, they were:

Scott Walker—I was interested in the early buzz around Scott Walker, having just finished his book that detailed the way he turned things around in Wisconsin (most notably, the way he took on the teachers' unions). I thought, here's a guy who could do this for the whole country. But it wasn't meant to be. For one thing, Walker was one of the last to enter the race (July 2015 shouldn't be considered "late" — but for the 2016 election, it was).

Rick Perry—Perry was the smart, popular and dynamic governor of the largest state in the continental U.S., but he was not without controversy. He had a property tax plan that funded a policy allowing illegal immigrants to attend state universities at the in-state tuition rate. The press called the property tax plan a "subject of confusion" that was "at the expense of renters," and conservatives were outraged that he gave the tuition break to non-citizens (even though, as Perry said, the students who were here illegally were paying sales and property taxes; remember, those are the only taxes anyone pays in Texas because there is no state income tax). Perry also didn't have the best luck as a presidential candidate the first time he ran in 2012, with a comical moment on the debate stage that revealed he didn't work well under pressure. When asked to name the three bureaucratic agencies he would eliminate as president, Perry could only name two. He literally said "oops" on the debate stage. That did him in, and he didn't come back with enough of a vengeance the next time around.

Dr. Ben Carson—When I saw Dr. Carson speak at an event in 2015, the first thing I recall him saying was, "Political correctness will be the end of the United States." That's to the best of my recollection – but if he did indeed say that, it was pretty damn correct as we are now seeing it happen with cancel culture and wokeism. His first time in front of a national audience was at the National Prayer Breakfast in 2013. That's where he got the attention of people, and he used his platform to promote a tax system that would be based on the biblical concept of tithing. After all: If God only wants 10% from us, why should the government want more?[163] I couldn't care less about a candidate's skin color. I care about intelligence. Ben Carson, who is an actual neurosurgeon, has it. There were plenty who mocked him for going on to work in the Trump cabinet, and maybe the *real* racists are those people.

Carly Fiorina—While she was still running Hewlett-Packard, Fiorina spoke at a business conference I attended. She didn't seem to have any presidential ambitions at the time. I had never heard of her before; all I knew was this lady made sense as a business leader, and I've always believed the country should be run like a business. She talked about using technology to advance federal policy. Holding up an iPhone, she said something like (and please understand this is based on my best recollection, "We didn't even have one of these things until seven years ago" (this was in 2014). She proceeded to talk about the power of technology in business and how our government could learn from that. Listening to Carly Fiorina, I thought this: If we're going to have a woman president, let's have a smart one.

Ted Cruz—He would have been in this slot, but for the fact that he was born in Canada. The argument was, does he qualify as a naturalized citizen? There was a lot of debate surrounding that based on the combination of Cruz's birthplace (Canada) and his father's birthplace (Cuba). Cruz's mother was born in the United States (Delaware). But I thought, if there was a question about Obama, then wouldn't there be a question here? And I stood by it, because I'm consistent.

Donald Trump—I didn't think he was serious at first. But I thought that if more people took him seriously, myself included, there was some incredible potential there. Recently, I was reminded of something I tweeted on June 2, 2015: *If people would take this man seriously, they would see jobs created, wealth built & freedom preserved.* Two weeks later on June 16, he announced his campaign. He was indeed serious, and I was pleasantly surprised.

I acknowledge that Trump was somewhat petty. But he was saying all the stuff that the rest of us already thought. There's a great line from the movie *The Contender*, where the fictitious president character says this:

"Napoleon once said, when asked to explain the lack of great statesmen in the world, that 'to get power you need to display absolute pettiness; to exercise power you need to show true greatness.' Such pettiness and such greatness are rarely found in one person."[164]

That pettiness, and that greatness, were found in Donald Trump.

By the time all the polished politicians had dropped out, he was the last one standing. The ones who promised they'd be "in it until the convention" (Fiorina) didn't keep that promise, despite how much money had been raised to stay the course (not to mention that Fiorina had her own giant net worth). Fiorina dropped out in February. The most polished politicians of the bunch, Cruz and Kasich, stayed in until May (mostly because they hated Trump). But they saw the writing on the wall.

I saw that Trump thinks like I think. He thinks like many of you think. Dr. Carson's remark about political correctness was something that Trump already understood. He was the only other person, out of 17 candidates, who really seemed to understand that while also saying what average Americans already had on their minds.

Those of us who were tired of being lectured by Barack Obama every time foreign terrorists killed our citizens (off *and* on our soil) and who saw how many of Obama's failures led to the rise of ISIS...those of us who were concerned about the criminal waves that came with illegal immigration...those of us who were tired of hearing the "giant sucking sound" Perot warned about back in the 90s as our jobs were being sent overseas...Trump made sense

to us. We understood that he didn't always say the most popular thing, but that sometimes you have to call a spade a spade.
Donald Trump called out all the spades, all the time.

Yes, he said everything that came into his head. I am also a guy
who says everything that comes into his head. I'm also not the
only American who identified with him. In 2016, there were
62,985,106 Americans who sent a message that they identified
with him, too.

For a lot of us, supporting Trump wasn't just about populism,
or wanting a president who understood business negotiations
— or, even the fact that we were craving a strong leader after
eight years of having a weak one. It was also about the fact that
Hillary Clinton is a terrible person. She just *is*. And obviously, her
husband is too. If you are the slightest bit inclined to feel sorry
for Hillary Clinton's loss (and the sad, embarrassing way she
explained it away for the entire four years Trump was president),
ponder these questions.

- How many people who have gotten in the Clintons' way
  over 30+ years have been "suicided"? We can't say for
  sure, but I have a pretty comprehensive list on my website. It was well-researched, and its count for the total
  mysterious deaths surrounding the Clintons is 55 (56
  if you count Jeffery Epstein). Go to EdHoffman.net/
  Clinton-Casualties, and prepare to be amazed. You may
  have seen some of this list before, but you don't find it
  in this well-organized format elsewhere.[165]
- How many Americans serving our country died in
  Benghazi, Libya on September 11, 2012? The answer
  is four: Ambassador Chris Stevens, Information
  Officer Sean Smith, and Navy SEALs Glen Doherty and
  Tyrone Woods.
- How many times did Hillary express her callousness
  toward the Obama administration's lies surrounding
  those deaths in Benghazi, to the point that she lashed
  out at a Republican senator: "What difference, at
  this point, does it make?"[166] The answer is one. It's
  one too many.

- How many Haitians, whose tiny country was devastated by a hurricane in 2010, were promised employment and housing opportunities that never came because of the failures of the Clinton Foundation? The answer is 60,000 that were promised employment, and 40,000 that were promised housing. Remember when Hillary Clinton said "just text this number" to send $10 to Haiti? Where did all that money go? The people of Haiti say it didn't go to them.[167]

- How many millions of dollars does the Clintons' daughter make to do...well, what exactly *does* she do? The actual amount she makes for being Vice Chair of the Clinton Foundation is technically zero[168] — but without that position, would she be "qualified" to sit on a corporate board for $9 million a year (which she does)?[169] You already know the answer. Even the New York Times allowed an op-ed before the election that admitted "the foundation is being used to further Chelsea's career and financial ambitions."[170] Of course, now we know that it isn't only the Clintons who do this. Joe Biden also figured out how to use this same model of using a charitable foundation as a front to enrich your family. But I guess that doesn't matter. It only matters what the president's kids do when the president is a Republican.

Unlike the Clintons, Trump couldn't be bought. Unlike Obama, Trump cared about America first. Unlike any president we've seen since Ronald Reagan, Trump operated from a position of strength.

Trump understood what Obama was too disloyal to our country to say: Although not all Muslims were terrorists killing Americans, all terrorists killing Americans were Muslims. Obama called ISIS a "death cult,"[171] but what about Al Qaeda? What about the Taliban? Trump tried to stop the bleeding (literally) by implementing a travel ban from eight Muslim-majority countries, and he was called racist for doing it (but by that time, his supporters were just used to everything he did being labeled as racist. That's why so many people embraced the term "deplorables").

As for running the country like a business, where do you start? Trump saw that if you're doing bad international trade, that's bad for everybody. In California, we saw what the original NAFTA agreement did to the people who grow our food. I personally know avocado farmers impacted by it. They're unable to harvest and sell their crops until Mexico has harvested and sold all of theirs, because Mexico undercuts their prices (something that's easy to do when your country doesn't have a Food and Drug Administration). That's how "free" the North American Free Trade Agreement is.

Look at the Accomplishments

Trump cut taxes for businesses and showed the critics that trickle-down economics really does work. He created 6.6 million jobs in his first three years, a 4.4% increase over the 152.2 million people working at the end of Obama's term. He bravely entered a trade war with China, because he understood that tariffs have a trickle-down effect too. He understood that by creating tax incentives to expand business, you create jobs; after all, you can't cut taxes for people who don't pay them in the first place (although Joe Biden sure is trying).

Trump reinstated American energy independence. Barack Obama went back and forth on drilling in the Arctic National Wildlife Refuge (ANWR) of Alaska multiple times, only to put an end to it for the remainder of his administration in 2015.[172] Alaska Senator Lisa Murkowski (often called a "Republican in Name Only" for her habit of siding with Democrats) did not take kindly to this move and its negative impact on the economy of her state. "I cannot understand why this administration is willing to negotiate with Iran, but not Alaska," she said.[173]

Former governor Sarah Palin – someone who knows a thing or two about Alaska – was asked about ANWR while running for vice president in 2008, right around the time she made "drill baby drill" a conservative catchphrase. "It's about 2,000 acres...2,000 acres out of 20 million acres," she told interviewer Maria Bartiromo. When Bartiromo asked her if comparing ANWR's footprint on Alaska to "a stamp on a football field" was a good analogy, Palin responded, "That's pretty accurate." She said there were "a lot of misconceptions about ANWR," such as the idea that drilling would impact the mating of the caribou. "Let's look at lessons learned over the last 30 years," she said, "when the Trans-Alaska oil pipeline was finally allowed to be built and there were the threats then, and the fears that the caribou herds would diminish and die off. No, the caribou herds are actually thriving. They're flourishing. There have not been adverse impacts on the caribou herds. So we anticipate the same thing as we tap more energy supplies up on the north slope in ANWR." Palin also pointed out that modern drilling technology allows for "directional drilling" that reduces the environmental impact of extracting oil.[174]

I thought Democrats *loved* technology. When it doesn't serve their purpose, they ignore it.

During his first year in office, Trump worked with Republicans to finally succeed at allowing the U.S. to drill for oil in ANWR. Republicans had been trying to make it happen since 1977 on their own, attempting to vote on it almost 50 times over 40 years.[175] Finally, they succeeded by including it in the Tax Cuts and Jobs Act of 2017— and they had Donald Trump to thank for it.

They can also thank him for removing restrictions on phase IV of the Keystone pipeline (the project phase that's become known as the Keystone XL pipeline). By doing this, Trump once again reversed one of Obama's previous attempts to stop America from becoming energy independent. Unfortunately, Joe Biden later reversed it right back.

Obama announced this attempt with a statement in the Roosevelt Room on November 6, 2015. It included this dubious sentiment: "The State Department has decided that the Keystone XL Pipeline would not serve the national interest of the United States. I agree with that decision." [176]

It *wouldn't serve our national interest?* Why not? It seems like a project that would create 11,000 American jobs is the very definition of serving our national interest. But not to Democrats, I guess. They'd much rather those people depended on the government for their living. At the time, the State Department was being led by John Kerry; today, he is Joe Biden's "Special Presidential Envoy for Climate" (nice job title). Today, we have him to thank for the current status of Keystone XL. More on that in a minute.

Under President Trump, our oil production increased in five key states: Texas, Oklahoma, New Mexico, North Dakota and Colorado.[177] In September 2019, we became a net exporter of petroleum (this includes crude oil and petroleum products used for distillate fuel, motor gasoline and jet fuel) because of Trump's energy reforms.[178] This was the first time our nation became a net petroleum exporter since monthly records began in 1973. By November 2019, the United States was exporting 772,000 barrels per day more petroleum than it imported.

This accomplishment was summed up nicely by Congressman John Joyce (R-PA), who represents Americans in the heart of the Coal Region. He celebrated the milestone in an op-ed, writing:

Under President Trump's leadership, America is energy independent for the first time in my lifetime. Rather than staying reliant on foreign nations, today we are a net exporter of American-made energy.[179]

Undoing with the Stroke of a Pen

Now, Joe Biden is undoing these accomplishments with the stroke of a pen. On his first day in office, the new president signed 17 executive orders. One of them placed a moratorium on drilling in ANWR *and* immediately halted construction of the Keystone XL pipeline by revoking the project's construction permit. The action is called Executive Order on Protecting Public Health and the Environment and Restoring Science to Tackle the Climate Crisis. Here are two excerpts:

1. (On ANWR): *The Secretary of the Interior shall...place a temporary moratorium on all activities of the Federal Government relating to the implementation of the Coastal Plain Oil and Gas Leasing Program...in the Arctic National Wildlife Refuge. The Secretary shall review the program and...conduct a new, comprehensive analysis*

of the potential environmental impacts of the oil and gas program.

2. (On Keystone XL): *The Permit is hereby revoked. Leaving the Keystone XL pipeline permit in place would not be consistent with my Administration's economic and climate imperatives.*[180]

Now we know what a Special Presidential Envoy for Climate does. Thanks, John Kerry.

The goal is to reverse Trump's policies one by one until his entire agenda is wiped out, and we're supposed to be *so* grateful it's happening. I don't know a single person who's grateful for any of it. Do you?

Like Ronald Reagan, Trump understood that government is the problem. That's why he removed government regulations. That's why he talked about draining the swamp. That's what he meant by making America great again.

I don't think Donald Trump stole that famous campaign slogan from Ronald Reagan. I think, in 1980, Reagan was forecasting the future. For those four years – the Trump years – that future was bright.

Why It All Matters

My passion for politics isn't really about politics at all. By definition, politics are just the activities involved with people making decisions in groups (and usually those groups involve government). What I'm actually passionate about is helping people see how what happens in government affects their real lives.

There's nothing wrong with caring about sports, but how do the things that happen with your team affect what happens with your life? Unless you actually work for the team, they don't. If people spent a little less time on that and redirected it toward what goes on with the people who run our government and make our laws, they'd understand their own situations a lot better. They might even have an easier time improving the way they live. In order to do that, you have to know how the government dictates the way we live. That includes the government of your state *and* our federal government.

Maybe you close your eyes to it because it puts you in a bad mood. It puts me in a bad mood, too. But these things are too important to ignore. The things of the present will affect the future — so if you aren't yet plugged in to what's going on in government and politics, now is the time to get plugged in. What happens there is what dictates some of the most important aspects of your life, your children's lives and their children's lives. If you care about that, you'll care about your government.

CHAPTER 28

"What the hell did I know about California? For some people it was still a place of hopes and dreams, a chance to start over. The idea was: if you could get there everything would be okay, and if it wasn't okay there, well, it probably wasn't going to be okay anywhere."[181]
- Kalifornia, 1993

NO MATTER HOW many homes my wife and I buy, California is still where our "headquarters" are.

I still believe it's the most all-around perfect state in terms of geographical beauty: weather, beaches, mountains...California has it all.

The problem is this: Along with all that, you get crazy people who live here with no concern for anything other than today and no concern for anyone but themselves. As for the politicians who govern this state, they continue to look the other way when it comes to California's homelessness and illegal immigration problems, both of which have gotten completely out of control.

I see five ways California can return to greatness:

1. Change the leadership. Now that virtually all of Southern California has pockets of tent cities that serve as offshoots of LA's Skid Row – and, people have finally had enough after more than a year of overreach on COVID restrictions – there's a recall election taking place to remove the out-of-touch, hypocritical Governor Gavin Newsom. Hopefully, it works — the problem is, that as of the time of this writing, we have nobody inspirational enough, strong enough or competent enough in the running.

2. Reverse us back to a law and order state. For those of us who work hard, live decent lives and follow the law, we see the criminals, the very people who have tanked our quality of life, running the show. Stop releasing them from prison in the name of social justice. Stop releasing them to keep things peaceful in the prisons. They need to *stay* in the prisons in order to keep things peaceful on our streets. Seriously, which is more important? And finally, do something about the criminal aliens who kill our residents. Some of them have been deported multiple times, only to return over and over before committing murder. Why don't we build prisons to keep them locked up *here*, never to hurt another Californian? That brings me to the next one.

3. Get control of illegal immigration. This is a nationwide problem, as anyone paying attention in Joe Biden's America can attest. But right now, the country's focus is on the border of Texas. Why not the border of California? Could it be because after decades of California governors who turned a blind eye to illegal immigration, we somehow "deserve" for our migrant crisis to be ignored? Right now, migrants who come over the border through San Diego County are being detained in "shelters" that are actually entertainment arenas, like the Long Beach Convention Center. As a kid, I used to go see bands like Journey, UFO, Styx and The Eagles play there. Now, it's a detention facility for unaccompanied kids whose parents paid the cartels to literally throw them over the border fence with no regard to safety (you may recall that fence could have been a wall, if federal judges in California weren't constantly blocking the last President from getting it done. It's harder to throw a child over a 50 foot wall than a 20 foot fence, but judges like to pretend that all migrant kids come here with caring parents who can't be separated from them. That's one of the biggest lies about illegal immigration there is). California's leaders do nothing about any of this, because it doesn't affect them. Here's an idea: Maybe the U.S. State Department should bus thousands of migrants up to Sacramento instead. It's amazing how people can change their minds once something is happening in their own backyards. But for the time being, in the towns where the current influx of migrants will ultimately settle (some of them in my local area of Riverside County), we will see crime skyrocket over the next two years. I'm counting on it.

4. Stop giving everything away to the unproductive and dishonest. In 2020, Gavin Newsom more than doubled the California Earned Income Tax Credit (CalEITC) for low income Californians. There was also a $600 payment available to those earning $75,000 or less who filed their taxes using an Individual Taxpayer Identification Number (an ITIN, which is an alternative to a Social Security number designed to enable illegal immigrants to work here). Tax breaks for middle income people are one thing — but in 2021, California tax filers who earned less than $30,000 in 2020 *also* got a one-time payment of $600 from a program called the Golden State Stimulus. You can work a $14 an hour job for 40 hours a week and make around $29,000. You can also lie on your taxes or make money illegally and have the same income on paper. Either way, it's costing California taxpayers $1.6 billion.

5. Make the state business friendly again. California needs to attract more businesses back here. Because trickle-down economics *does in fact work*, a healthy economy will trickle down to new workers employed by these businesses. But businesses are being driven out by high taxes, insane regulations and unreasonable employment laws that do nothing to protect employers from unscrupulous employees. I have personally spent $40,000 to settle a single employee grievance, and I'm not a bad employer. Plus, the rampant homelessness all over the state is forcing businesses to close (as it turns out, people don't like to shop and dine at establishments with full blown tent cities on their sidewalks). How did it get this way? You can blame it on the "war on drugs" all you want, but other factors are in play here too. One friend told me a story about looking at properties in San Antonio, Texas. He asked a local how they deal with their homelessness problems. "We don't have a homeless problem," the person said. "Instead of 20 people giving the homeless $5, we put our money together and buy them a $98 bus ticket to California." He was dead serious, and I'm willing to bet that if people are doing that in Texas, they're doing it in Arizona and New Mexico too.

Everyone likes to think about what they'd do if they were in charge of the company they work for or the places they live in. If I were governor of California, I would:

1. Triple the number of law enforcement officers in the state. No one wants to live in a lawless shithole where you can't go to the grocery store at night without a concealed firearm, except for gang members. They're the ones making it that way.

2. Make it an open carry state. Bad guys with guns can't get away with crime when they're surrounded by good guys with guns. It works in Arizona, Texas and other open carry states.

3. Overhaul the tax code. Get rid of ridiculous tax rates, the gas tax and the state income tax. I would create a statewide sales tax where no one has to pay 13.3% to the state, but no one gets to pay zero either. This would stop people from cheating on their taxes virtually overnight, and the federal government should adopt the same policy.

4. Break off the contract with California Teachers Association. This is what Scott Walker did with the teachers unions in Wisconsin back in 2011. It's as simple as this: Make teachers accountable for teaching. If they don't teach, they get fired.

5. No more fake droughts. No one is buying it; we have the Pacific Ocean right next to us. Stop dumping cash into some high speed rail to nowhere train, and invest in desalination so we never have a water shortage again. Keep the Central Valley watered so it produces fruits and vegetables to feed our people and uphold California's well-earned title of "the breadbasket of the world." Every time there's a statewide campaign where we're encouraged to kill our lawns, cities like Beverly Hills are exempt. Gee, I wonder why?

6. Fix our terrible roads. Hire private companies to repair our crumbling, pothole-ridden roads. Incentivize them to do it quickly and with minimal disruption to traffic, since Cal-Trans can't seem to accomplish this. Everything the government does takes 10 times as long for 100 hundred times the price, while private companies can be incentivized to execute projects more efficiently. Here's an example: In 1993, Orange County hired private contractors to construct The Toll Roads (the Transportation Authority's marketing name for California State Route 241). The county incentivized the contractors to complete the project early with this arrangement: For every day they finished early, they would be able to keep that many days' worth of toll fees. In 1997, the annual toll revenue was $6,636,326. If they finished the project one year early, I'd say that's a pretty good incentive — and I have it on good authority that they finished more than a year early, so that's an even *better* incentive.

7. Support our police. Stop paying off the families of criminals who think death by cop is a cheap life insurance policy for their families to cash in on.

These are just off the top of my head. I'm sure I could come up with more; lots of thinking Californians could, because we are all fed up. Dawn and I now have homes in Arizona and Montana, so we can get out anytime we need to for as long as we want to in order to escape the insanity. But most Californians don't have that luxury.

And no, I'm not running for governor. But anyone who does needs to embrace these objectives in order to have a fighting chance of winning the election and saving this state.

CHAPTER 29

SOME PEOPLE VIEW success like the Emerald City, a place where they envision:

- All their work will be done.
- All their dreams will have come true.
- And a lifetime of wisdom will have been accumulated.

But the truth is, success is achieved along the yellow brick road. It's the journey, not the destination. It's learning from all experiences – your own *and* those of others – as you travel along the path.

Over my six decades of life, I've come to understand that success comes down to some simple strategies. Here they are, in order of importance.

Be Healthy.

You want to provide for your family, and that means making money. But you can't make money if you can't influence people, and you can't influence people if your brain isn't healthy, and your brain isn't healthy if your body isn't healthy. So you have to eat well and exercise, and do it consistently. It sounds simple, but how many people don't do it? Exactly. That's why it comes first.

Additionally, part of staying healthy (mentally, emotionally and spiritually healthy) is spending time with your family and friends while doing things you enjoy. If your life is out of balance, your body isn't healthy. I guarantee it. I also guarantee that while you're working on becoming successful, a portion of your life *will* be out of balance. So be aware of that.

Make Money.

After accomplishing physical health, you can start making money. If you're a big picture person, that's great – but remember that you can't change the world if you can't afford to eat.

So, focus on your end game and what it will take to get you there.

- Don't make decisions too quickly.
- Think things through, but be actionable.
- Stick to your plan, but be flexible.
- Understand some things are fluid, and you may need to adjust the plan if something isn't working out.

No matter what your career field is, that's the mindset you need to be in to start succeeding financially. And remember: You don't *need* money. You only need the things money can provide. Understanding that distinction can help you stay on track.

Pay Attention.

Success requires you to stay plugged in to what's going on around you – in your family, in your industry and in the world. So, keep your eyes open and your brain turned on. There are many small ways you can practice this in your daily life. Some easy examples:

- If you see a social media headline, read the full story. Don't comment or share it until you have read it in its entirety and are sure you fully understand the content.
- Watch the news. If you love sports, fine; watch the news *before* you watch sports. If this becomes your routine, you might start enjoying it.
- When you're watching the news, listen to what's being said. Who cares what the anchor is wearing? Who cares what's running on the ticker at the bottom of the screen? If it was important, they'd be talking about it. Focus on the reporting, and learn to separate facts

from opinion. Learn to look at the facts on all sides, and then *you* decide what the truth is based on what makes sense to you. Always consider the source, and don't drink the Kool-Aid. Just because it's on the internet (or yes, even on TV) doesn't mean it's true.

Finally, success is about taking action. Remember the guy I met at my first conference – the one who banged out pages and pages of notes on his clipboard and bragged that he'd been to "hundreds" of events...then, admitted he was still "getting ready" to buy his first property?

Don't be like him. He's always "getting ready" to do something. He says things like, "I'm almost ready...I'm almost there."

"Almost" is a way of life for almost everyone in America. You can be the exception — the one who *does* something, who *is* ready, and who *gets* there.

You've heard the expression "the fruits of my labor." Everybody wants the fruits, but not everybody wants to put in the labor. If you can put the labor in, you'll get the fruits. And you'll enjoy them more, because you earned them. I'll bet on someone with people skills and work ethic to beat out someone with a college degree and talent any day. Hard work wins when talent won't work hard.

Hopefully, the experiences here can guide you on your way.

ENDNOTES

1. Danny DeVito, Other People's Money, directed by Norman Jewison (1991; Burbank, CA: Warner Brothers), DVD.
2. Steve Martin, Grand Canyon, directed by Lawrence Kasdan (1991; Century City, CA: 20th Century Fox), DVD.
3. Rudy Ruettiger, "Motivational Keynote Presentation" (speech, Scottsdale, AZ, August 2012).
4. Andy Garcia, Hero, directed by Stephen Frears (1992; Culver City, CA: Columbia Pictures), DVD.
5. Jack Nicholson, A Few Good Men, directed by Aaron Sorkin (1992; Beverly Hills, CA: Castle Rock Entertainment), DVD.
6. Steve Martin, Leap of Faith, directed by Richard Pearce (1992; Hollywood, CA: Paramount Pictures), DVD.
7. Tom Hanks, A League of Their Own, directed by Penny Marshall (1992; Culver City, CA: Columbia Pictures), DVD.
8. Ann Margaret, Grumpy Old Men, directed by Donald Petrie (1993; Burbank, CA: Warner Bros.), DVD.
9. Michael J. Fox, The American President, directed by Rob Reiner (1995; Universal City, CA: Universal Pictures), DVD.
10. Ed Harris, The Truman Show, directed by Peter Weir (1998; Hollywood, CA: Paramount Pictures), DVD.
11. Al Pacino, Any Given Sunday, directed by Oliver Stone (1999; Burbank, CA: Warner Bros.), DVD.
12. Joan Allen, The Contender, directed by Rod Lurie (2000; Universal City, CA: DreamWorks), DVD.
13. Barry Pepper, The 25th Hour, directed by Spike Lee (2002, Burbank, CA: Buena Vista Pictures/Disney), DVD.
14. Kevin Kline, The Emperor's Club, directed by Michael Hoffman (2002; Universal City, CA: Universal Pictures), DVD.
15. Albert Finney, Big Fish, directed by Tim Burton (2003; Culver City, CA: Columbia Pictures), DVD.
16. Tom Cruise, The Last Samurai, directed by Edward Zwick (2003; Burbank, CA: Warner Bros.), DVD.
17. Billy Bob Thornton, Friday Night Lights, directed by Peter Berg (2004; Universal City, CA: Universal Pictures), DVD.
18. Leonardo DiCaprio, The Aviator, directed by Martin Scorsese (2004; Burbank, CA: Warner Bros.), DVD.
19. Kirsten Dunst, Elizabethtown, directed by Cameron Crowe (2005; Hollywood, CA: Paramount Pictures), DVD.
20. Albert Finney, A Good Year, directed by Ridley Scott (2006; Century City, CA: 20th Century Fox), DVD.
21. Greg Kinnear and Paige Turco, Invincible, directed by Ericson Core (2006; Burbank, CA: Buena Vista Pictures/Disney), DVD.
22. Denzel Washington, The Great Debaters, directed by Robert, Eisele (2007; Chicago, Illinois: Harpo Productions), DVD.

23. Bruce McGill, Law Abiding Citizen, directed by F. Gary Gray (2009; Beverly Hills, CA: Overture Films), DVD.

24. Sandra Bullock, The Blind Side, directed by John Lee Hancock (2009; Burbank, CA: Warner Bros.), DVD.

25. Meryl Streep, The Iron Lady, directed by Phyllida Lloyd (2011; Century City, CA: 20th Century Fox), DVD.

26. Gerard Butler, Chasing Mavericks, directed by Michael Apted (2012; Century City, CA: 20th Century Fox), DVD.

27. Ben Reed, American Sniper, directed by Clint Eastwood (2014; Burbank, CA: Warner Bros.), DVD.

28. Emma Stone, The Birdman, directed by Alejandro G. Iñárritu (2014; Los Angeles, CA: Searchlight Pictures Corporation), DVD.

29. Brad Pitt, The Big Short, directed by Adam McKay (2015; Hollywood, CA: Paramount Pictures), DVD.

30. James Badge Dale, 13 Hours: The Secret Soldiers of Benghazi, directed by Michael Bay (2016; Hollywood, CA: Paramount Pictures), DVD.

31. Julia Butters, Once Upon a Time in Hollywood, directed by Quentin Tarantino (2019; Culver City, CA: Sony Pictures Releasing), DVD.

32.-33. Sylvester Stallone, Rocky, directed by John G. Avildsen (1976; Beverly Hills, CA: United Artists), DVD.

34.-35. Sylvester Stallone, Rocky IV, directed by Sylvester Stallone (1985; Beverly Hills, CA; MGM), DVD.

36. Carl Weathers, Rocky IV, directed by Sylvester Stallone (1985; Beverly Hills, CA; MGM), DVD.

37. Sylvester Stallone, Rocky Balboa, directed by Sylvester Stallone (2006; Culver City, CA: Sony Pictures Releasing), DVD.

38. Jack Nicholson, A Few Good Men, directed by Aaron Sorkin (1992; Beverly Hills, CA: Castle Rock Entertainment), DVD.

39. George Clooney, Up in the Air, directed by Jason Reitman (2009; Universal City, CA: DreamWorks), DVD.

40. Rami Malek, Bohemian Rhapsody, directed by Bryan Singer (2018; Century City, CA: 20th Century Fox), DVD.

41. Lou Ferrigno, Speakers Inc. Speakers Bureau, https://www.speakinc.com/speakers/lou-ferrigno/

42. Bill Pullman, Independence Day, directed by Roland Emmerich (1996; Century City, CA: 20th Century Fox), DVD.

43. Thomas Jefferson, et al, Copy of Declaration of Independence (1776).

44. Mark Olsen, "'Wolf of Wall Street's' excess, corruption hit a nerve," Los Angeles Times, January 1, 2014.

45. Booth, Philip. "…And the Pursuit of Happiness; Wellbeing and the Role of Government." The Institute for Economic Affairs, January 2012, https://www.researchgate.net/publication/228198469_and_the_Pursuit_of_Happiness_-_Wellbeing_and_the_Role_of_Government.

46. David Cameron, Google Zeitgeist Europe conference, Watford, UK, 2006.

47. Stossel, "Pursuit of Happiness," 2012, https://www.youtube.com/watch?v=pBr73Q13kE4.

48. David Spade, Tommy Boy, directed by Peter Segal (1995; Hollywood, CA: Paramount Pictures), DVD.

49. Karen Hutto, "How A.L. Williams Changed the Life Insurance Industry," review of Coach: The A.L. Williams Story by Arthur Williams, Amazon, August 2006.

50. Ron Dean, Cocktail, directed by Roger Donaldson (1988; Burbank, CA: Buena Vista Pictures/Disney), DVD.

51. Ron White, I Had the Right to Remain Silent, But I Didn't Have the Ability. New York: Dutton Books, 2006.

52. Anthony Hopkins, The Edge, directed by Lee Tamahori (1997; Century City, CA: 20th Century Fox), DVD.

53. Ray Liotta, Field of Dreams, directed by Phil Alden Robinson (1989; Universal City, CA: Universal Pictures), DVD.

54. "What is Consultative Selling?", Richardson Sales Performance, https://www.richardson.com/sales-resources/defining-consultative-sales/.

55. Dale Dauten, "Master Seller Tells Pully Success Secret, for a Price," Chicago Tribune, February 12, 1996.

56. Jeff Goldblum, Jurassic Park, directed by Steven Spielberg (1993; Universal City, CA: Universal Pictures), DVD.

57. "About NMLS," NMLS Resource Center, Nationwide Multistate Licensing System, https://nationwidelicensingsystem.org/about.

58. Leo Anthony Gallagher Jr., Gallagher: Over Your Head, directed by Joe Hostettler (1984; Beaumont, Texas), DVD.

59. Charles S. Dutton, Against the Ropes, directed by Charles S. Dutton (2004; Universal City, CA: Universal Pictures), DVD.

60. Josh Sanburn, "A Famous Quote Misquoted," TIME magazine, February 4, 2011, http://content.time.com/time/specials/packages/article/0,28804,2046390_2046393_2046512,00.html.

61. Alec Baldwin, Glengarry Glen Ross, directed by James Foley (1992; Burbank, CA: New Line Cinema, DVD).

62. Michael Douglas, Wall Street, directed by Oliver Stone (1987; Century City, CA: 20th Century Fox), DVD.

63. Hillary Clinton, campaign event for Martha Coakley, October 2014.

64. Danny DeVito, Other People's Money, directed by Norman Jewison (1991; Burbank, CA: Warner Brothers), DVD.

65. Eddie Kay Thomas, American Pie, directed by Paul Weitz (1999; Universal City, CA: Universal Pictures), DVD.

66. Reg Rogers, Primal Fear, directed by Gregory Hobbit (1996; Hollywood, CA: Paramount Pictures), DVD.

67. Robert Guillaume, The Lion King, directed by Roger Allers and Rob Minkoff (1994; Burbank, CA: Buena Vista Pictures/Disney), DVD.

68.-69. Danny DeVito, Other People's Money, directed by Norman Jewison (1991; Burbank, CA: Warner Brothers), DVD.

70. Al Pacino, Two for the Money, directed by D.J. Caruso (2005; Universal City, CA: Universal Pictures), DVD.

71. Tagline, movie poster. Tommy Boy, directed by Peter Segal (1995; Hollywood, CA: Paramount Pictures), DVD.

72. "Setting the Record Straight: Six Years of Unheeded Warnings for GSE Reform," President George W. Bush, White House Archives, last modified October 2008, https://georgew-bush-whitehouse.archives.gov/news/releases/2008/10/20081009-10.html.

73. Karl Rove, "President Bush Tried to Rein in Fan and Fred," Wall Street Journal, January 8, 2009, https://www.wsj.com/articles/SB123137220550562585.

74. "No. 23 of the Subprime 25: Greenpoint Mortgage Funding Inc./Capital One Financial Corp," Who's Behind the Financial Meltdown?, The Center for Public Integrity, last modified May 19, 2014, https://publicintegrity.org/inequality-poverty-opportunity/no-23-of-the-subprime-25-greenpoint-mortgage-funding-inc-capital-one-financial-corp/.

75. Al Yoon, "Alt-A pioneer lays low as mortgage market seizes," Reuters, August 10, 2007, https://www.reuters.com/article/instant-article/idUSN1021905920070810.

76. Chris Isidore, "10 years ago: IndyMac collapses and starts a flood of bank failures," A Decade Later, CNN Money, July 11, 2018, https://money.cnn.com/2018/07/11/news/companies/indymac-failure/index.html.

77. Peter Wallison, "Hey, Barney Frank: The Government Did Cause the Housing Crisis," The Atlantic, December 13, 2011, https://www.theatlantic.com/business/archive/2011/12/hey-barney-frank-the-government-did-cause-the-housing-crisis/249903/.

78. Phil Gramm and Mike Solon, "The Clinton-Era Roots of the Financial Crisis," Wall Street Journal, August 12, 2013, https://www.wsj.com/articles/SB10001424127887323477604579000571 334113350.
79. Karl Rove, Mortgage Bankers Conference address, San Francisco, 2008.
80. Andrew Miga, "Rep. Frank helped partner land Fannie Mae job," Associated Press, May 26, 2011, http://archive.boston.com/news/local/massachusetts/articles/2011/05/26/rep_frank_helped_partner_land_fannie_mae_job/.
81. "DC's Most Influential Gay Couple Calls it Quits," Associated Press, July 3, 1998.
82. Morgenr, "Barney Frank in 2005: What Housing Bubble?, https://www.youtube.com/watch?v=iW5qKYfqALE.
83. Jeff Jacoby, "Frank's fingerprints are all over the financial fiasco," Boston Globe, September 28, 2008, http://archive.boston.com/bostonglobe/editorial_opinion/oped/articles/2008/09/28/franks_fingerprints_are_all_over_the_financial_fiasco/.
84. Michael Douglas, Wall Street, directed by Oliver Stone (1987; Century City, CA: 20th Century Fox), DVD.
85. Noelle Knox, "43% of first-time homebuyers put no money down," USA Today, January 18, 2006, https://usatoday30.usatoday.com/money/perfi/housing/2006-01-17-real-estate-us-at_x.htm.
86. Edmund L. Andrews and Louis Uchitelle, "Rescues for Homeowners in Debt Weighed," New York Times, February 22, 2008, https://www.nytimes.com/2008/02/22/business/22homes.html.
87. Russell Crowe, A Good Year, directed by Ridley Scott (2006; Century City, CA: 20th Century Fox), DVD.
88. Les Christie, "Foreclosures up a record 81% in 2008," CNN Money, January 15, 2009, https://money.cnn.com/2009/01/15/real_estate/millions_in_foreclosure/.
89. Robert Kiosaki, "Pay Yourself First (But Don't Save the Money)," last modified March 24, 2020, https://www.richdad.com/pay-yourself-first.
90. National Association of Realtors, "Housing Affordability Slips in June 2020 as Median Family Income Falls," August 2020, https://www.nar.realtor/blogs/economists-outlook/housing-affordability-slips-in-june-2020-as-median-family-income-falls.
91. "Rules that Warren Buffett Lives By," Stephanie Loiacono, Investopedia, last modified January 2021, https://www.investopedia.com/financial-edge/0210/rules-that-warren-buffett-lives-by.aspx.
92. Gerard Butler, Chasing Mavericks, directed by Michael Apted (2012; Century City, CA: 20th Century Fox), DVD.
93. Albert Finney, A Good Year, directed by Ridley Scott (2006; Century City, CA: 20th Century Fox), DVD.
94. Ellen DeGeneres, Finding Nemo, directed by Andrew Stanton (2003; Burbank, CA: Buena Vista Pictures/Disney), DVD.
95. Adam Sandler, The Wedding Singer, directed by Frank Coraci (1998; Burbank, CA: New Line Cinema), DVD.
96. Christopher Reed, Rudy, directed by David Anspaugh (1993; Culver City, CA: Tri-Star Pictures), DVD.
97. Tomasz Wisniowski, "Over the Top World Championship," The Arm Wrestling Archives, 2011. https://www.thearmwrestlingarchives.com/over-the-top-world-championship.html
98. William Fichtner,12 Strong, directed by Nicolai Fuglsig (2018; Burbank, CA: Warner Brothers), DVD.
99. Randall Duk Kim, Kung Fu Panda, directed by Jennifer Yuh Nelson (2008: Universal City, CA: DreamWorks), DVD.
100. Emma Margolin, "Make America Great Again- Who Said it First?", NBC News, September 9, 2016, https://www.nbcnews.com/politics/2016-election/make-america-great-again-who-said-it-first-n645716.

101.-102. President Ronald W. Reagan, "Explosion of the Space Shuttle Challenger Address to the Nation," January 28, 1986, National Aeronautics and Space Administration, NASA History Office, https://history.nasa.gov/reagan12886.html.

103. "The End of the Innocence," Track 1: The End of the Innocence. Geffen Records, 1989. Written by Don Henley and Bruce Hornsby, performed by Don Henley.

104. "1988 flashback: George H.W. Bush says, 'Read my lips: No new taxes'," NBC News, December 4, 2018, https://www.nbcnews.com/video/1988-flashback-george-h-w-bush-says-read-my-lips-no-new-taxes-1388261955924.

105. Lev Grossman, "Did the U.S. Betray Iraqis in 1991?", CNN, April 3, 2003, https://www.cnn.com/2003/ALLPOLITICS/04/07/timep.betray.tm/.

106. Maureen Dowd, "WAR IN THE GULF: The President; Bush, Scorning Offer, Suggests Iraqis Topple Hussein," New York Times, February 16, 1991, https://www.nytimes.com/1991/02/16/world/war-in-the-gulf-the-president-bush-scorning-offer-suggests-iraq-is-topple-hussein.html.

107. "Perot in 1992 warned NAFTA would create 'giant sucking sound'," Washington Post, July 9, 2019, https://www.washingtonpost.com/video/politics/perot-in-1992-warned-nafta-would-create-giant-sucking-sound/2019/07/09/1f2a84e9-a56c-4487-9c43-892ab1b0c782_video.html.

108. Ed Rollins, "Rollins: Ross Perot was a patriot who paid attention to globalization and deficits," USA Today, July 10, 2019, https://www.usatoday.com/story/opinion/2019/07/10/ross-perot-dies-put-deficits-trade-on-national-agenda-column/1690924001/.

109. Dana Carvey, "Joyride With Perot," Saturday Night Live, October 24, 1992, NBC, https://www.nbc.com/saturday-night-live/video/joyride-with-perot/n10313.

110. Admiral James Stockdale, "1992: Who am I? Why am I here?", CNN, June 9, 2011, https://www.youtube.com/watch?v=hk53qOhq40M.

111. Glenn Kessler, "Bill Clinton and the missed opportunities to kill Osama bin Laden," February 16, 2016, https://www.washingtonpost.com/news/fact-checker/wp/2016/02/16/bill-clinton-and-the-missed-opportunities-to-kill-osama-bin-laden/.

112. The 9/11 Commission Report, National Commission on Terrorist Attacks Upon the United States. July 22, 2004.

113. Jules Witcover, Jack W. Germond, "Democrats hit Rogan to avenge Clinton," originally published in Baltimore Sun (not archived), 2019, https://muckrack.com/jack-w-germond.

114. T. Christian Miller, "Schiff Announces Intent to Run for Rogan's House Seat," Los Angeles Times, April 10, 1999, https://www.latimes.com/archives/la-xpm-1999-apr-10-me-26065-story.html.

115. Leah Burrows, "How future volcanic eruptions will impact Earth's ozone layer," News & Events, Harvard John A. Paulson School of Engineering and Applied Sciences, August 16, 2017, https://www.seas.harvard.edu/news/2017/08/how-future-volcanic-eruptions-will-impact-earths-ozone-layer.

116. Laura Lambert, Ramzi Ahmed Yousef, Britannica, 2011, https://www.britannica.com/biography/Ramzi-Ahmed-Yousef.

117. "Flight 93," National Memorial Pennsylvania, National Park Service, https://www.nps.gov/flni/learn/historyculture/sources-and-detailed-information.htm

118. "Statement by the President in His Address to the Nation," President George W. Bush, White House Archives, September 11, 2001, https://georgewbush-whitehouse.archives.gov/news/releases/2001/09/20010911-16.html.

119. Afsin Yurdakl, "He told Bush that 'America is under attack'," NBC News, September 10, 2009, https://www.nbcnews.com/id/wbna32782623.

120. George W. Bush, "Bullhorn Address to Ground Zero Rescue Workers," American Rhetoric, September 14, 2001, https://www.americanrhetoric.com/speeches/gwbush911groundzerobullhorn.htm.

121. "Congress spontaneous sings God Bless America 9/11/01," C-SPAN, user-created clip by EmilyMillerDC, September 11, 2019, https://www.c-span.org/video/?c4816002/user-clip-congress-spontaneous-sings-god-bless-america-91101#.

122. Shanthi Bharatwaj, "5 Historic Days on the NYSE," The Street, July 7, 2011, https://www.thestreet.com/investing/stocks/5-historic-days-on-the-nyse-11176391.

123.-124. "This Day In Market History: NYSE Reopens For First Time After 9/11 Attacks," We Bull, September 13, 2020, https://www.webull.com/news/24130049.

125. David W. Moore, "Bush Job Approval Highest in Gallup History," Gallup News Service, September 24, 2001, https://news.gallup.com/poll/4924/bush-job-approval-highest-gallup-history.aspx.

126. George W. Bush, "President Bush Addresses the Nation," Washington Post, September 21, 2001, https://www.washingtonpost.com/wp-srv/nation/specials/attacked/transcripts/bushaddress_092001.html.

127. Alexander Mooney, "Bush: 'Mission Accomplished' a Mistake," CNN, November 12, 2008, https://www.cnn.com/2008/POLITICS/11/12/bush.regrets/index.html.

128.-129. George W. Bush, Decision Points, (New York: Crown Publishing Group, 2010), 394.

130. "Camp David, The President's Country Residence," The Grounds, The White House, https://www.whitehouse.gov/about-the-white-house/the-grounds/camp-david/.

131. Unknown, "Obama Travel Cost Now $105,662,975.27," Judicial Watch, September 14, 2017 https://www.judicialwatch.org/press-releases/judicial-watch-obama-travel-cost-now-105662975-27/.

132. Personal conversation at Mortgage Banker's Conference, 2017.

133. Unknown, "Biden's description of Obama draws scrutiny," CNN, February 9, 2007, https://www.cnn.com/2007/POLITICS/01/31/biden.obama/.

134. "Four Years of Speeches, One Signature Phrase," YouTube, 2:57, TIME, December 21, 2012, https://www.youtube.com/watch?v=5oNcHS0c5W8.

135. Jillian Fama, "Obama: (Insert Issue Here), 'It's the Right Thing to Do'," ABC News, June 27, 2012, https://abcnews.go.com/blogs/politics/2012/06/obama-insert-issue-here-its-the-right-thing-to-do.

136. Christopher J. Scalia, "Why Obama Says, 'That's Not Who We Are': Column," USA Today, February 8, 2016, https://www.usatoday.com/story/opinion/2016/02/08/barack-obama-thats-not-who-we-are-rhetoric-patriotism-column/79971138/.

137. Barack Obama, "President Obama Campaign Rally in Roanoke, Virginia," July 13, 2012, https://www.factcheck.org/2012/07/you-didnt-build-that-uncut-and-unedited/.

138. Ben Smith, "Obama: Cambridge police acted stupidly," Ben Smith Blog, July 22, 2009, https://www.politico.com/blogs/ben-smith/2009/07/obama-cambridge-police-acted-stupidly-020099.

139. Krissah Thompson and Scott Wilson, "Obama on Trayvon Martin: 'If I had a son, he'd look like Trayvon'," Washington Post, March 23, 2012, https://www.washingtonpost.com/politics/obama-if-i-had-a-son-hed-look-like-trayvon/2012/03/23/gIQApKPpVS_story.html.

140. Cindy Boren, "Obama Uncertain if He'd Let a Son Play Football," Washington Post, January 28, 2013, https://www.washingtonpost.com/news/early-lead/wp/2013/01/28/obama-uncertain-if-hed-let-a-son-play-football/.

141. Peter Baker and Julie Hirschfeld Davis, "A Terrorist Horror, Then Golf: Incongruity Fuels Obama Critics," New York Times, August 21, 2014, https://www.nytimes.com/2014/08/22/us/politics/a-terrorist-horror-then-golf-incongruity-fuels-obama-critics.html.

142. "Address to the Nation by the President," President Barack Obama, White House Archives, December 6, 2015, https://obamawhitehouse.archives.gov/the-press-office/2015/12/06/address-nation-president.

143. Lindsay Holst, "President Obama Delivers a Statement on the Ferguson Grand Jury's Decision," President Barack Obama, White House Archives, November 24, 2014, https://obamawhitehouse.archives.gov/blog/2014/11/24/president-obama-delivers-statement-ferguson-grand-jurys-decision.

144. U.S. Department of Justice Civil Rights Division, Federal Reports on Police Killings: Ferguson, Cleveland, Baltimore and Chicago, June 2017.

145. Unknown, "'Pigs in a blanket' chant at Minnesota fair riles police," CBS News, August 31, 2015, https://www.cbsnews.com/news/pigs-in-a-blanket-chant-at-minnesota-fair-riles-police/.

146. "60% Say Race Relations Have Gotten Worse Since Obama's Election," Rasmussen Reports, July 19, 2016, https://www.rasmussenreports.com/public_content/politics/current_events/social_issues/60_say_race_relations_have_gotten_worse_since_obama_s_election.

147. Brian Ross and Rehab El-Buri, "Obama's Pastor: God Damn America, U.S. to Blame for 9/11," ABC News, May 7, 2008, https://abcnews.go.com/Blotter/DemocraticDebate/story?id=4443788&page=1.

148. Reverend Wright Transcript: "From the Day of Jerusalem's Fall," ABC News, April 27, 2008, https://abcnews.go.com/Blotter/story?id=4719157&page=1.

149. Daniel Nasaw, "Controversial Comments Made by Rev Jeremiah Wright," The Guardian, March 18, 2008, https://www.theguardian.com/world/2008/mar/18/barackobama.uselections20083.

150. Press release, "Judicial Watch: Obama Travel Cost Now $105,662,975.27," Standard Newswire, September 14, 2017, http://standardnewswire.com/news/5626012995.html.

151. Nick Gass, "The White House press corps' strange Hawaii vacation," Politico, December 28, 2015, https://www.politico.com/story/2015/12/barack-obama-hawaii-vacation-press-corps-report-217157.

152. "Judicial Watch: President Obama's 2015 Golf and Family Vacation Trips Cost Taxpayers $3,115,688.70 in Travel Expenses Alone," Judicial Watch, November 17, 2015,
https://www.judicialwatch.org/press-releases/judicial-watch-president-obamas-2015-golf-and-family-vacation-trips-cost-taxpayers-3115688-70-in-travel-expenses-alone/.

153. Jack Nicholson, A Few Good Men, directed by Aaron Sorkin (1992; Beverly Hills, CA: Castle Rock Entertainment), DVD.

154. Unknown, "Did Mitt Romney Really Ask for 'Binders Full of Women'?", The Guardian, October 2012.

155. Reuters staff, "Energized by Debate, Obama Knocks Romney on Women's Issues," Reuters, October 17, 2012, https://www.reuters.com/article/usa-campaign-obama/energized-by-debate-obama-knocks-romney-on-womens-issues-idUSL1E8LHH2O20121017.

156. Arlette Saenz, "Biden Knocks Romney for Binder Comment, '1950s Time Warp' on Women," ABC News, October 17, 2012, https://abcnews.go.com/blogs/politics/2012/10/biden-knocks-romney-for-binder-comment-1950s-time-warp-on-women.

157. Michael D. Shear and Michael Barbaro, "In Video Clip, Romney Calls 47% 'Dependent' and Feeling Entitled," The Caucus Blog, New York Times, September 17. 2012, https://thecaucus.blogs.nytimes.com/2012/09/17/romney-faults-those-dependent-on-government/.

158. Unknown, "Romney's '47 Percent Slur' Reverberates On Social Media," WBUR, September 18, 2012, https://www.wbur.org/hereandnow/2012/09/18/romney-twitter-percent.

159. Aaron Blake, "Romney's '47 percent' comment and the importance of the echo chamber," Washington Post, September 19, 2012, https://www.washingtonpost.com/news/the-fix/wp/2012/09/19/romneys-47-percent-comment-and-the-importance-of-the-echo-chamber/.

160. Juli Weiner, "Romney's 10 Percent Apology for His 47 Percent Comment," Vanity Fair, October 5, 2012, https://www.vanityfair.com/news/2012/10/Romneys-10-Percent-Sincere-Apology-for-His-47-Percent-Comment.

161. Kevin Kline, Dave, directed by Ivan Reitman (1993: Burbank, CA: Warner Brothers), DVD.

162. Cheyenne Haslett, "Mitt Romney Finally Gets Credit Years Later for His Warnings on Russia," ABC News, February 26, 2019, https://abcnews.go.com/Politics/years-mitt-romney-finally-credit-warnings-russia/story?id=61330530.

163. Julia Limitone, "Ben Carson's 10% Flat Tax Plan," Fox Business, January 9, 2017, https://www.foxbusiness.com/politics/dr-ben-carsons-10-flat-tax-plan.

164. Jeff Bridges, directed by Rod Lurie (2000; Universal City, CA: DreamWorks), DVD.

165. Ed Hoffman, "Clinton Casualties," EdHoffman.net, last modified June 2021, https://edhoffman.net/clinton-casualties/.

166. Janell Ross, "Why Hillary Clinton needs to avoid another 'What difference does it make?' moment on Benghazi," Washington Post, October 22, 2015, https://www.washingtonpost.com/news/the-fix/wp/2015/10/22/why-hillary-clinton-needs-to-avoid-another-what-difference-does-it-make-moment-on-benghazi/.

167. Jonathan M. Katz, "The Clintons' Haiti Screw-Up, As Told By Hillary's Emails," Politico, September 2, 2015, https://www.politico.com/magazine/story/2015/09/hillary-clinton-email-213110/.

168. William J. Clinton Foundation Independent Accountants' Report and Consolidated Financial Statements, December 31, 2011 and 2010, https://www.clintonfoundation.org/sites/default/files/clinton-foundation-financial-report-2011.pdf.

169. Alexander Bolton, "Chelsea Clinton reaps $9 million from corporate board position," The Hill, January 6, 2020, https://thehill.com/homenews/senate/476894-chelsea-clinton-reaps-9-million-from-corporate-board-position.

170. Richard W. Painter, "The Real Clinton Foundation Revelation," New York Times, August 31, 2016, https://www.nytimes.com/2016/08/31/opinion/the-real-clinton-foundation-revelation.html?_r=0.

171. Byron Tau, "Obama Calls ISIS a 'Vicious Death Cult' at National Prayer Breakfast," Wall Street Journal, February 5, 2015, https://www.wsj.com/articles/BL-WB-52806.

172. Timothy Gardner, "Here's Why Obama is Approving Arctic Drilling Again," Scientific American, April 1, 2015, https://www.scientificamerican.com/article/here-s-why-obama-is-approving-arctic-drilling-again/.

173. Sam Sanders, "Obama Proposes New Protections For Arctic National Wildlife Refuge," NPR, January 25, 2015, https://www.npr.org/sections/thetwo-way/2015/01/25/379795695/obama-proposes-new-protections-for-arctic-national-wildlife-refuge.

174. Christopher Solomon, "The ANWR Drilling Rights in the Tax-Reform Bill," Outside, November 16, 2017, https://www.outsideonline.com/outdoor-adventure/environment/drilling-crown-jewel-arctic-refuge-grows-closer/.

175. "AT LAST: Congress Approves Legislation to Open Alaska's 1002 Area," Republican News, Senate Committee on Energy & Natural Resources, December 20, 2017, https://www.energy.senate.gov/2017/12/at-last-congress-approves-legislation-to-open-alaska-s-1002-area.

176. "Statement by the President on the Keystone XL Pipeline," President Barack Obama, White House Archives, November 6, 2015, https://obamawhitehouse.archives.gov/the-press-office/2015/11/06/statement-president-keystone-xl-pipeline.

177. "Oil and Petroleum Products Explained," U.S. Energy Information Administration, last modified April 8, 2021, https://www.eia.gov/energyexplained/oil-and-petroleum-products/where-our-oil-comes-from.php.

178. "Despite the U.S. becoming a net petroleum exporter, most regions are still net importers," Today in Energy, U.S. Energy Information Administration, February 6. 2020. https://www.eia.gov/todayinenergy/detail.php?id=42735

179. Rep. John Joyce, M.D., "Under President Trump, America is energy independent," Opinion, Penn Live, September 25, 2020, https://www.pennlive.com/opinion/2020/09/under-president-trump-america-is-energy-independent-opinion.html.

180. "Executive Order on Protecting Public Health and the Environment and Restoring Science to Tackle the Climate Crisis," Presidential Actions, The White House, January 20, 2021, https://www.whitehouse.gov/briefing-room/presidential-actions/2021/01/20/executive-order-protecting-public-health-and-environment-and-restoring-science-to-tackle-climate-crisis/.

181. David Duchovny, Kalifornia, directed by Dominic Sena (1993: Universal City, CA, Gramercy Pictures), DVD.

182. Robert DeNiro, Limitless, directed by Neil Burger (2011: Beverly Hills, CA, Relativity Media), DVD.

CPSIA information can be obtained
at www.ICGtesting.com
Printed in the USA
BVHW070116030921
615902BV00013B/382